An Officer's Story

An Officer's Story

A Politico-Military Journey

Steve Kime

authorHOUSE®

AuthorHouse™
1663 Liberty Drive
Bloomington, IN 47403
www.authorhouse.com
Phone: 1 (800) 839-8640

Published by AuthorHouse 09/09/2015

ISBN: 978-1-5049-4975-0 (sc)
ISBN: 978-1-5049-4976-7 (hc)
ISBN: 978-1-5049-4974-3 (e)

Library of Congress Control Number: 2015914950

Print information available on the last page.

Acknowledgements

Role models and mentors helped me at every stage of my life. In childhood and boyhood, some had a profound impact on me and are singled out. In the Navy, in higher education, and when I was involved in Russian and military matters, a legion of officers, scholars and policymakers taught and guided me. Some were, like me, ordinary folks, but the reader might recognize others. I have identified many, and I will never forget the debt I owe each of them. Please salute them as you meet them in my Story.

Not all in my generation would accept my judgments. Some would loudly dissent, but I have tried in this Story to reflect reasonably accurately the views of my generation. To be certain that I am not distorting those views, some contemporaries and colleagues with varying experiences and outlooks reviewed parts of this Story. Dave Barksdale, County Historian in New Albany, Indiana, verified some historical information. Some reviewers made suggestions that I heeded. Three contributors, for example, noted that Democrats of our era included both the blue-collar FDR Democrats and more conservative democrats, more like old Southern Democrats, who never accepted FDR. They are correct: one of my role models thought FDR was a Communist.

A couple of my reviewers think that lingering racism in the U.S. is stronger than I think it is and that the racial elements in reactions to the events of the Sixties and Seventies were stronger than I estimate them to have been. Robin Phillips, a retired Army Lieutenant Colonel and Russian expert, was an insightful and substantive reviewer and editor. All of my contributors are perceptive observers with key perspectives, and I have adjusted my draft in some places to take their views into account. We would still disagree on some things. In the end it is my Story and I'm sticking to it!

The American Family has been at the core of American culture and values. Military families exude that culture and those values. This Story concentrates on my professional life and political-military issues and thus may not sufficiently reflect that my family was involved at every stage. No decision was made, action taken, or opinion arrived at without the influence and consideration of the Family I was born into or the Family that my wife, Wilma, and I built. This book is dedicated to those families.

Contents

Foreword

All of us are going to die. Some of us grow old. A lucky few get to be in the Navy.

Naval Officers come from everywhere and good ones can do just about anything. Most could have gratified their egos and made a lot more money as civilians. Virtually all, including me, would join the Navy again today. In spite of the public image of handsome, spoiled, and "entitled" graduates of Annapolis tossing their hats in the air, a careful observer would find common roots and simple beginnings for many of those who don the Naval uniform. There is an elite heritage, of course, but the Navy is looking for hard workers with brains and personal courage, and it vigorously sorts people out over a Naval career. Even sons of the rich and high-ranking have to pass through a decades-long vetting process. The survivors, regardless of rank achieved, are almost all winners.

Some officers are certainly better than others. This is only roughly reflected by rank. With the exceptions of the occasional rock star or dud, what distinguishes between them over twenty or thirty years is sometimes more about accidents of time and place, luck of the draw, and the ability to fit the prevailing notion of what the Navy wants and needs, than it is about character or even competence. Some fine Naval Officers become Captains and Admirals, and some do not. It is an honor just to be one of them.

My cohort of Naval Officers commissioned in 1962 brought a lot of social, political and economic baggage with them. Of course, every cohort does, but those that spent their formative years in the Fifties would be inoculated in fundamental ways against the assaults on American polity and society of the Sixties and Seventies. Our Depression-era and Greatest Generation role models taught us some important things about character and about American politics. We had learned those things while living in an America that was proud and productive. We had some solid underpinnings that would allow us to accept some change but hang on to things that really counted.

The formative experiences that my generation had and the context in which it passed childhood and entered adulthood are key to understanding the last half of the twentieth century. They are reflected here. I am convinced that the worldviews and perspectives in this book reside deep in today's social fabric and will rise up and impact the future of America in the mid Twenty-First century. We are already seeing the first signs.

America may face serious turmoil in the next few decades. The emerging backlash of the Twenty-first Century, manifested by political extremes on both Left and Right and the failure of political parties and government in general to embrace the American mindset, much of which was formed in places and times

that are discussed here, seems to have surprised historians and social scientists. This is because they were not paying attention to the unremarkable people in all walks of American life who embody deeply held opinions and values. I was an unremarkable Naval Officer with a middle-American heritage who was blessed with some interesting perches from which to view a key period of history. The political undercurrents that impacted me are still flowing in the early twenty-first century. They are why this book was written.

As I relate what happened to me, I will pause at times to explain the attitudes and opinions that my generation developed and the implications of their views on the socio-political currents and events of the last half century. This will annoy some readers, and they may choose to dismiss my views as the screed of an old officer or to claim that my generation was merely an aberration between the Greatest Generation and the Baby Boomers, but I submit that my views reflect the outlook of most of those I knew in my time, that their views had crucial impact, and that much of their perspective still exists today.

I was privileged to serve in several arenas, some of them controversial. Russian military and social history, submarines, nuclear and conventional military strategy and policy, national and military intelligence, and higher education are all areas in which I served. Officers serve long active duty years unable to express opinions that would upset the civilians elected and appointed to run the country. That is as it should be, and I never met an officer who thought otherwise. For better or worse, I developed strong views based on first-hand experience and responsibility in several areas. Some of these views were contrary to those of the political establishment.

I share those views now in retirement without equivocation, and I expect disagreement. At the end of my journey, and the end of this book, I present assessments in the areas where I participated that are most important: Russia, and America's national security outlook

This is an American journey from roots in the Heartland through vistas that the Navy opened for me. It is a story that any American might live. In this sense, though the life of the naval officer presented here is different from the Navy norm, it is not a remarkable one. There are extraordinary lives in and out of the Navy, but most lives are only part of a great social fabric and end unremarkably. Their stories fade into the sweep of history. Lessons learned and perspectives developed, especially in unusual careers like mine, are gone forever unless someone writes them down.

I did not follow a standard career pathway because of my willful nature, but also because the Navy was wise and flexible enough to let me contribute where I could help the most. I am grateful. I made career tradeoffs and did not always do what the Navy preferred. I ended up with no regrets and a profound love of and respect for the United States Navy.

Along the way, I enjoyed a view of America's development during a tumultuous half century and got to participate in some interesting parts of it.

This is one officer's Story about his journey.

Chapter I

Home:
Life and Thought
in the Forties

1917 sheet music cover
of the Tin Pan Alley
pop-song "Back Home
Again in Indiana"

New Albany, Indiana, is the epitome of Middle America. It would be difficult to find a more typical place to swim in the mainstream of the country. A modest community across the Ohio River from Louisville, Kentucky, it was a town of about 30,000 when I was born there in 1940. The region, known locally as "Kentuckiana," has an interesting history.

"Kentuckiana"

source: https://upload.wikimedia.org/wikipedia/commons/4/4e/Map_of_Kentuckiana.png

Shawnee and Iroquois tribes had bustling communities in the region for centuries. Pioneers in the 18th century, including Daniel Boone, came through the Cumberland Gap into the Indian territory of what was then a part of Virginia called "Kain Tuk." Many of these settlers, including Abraham Lincoln's family and mine, headed north across the Ohio River

1

into fertile Indiana farming land. Traffic up and down the Ohio River attracted white settlers throughout the 18th and 19th centuries.

George Rogers Clark had led forces that gained control of the area in 1779. Virginia then granted Clark 150,000 acres of land, which encompassed what is now Clark County, Indiana, and parts of the surrounding counties. President Jefferson sent Clark and his party from this area to explore the Northwest Territory after the Louisiana Purchase in 1803. Clark sold much of Clark County to his men, and what became New Albany was in turn sold by one of Clark's Colonels to three Scribner Brothers from New York who sold plots and established the town of New Albany in 1813. Within a few decades, it became a boomtown. Towns established to the East, like Providence and Silver Grove where I was born, eventually became part of New Albany. Floyd County was eventually separated from Clark County, with New Albany as the county seat.

My paternal grandmother's family, the Durbins, were early settlers of Kentucky and many made the trek north across the Ohio. My great-grandfather, Wilhelm Martin Kime, was born in Pennsylvania and served in the Mexican War. On the way back up the river system to get home after the war, his boat went aground at the Falls of the Ohio and he swam ashore. He married a miller's daughter from Kentucky and stayed in southern Indiana the rest of his life.

The Ohio River, and the Falls, made New Albany a key geographical location as the country expanded westward following the rivers. Its heyday was the mid-19th Century, and New Albany became one of the richest and biggest towns in the Midwest. The first plate glass in America was manufactured in New Albany.

SOUTHERN PART OF NEW ALBANY, INDIANA   FALLS OF THE OHIO, BETWEEN

The first high school in Indiana, established in1853, was New Albany High School. A Carnegie Library was built in the town. There was a significant boat-building period, including steamboats such as the *Robert E. Lee,* of The Great Steamboat Race fame. New Albany's Main Street to this day is lined with handsome old houses that have widow's walks on top of them.

NEW ALBANY industries:
Boilermaker Shops
Steamboat Industry
Glass works
Iron works
Tin Manufacturing
Hames, Chains and Single-Trees
Grain and Milling:
Textiles & Clothing Mfg
Merchant Tailoring:
Leather
Breweries & Bottling Works
Brick Works
Stone, Marble and Granite Works
Concrete Construction
Woodworking
Plywood and Veneer
Prefabricated Houses
Carriage and Wagon Mfg. &Furniture Mfg
Wholesale Florist
Fertilizer
Automobile Mfg in the early 1900s
Slaughter Houses and Meat Packers
Cigar Mfg
Wholesale Grocers, Druggists, Liquor &
Bitters Distributors & Bakers&
Confectioners

The town became a commercial Mecca in the Midwest by the mid-19th Century when there were a number of thriving industries. New Albany's boom time ended at the turn of the 20th Century, and the town morphed into a working community and bedroom town for Louisville, which grew into a major city after the locks around the Falls were built on the Kentucky side of the Ohio.

New Albany remained a center of plywood and veneer production for many years. Cabinetmaking and woodworking were major local industries. Ford and International Harvester, legendary Kentucky whiskey makers, a smelly tannery and glue factory, a foundry, and Purina Feeds provided jobs. So did canneries, a box factory, and several woolen mills and clothing factories. All this meant railroads were vital to the busy crossroads that the region became. The men in my family were railroaders

"Kentuckiana" became a social prototype of America. There is a fairly large city, small towns and plenty of farming countryside, all places where hard working immigrants worked the land and operated buzzing factories. Former slaves made their homes there. Railroads intersected there.

William Martin Kime, my paternal great grandfather, an ordinary fellow who lived an ordinary life, chose to raise his family there. It was a place and time where "The American Way of Life" evolved.

House Calls and War

The Kime household in 1948
Author's photo

Harry E. Voyles was a small-town doctor in New Albany at a time when house calls were made and babies were born at home. His time and comfort were not as important as the eighth and ninth babies of a railroad brakeman. Doc Voyles made house calls before lawyers made his kind of family medicine impossible. I was one of twins emerged alive in the wee hours of the 3rd of December in 1940. Two months after delivering me, a half mile away, he would deliver Wilma Snook, who accompanies me throughout this Story.

Steve Francis Kime was born at about 2:30 A.M. on December 3rd. Doc Voyles inaccurately scrawled the birth of a Stephan Francis Kime on December 2nd. When the ninth baby arrived a year later, he was named "Harry Eugene" after the venerable sawbones. Doc Voyles got that name right.

My generation began to appear as war clouds gathered about four decades after the boom ended in New Albany. My generation is distinct from The Greatest Generation that fought World War II, and from their parents who were adults in the Roaring Twenties and the Depression

Thirties. We were born in the Thirties and Forties, before the Baby Boomers. We grew up between a "deprived" and heroic generation and an "entitled" one.

Our early childhood war was The Big One. World War II consumed the society and the economy. The Big One may have saved the economy, but all that children like me knew was that there was a shortage of everything, everyone was in a big fight together, and young men were off killing Germans and Japs. At first, Germans were the bad guys, though almost everyone we knew was from German stock. It was weird to hate German people who were our cousins, ancestors and close neighbors, and to love English people whose grandfathers fought our grandfathers in the Revolution and in 1812, but since adults did not seem to reflect on it much, it made sense at the time. Of course, WWI veterans already hated Germans, who seemed intent on doing things so outrageous that they continued to alienate Americans with strong German roots.

It was easier to hate "Japs" than Germans. Americans certainly worked up a bigger lather over the Japs than over the Germans, and not just because of Pearl Harbor and the murder of 2400 sailors. The racism discussed below made it easy to hate Japs. Kids "shot" them in neighborhood games as quickly as little Cowboys shot little Indians. No one in New Albany doubted for a second that Japanese-Americans were likely traitors and had to be kept in camps. It was not the first time that manifest injustice was accepted in America's race from wilderness to superpower. Ask Native Americans. Manifest Destiny trumped much of what we sometimes describe as "American Values" today. It is hypocritical now to apply Political Correctness and act like those who built internment camps were wrong. It is a sad part of our history not compatible with our values and with what we know now to be facts about the unfortunate people imprisoned there, but the decision was made in a totally different time and circumstance. The same is true of Truman's use of the Atom Bomb, a sad event that must be understood in terms of its time and situation. Of course we would not intern Japanese-Americans today, but we should not have to distort history to validate the present.

The Bag Plant in Jeffersonville sent gunpowder to the Front. Thousands worked there and got lots of overtime. Overtime was a good thing. Women sewed uniforms. Gas and sugar were short. There were no new cars. The War, which paradoxically helped pull the economy out of its doldrums, consumed everything and affected everybody.

For toddlers, terrible twos, and little guys like me, the radio was dramatic and scary sometimes, interrupting Fibber McGee and Molly, Ma and Pa Kettle and Amos and Andy to bring chilling news read in stentorian tones.

Brothers were heroes in their Navy and Marine uniforms. Brother Junior brought home a rifle on furlough before heading to the horrors of the Pacific at Peleliu (Palau) and Iwo Jima. He hung his rifle on a beam in the basement and took it when he went to war. Mom cried.

My memories from those childhood years are war-related. I remember seeing young Martin Kime, Jr. at the front door in his Marine uniform. It was odd that he knocked on the door as if he had become someone else. I remember Mom, a gray-haired mother of nine in a housedress at age 38, crying at the sight of him. Junior, a delightful young man with a great sense of humor, cooked Christmas dinner before deployment. There was sadness and amazement when the cover of Life Magazine revealed what she insisted was her boy with bombs exploding in the background.

When it was over, children and adults alike felt the post-war relief that swept the nation. Everyone saw Eisenstaedt's photo of a sailor kissing a girl on VJ day in August of 1945. A nation rejoiced.

Six decades later, my big brother Junior, in his eighties, finally talked about the horrors of the Pacific. He cried. Junior had not ever talked about it, but he got it off his chest to his little brother, who was then a retired senior naval officer. He had befriended a Life Magazine photographer who took thousands of photos. One appeared in Life Magazine. Junior showed me about a hundred photos. Some showed bodies stacked like cordwood. Junior was tasked to bayonet any that still moved. He had seen a childhood friend die, and he was haunted by the notion that it was "friendly fire" in a hellish situation that killed the boy.

PTSD was unknown at a macho time when any lingering sadness was considered a shameful weakness. A family prankster as a boy, Junior returned from the Big One to avoid family and live in the country. He must have burned the photos after showing them to me. They could not be found after his death in 2009.

Reawakening

"I Hear America singing, the varied carols I hear"
Walt Whitman

A sense of general wellbeing grew among working families of the late Forties as America emerged from war and depression to become, for a few years, the only superpower on Earth. This Gulliver-like awakening was a breath of fresh air for the population.

The political class soon used this postwar awakening of the American Gulliver to distort the role our country would play in the world. Both the Left and the Right found reasons to promote a global, internationalist role for America. Both went too far. This reawakening also brought domestic social issues deeply imbedded in American culture to the forefront of America's consciousness. In a highly visible symbol of this domestic stirring, President Truman integrated the Armed Forces. The Dodgers started Jackie Robison, who had been a lieutenant in a segregated Army, at first base on April 15, 1947.

Working families still did not have much, but we did not know that it was not enough. Today someone would tell us that we are below some US poverty level that is higher than the economic level of the vast majority of humanity. Work was not always easy for the men and was sometimes overwhelming for women, even in burgeoning postwar America. We ate an inordinate amount of oatmeal, and Roosevelt's "chicken in every pot" was a rare bird in working men's families. But life was good! The iceman sometimes gave the kids a chunk of ice to suck on, the quart of milk with cream on top somehow served eight or nine people, and the Rag Man, who presumably had less than we did, patrolled the alleys in an old wagon pulled by a horse. Who knew we were poor?

An important part of the awakening of ordinary Americans after WWII was increased mobility. People moved and they moved around. It was as if they had been unleashed to demonstrate their freedom. The love affair with the internal combustion engine, unrequited during the Depression and War, was reinvigorated. Suburbs appeared and grew. Soon there would be an interstate highway system that was a modern Wonder of the World. Small businesses thrived. Every nook and cranny of the country became accessible.

Rapid change brought growing pains, but most people saw more good then bad. The growing American pie meant that more people wanted a piece of that pie. Long simmering denial of access to the fruits of American prosperity, most obviously denial of access to blacks, who had endured generations of indignity and deprivation since the Emancipation, began to boil up in the early Fifties. In white America, where I was raised, it was sensed then but did not become palpable until later. There were shoes yet to drop.

One of the negative impacts of the automobile and highway revolutions was the decline of the railroads. This was hard on families like mine that had finally seen a little financial progress. For the nation, it meant a dependence on oil that would in turn result in some domestic and foreign policies now clearly wrong and shortsighted, but compatible with Progressive and Internationalist goals. Oil made big businessmen strange bedfellows to the Progressives and Internationalists.

The mistaken shift from rails to highways also caused the rise of the Teamsters Union, mobbed up and mean as Hell. The Teamsters and the truckers made the Brotherhood of Railroad Trainmen look like girl scouts. The union movement, in fact, began to diverge from the kind of relationship that most American workers, who were not militant revolutionaries, wanted with management. This period marked the beginning of a steady decline in unionism. The unions outlived their short-term purposes, but faded as the incompatibility of mob rule and basic values became clear. The unions have prolonged their demise by collecting dues and using them to support Progressive politicians who, in turn, serve union goals, but this gambit is wearing thin in the 21st Century.

After the war, when he had some gas, Dad visited our family roots in a resoundingly Catholic area of Western Kentucky where hardscrabble farms and devout families of innumerable children dwelt. Dad's older brother, John, lived there with 14 kids. It was an epic 85-mile journey to Sunfish, Kentucky in the '39 Chevy. Dad thought 35 miles an hour was the speed of light. Kids worked hard first in these families and went to school second. Cows were milked at 4 AM. Biscuits with slabs of freshly churned butter and fresh eggs were served at five. There was no heat at night. Several kids shared a bed to keep warm.

One morning I was sent with a 13-year-old cousin to go hunting for squirrel before sunup. He bagged three squirrels with a .22 caliber rifle from the same tree as they scurried from limb to limb. We had squirrel for supper. On the way home, he warned me that The Crazy Lady would have heard the shooting and be looking for us. Sure enough, an old lady came out of a shack, yelling and waving an enormous revolver. She fired twice, and we did not linger to determine what direction she fired in. Some of pioneer Kentucky still lived!

Sixty years later, I returned to Sunfish during genealogy research on family roots. Overlooking the church my ancestors built and where my grandma was baptized, I found cousins whose families, experiences and perspectives were exactly what someone like me would have guessed. It was as if that place was where the country's thinking had taken root. Of course, this feeling will disturb the folks in New England and Virginia where our Founding Fathers planted fertile seeds, but I have often wondered if Daniel Boone did not transplant many of those seeds when he led those pioneers through the Gap to Kain Tuck.

In the valley at Sunfish the churchyard was filled with graves of my ancestors, including Uncle John and his boy who got the Silver Star posthumously in WWII. Several other heroes were buried in that serene and lovely place.

Author's photos

Fun and Family

Twice a year our family had some fun. On July 4th we drove into the country to the shack that Dad's elder sister, Esther, lived in near Pekin, Indiana. It was only 35 miles away, but it took Dad two hours to get there in the old '39 Chevrolet that had to go up some of the hills in reverse gear. Uncles, aunts and a throng of cousins put together a makeshift table and all would share a huge potluck picnic.

Aunt Esther would whack off the heads of a few chickens and awestruck kids would watch them run around the barnyard before they were hung up on the clothesline. (This helped me later to understand behavior in the Pentagon.) The chickens were then scalded and plucked before Esther chopped them up. She used the same menacing big, flat butcher knife for all occasions. Esther ordered the other women, and the burly railroaders, around like little kids. You did not mess around with Aunt Esther. The kids played in the old barn where moonshine was made during prohibition, rolled down a huge hill inside a big tire, and ate the fried chicken.

Dad was a notorious tightwad. Money was hard to come by, and he did not part with it lightly. His favorite sayings were "don't take any wooden nickels" and "a fool and his money are soon parted." I still have the moneybox where my mom would put the few dollars she was given to feed the family. She often ran out, and we ate a lot of oatmeal. Dad took care of his mother before he parted with money for our household; but Aunt Esther needed help, too, so Dad would pay for feed to raise two or three hogs and then paid to butcher them. In return, we got fresh pork from one of the hogs. I saw more of the lower and internal parts of the animal than anything else. Dad would complain that it was the most expensive meat on the planet. When Dad died in 1965, we could not find an unpaid bill.

Aunt Esther hardly noticed me among the army of nieces and nephews. When she got infirm and moved in with her sister in New Albany for her final years, I visited them once or twice. She had never written a note or talked to me on the phone, but when I graduated from college she mailed me a note and a dollar bill.

The second thing we did to have fun was an annual visit to Fontaine Ferry Park in Louisville on Nickel Day. We looked forward to this all year. Dad, who was frugal at the usual holidays, saved money for this outing each year. He loved the amusement park as much as we did. We could only go there when most rides and cotton candy, which normally cost 12 cents, cost a nickel. Each child got a $2 roll of nickels, which were doled out with great solemnity. When the nickels were gone, you were through. It cost a quarter to ride the roller coaster or go to a place called Hilarity Hall where there were a number of activities. The strategy was to ride the rides until you had five nickels left: then, after a picnic lunch, stay in the Hilarity Hall for the rest of the day. Unless you were independently wealthy, you could not afford the roller coaster.

The Park was located at the end of a trolley line, like such amusement parks of the time in other cities, to draw trolley business on weekends. It was also approachable by a steamboat ride down the Ohio from downtown Louisville.

Families like mine could never afford the steamboat ride, but there was a charming ride by automobile past big, beautiful homes. The place was an idyllic and magical place to our family.

Our annual low-budget frolic at Fontaine Ferry turned out to be a childhood illusion that would be exploded during America's Time of Troubles in the late Sixties. It never occurred to kids like me that the place was segregated. After many protests, Fontaine Ferry, and the nearby neighborhood of big, beautiful homes, was integrated in 1964.

In 1968 the West End of Louisville was struck by ferocious race riots. By 1969, Fontaine Ferry Park was not a safe place. In the spring of 1969, racial protestors wreaked huge damage. Attempts to repair, rename and reopen the Park for the next decade were rewarded by vandalism and fires. In 1981, the city gave up. The grand old 1910-vintage carousel was sent to Chicago. The fate of Fontaine Ferry left a bitter taste in the mouths of both sides of the racial divide. Its demise was a local tragedy.

At the end of the 1940s, while America was adjusting to its new identity as a superpower, I was a little boy coping with school and neighborhood kids who all seemed bigger than I was. There was no kindergarten then, and I was enrolled in first grade at age five. I peed my pants the first day.

As the 8th child in a family of assertive individuals, I was not yet a Type A. My sisters ruled at home. Mom was often ill, Dad "pounded cinders" on the railroad every hour he could, and my elder sister, Amelia, was the Alpha dog. If I did not behave, Millie said I would be sold to the Rag Man. I believed her.

In fact, the Rag Man was one of two brothers who kept a little farm a few hundred yards from our house. These two anachronisms of the Fifties stubbornly held out against progress. They kept an old horse and a couple of milk cows. They had a wonderful grape arbor and I suspect they made some wine. Families like mine bought the milk. Once a month the old horse was hitched up and a wagon passed through the town's alleys to collect old iron, rags and any junk that could be sold. This was recycling, Fifties style.

After the brothers died in the Fifties, houses sprung up in their fields. In a way, the new development marked the beginning of the end of the postwar Happy Days that leftists today are quick to criticize but too lazy to try to understand.

Chapter II
The Fifties:
Hoosier Roots, Role Models,
and Lessons Learned

1950 brought a calamity bigger to a little boy than the Korean War. Mom died. She was not yet 44 years old, but she died an old lady. This was not unusual in America's short but frenetic history. Women worked themselves to death as the frontier was settled, the factories and railroads built, and the land tilled. Wives and mothers were used up in the millions to build this country. The cost was enormous. In later years, as I adopted genealogy as a hobby and saw how many wives a man would go through, I wondered why this had not been improved in working families by the middle of the twentieth century. Of course, in 1950 I was just a little boy and did not know history. I just missed my mom.

Teenagers Amelia, Lila and Henry were devastated. Each made dramatic life choices based on the loss of their Mom. Millie and Lila got married too quickly. Henry would not go to school. He was found several times sobbing at Mom's grave. Henry, who had trouble with high school academics, married a sweet girl of similar ability. Henry worked hard, long hours at whatever jobs he could find until he died at 60. He never accepted charity, paid his own way, and was clear on what was right and wrong. Leftists today would be recruiting him to accept disability pay or some other kind of entitlement. Henry would have refused. We need more Americans like him.

Mom's last words were "take care of my babies." I was told this the day she died by my eldest brother, Roy. As I grew older I realized that this charge of responsibility for her kids somehow applied more *to* me than it was *about* me. My younger brother, Harry, the delight and favorite of all of us, was really the only "baby" of the family. Roy was all about family and Roy and I both grew to understand as years passed that some in a family end up with the responsibility. He took responsibility until his old age, and then it was passed to me.

Silver Street Elementary School in New Albany is across the street from a national cemetery established by Abraham Lincoln to bury Civil War dead. In 1951 and 1952, children and teachers paused every time sweet and mournful taps were played and three shots fired in honor of some young man who had fallen in Korea, or some World War veteran. By 1953, taps and the gunshots for Korean War dead had become so common that it was hardly noticed. Kids collected the brass in the cemetery after school

Once, when collecting brass at the cemetery, I bet a friend that I could jump off the wall and grab a tree limb. I lost the bet, and broke my arm in three places. When I got off the ground, my arm flapped so wildly that the back of my hand touched the back of my head. There was no such thing as prepaid health care and, if there were, we wouldn't have had it. They took care of it as cheaply as possible, but it cost a whopping $75 that probably came straight from household money. Dad showed me the bill.

There was no coddling at the Catholic hospital. The arm was put in a hot, heavy cast, which was taken off six weeks later. When it was removed, there were angry-looking inch-high blisters inside the elbow. A nun held my arm while another nun ripped the blisters open and cleaned out the wound with alcohol. I was told not to cry, so I didn't. I escaped a rigorous Catholic upbringing because my Mom's family was, to put it mildly, not enthusiastic about the Pope. But I knew not to mess with the Sisters of St. Francis of Perpetual Adoration.

There was one advantage of having the heavy cast on my arm. The school bully when I was in 5th Grade pushed me around a lot. Miss Mace (I'm not making this up) was our 110-year old teacher who favored long black dresses. She did not particularly like me but she hated James McDonald, a fat, obnoxious brat who was a head taller than the other kids. She saw me catch him across the nose with the elbow of the cast and put him, bleeding, squarely on his ass. She turned her back.

Playgrounds were different in those days. I can't imagine Miss Mace cancelling recess because her little dears might get cold.

Dr. John Reisert was my sixth grade teacher. I might have been the first student he ever had. He was a local high school graduate who became a prominent community leader and educator and a member of the New Albany High School Hall of Fame. He asked me to cut his grass as part of the lawn business that I had. A firm teacher, he and his wife Carolyn were kind and understanding people. John Reisert was one of those teachers that kids remember in their later years. He was the kind of role model that schools, and boys everywhere, desperately need today. He chose me as leader of the grade school patrol. I hope that some of his character and values rubbed off on me. A bonus is that we later became good friends as adults and fellow educators.

The adults that influenced me most were serious professionals who also had a wicked sense of humor. As I grew up, I began to understand that this was a trait of bright people. John Reisert tells a story of the time when he was principal of an elementary school. He and another friend Jack Seville, a future boss of mine, were at a shelter near John's school. Scrawled on the building was "Mister Reisert eats shit." Jack remarked: "what a compliment! No one calls me mister!"

Dad remarried soon after Mom died. His new wife was the widow of a fellow railroader with two children who had been placed temporarily in an orphanage. Some of Dad's kids did not accept this marriage, but he was Old School and did not ask their opinion. A baby daughter soon appeared. Sisters and brothers in their teens left home and got married. The older siblings distanced themselves from the new family. Life went on.

Role Models and life lessons in The Fifties

> *"It takes a village to raise a child*
> *African Proverb*

The African proverb above, which contains much wisdom, has been corrupted to claim that families are not critical to American culture and that "society" and government must fill a void left by the failure of the

American family to do its job. This is exactly wrong. The family is the very heart of the American Village and family values are at the center of social values. But the family is not alone in

America, and it should not be. Neighborhoods, churches, and communities are also important. In my case, a few American individuals, each quite different from the other, emerged from the community to have a profound impact on my life. Each represents facets of America in the Fifties. In addition to others mentioned here, they, and the prototypical Working Man, my Dad, provided insights into the values and philosophies of middle America that are shared in this book.

Unc

"From the day you are born 'till you ride in a hearse,
there ain't nothin' so bad it can't get worse"
John Denny, aka "Unc"

Neighbors took a special interest in me in the Fifties. I had mowed the lawn of Mildred and John Denny since shortly after losing my mother. John Denny, "Unc" to everyone, was Vice-President of a machine manufacturing plant in Louisville that he had helped to build and that had prospered. Unc was one of those American geniuses that made this country an industrial behemoth. After the war, the boss bought him a big black Cadillac that only barely fit into the garage at his home on Lake Street, a block from where Dr. Voyles delivered Kime babies.

Unc could make anything and could see the way to fix things before normal people understood why they were broken. He was not cut out to manage people; especially the ungrateful union-directed workers that began to destroy U.S. productivity in the Fifties. He did his duty, grappling gamely with the unions from Monday through Friday. Sadly, he drank on weekends.

Unc was actually two people. I never had a conversation with him during the week even though I saw him often. He would come home at exactly the same time every day, sit down alone to a meal always ready for him and say not a word. I quickly learned not to be there then. On the weekend, Unc became the fishing, turkey shooting, camping, and canoeing outdoorsman that everyone loved and, hopefully, remembers. His generosity knew no bounds.

He would take a child who cut his grass to a turkey shoot, pay the dollar for every shot and, when a turkey was won, give the turkey to the railroader's family on the next block. Sometimes, after too much bourbon, he won when he could barely hold his 16-gauge shotgun up to fire it. But he remembered the birthdays of old people from his youth no one else seemed to know, who were living in remote places sometimes difficult to find. He would bring flowers and unabashedly offer a few dollars. Sometimes, well before state law would allow it, I got to drive home.

In 1953, seven-year-old Denny Cox, Unc's nephew, came to live with Unc and Aunt Mil. Denny had lost both his parents in a year. I had cut his family's grass for a while and knew "Little Denny," as he was known then. About 1955 Unc bought a cabin and several acres on Blue River in Indiana. These events were very important in my life.

Virtually every weekend was spent at camp on Blue River where work and fun flowed freely together. It was not easy. Unc insisted that the place be kept well, and that meant long hours cutting grass, chopping wood, or doing anything else that needed doing. Denny and I cooked and cleaned. If equipment needed to be operated or fixed, we learned how to do it. We laid tiles on the cabin floor, made one hell of a mess of it, and got to clean it up. When I broke my left hand, I learned to chop wood with one arm.

Rowboats, canoes, and fishing gear were always at hand. We knew every rock in Blue River for miles, and we frequently would carry a canoe miles upstream and float for hours through rapids and fish as the Blue River fell toward the Ohio.

We learned how guns and culture were intertwined. We would hunt frogs all night and eat them before noon. We had to do all these things right. No discussions: just learn the right way and do it. Unc's way was the right way. If he disapproved, he was not subtle about it. If he liked what you did, it was high praise indeed. By the way, the right way to cook bacon and eggs is to rise before sunup, get a fire under an iron skillet as low as possible, and turn the bacon in slow motion, zombie-like, for two hours. No talking. It has to be thick-sliced bacon from deep in Kentucky or West Virginia. When it is golden brown and stiff as a board, pull it out. (There is a 15-second window.) Eggs are cooked to order in the bacon grease and served with toast and slabs of creamery butter. Coffee has to have been cooking slowly until it is almost no longer in liquid state.

The Blue River Valley in Southern Indiana is quintessential America. It flows through farmland settled by immigrants and cherished by families that gave their lives to working the land. They sent their sons to war for America. Denny Cox served for years on the Blue River Commission that worked hard to keep the river unspoiled. These were Constructive Environmentalists, like Lady Bird Johnson, who really cared about America and didn't have to be angry about it.

Unc's Camp on Blue River   *Unc - on a weekend*

Author's photos

Aunt Mil

Unc was not an easy character to live with, but he was incredibly lucky: he married Mildred McKinley, who was quite a character herself. A flapper in the Roaring Twenties who had had a brief marriage to a gambler, she somehow turned into a perfect fit for the mercurial and temperamental Unc. She made him exactly the home he wanted without yielding one whit of her own remarkable personality. If Unc wanted to cook a possum, she made it into a delicious dish. If he said something stupid, she told him it was stupid.

It would be tempting to say that Mildred Denny was a closet Womens' Libber, but as I grew up, I realized that she was a prototypical American Libertarian. She was no crazy Jane-One-Note like Kate Millett, and she would have rejected the radical feminists who proclaimed that "There is no God and Mary was his mother!" She would have hated the rabble-rousers in the National Organization of Women. Aunt Mil, as she was universally known, thought *everyone* should be free. And she liked guys. Ninety pounds soaking wet, she could arm-wrestle most of them to the ground.

She also thought that work was important, and she was a stickler for getting things right. Her lawn and gardens were a source of pride to her, and she insisted on good work. Her gutters needed cleaning, her porch needed mopping, and sometimes her carpet needed vacuuming. She did not distinguish between girl jobs and boy jobs. There was always something to do. She paid well and was quick to compliment. Her praise was worth the effort.

Aunt Mil had a huge following. This was not visible to the casual observer, because she rarely left home. People came to her. She held court on Lake Street. Her opinions were heeded, and she was never found short of opinions. The remarkable thing is that this lady, with no particular formal education or unusual amount of experience, knew stuff! She not only was incredibly well informed, she made sense of what she knew, and she did it with a sense of humor and sometimes with a little profanity. She was no bully. If you had an argument, she would hear it. If you disagreed with her, she could deal with it. No subject was out of bounds. She suffered no fools of any age but was kind to everyone. She served up her views with large portions of cakes, pies, and huge dollops of ice cream.

She did not make distinctions between kids and adults. In Aunt Mil's court, all were equal. Whether in a card game or a discussion, you had to hold up your end. You could win or get crushed. Aunt Mil could count cards, so she was much sought after as a partner in Euchre or Pinochle, which were played for blood at her kitchen table. She spent hours with this writer at cribbage and scrabble, often after a trip to the grocery store or some other chore for her. She gave no quarter and did not permit dictionaries at a scrabble game except to prove you were right. It was many games before I registered a win. Aunt Mil was a voracious reader and belonged to the Book of the Month Club. I was given books as she completed them. In a few days, she would start to ask questions and probe for my opinions about what I had read. Again, no themes were out of bounds, and she hated sloppy thinking.

Almost every day, I would make a run to the little neighborhood grocery for Aunt Mil. I was fond of the cheddar cheese there. She let me get a 5-cent slice with her groceries until it became impossible to slice it that thin. Then she allowed a 10-cent slice. It did not occur to me until much later that Aunt Mil did not need groceries every day, and that a trip to the grocery to buy a tomato or a loaf of bread did not always make sense. I am sure that she invented jobs for me to do.

Mil's thoughtfulness and generosity extended well into my youth. She had an old suit of Unc's tailored to fit me so I could dress for some events. She replaced my old $125 car, a 1947 Olds that was totaled by a drunk driver running a stop sign when taking Unc to the ice cream store. When the used '54 Chevy failed, she insisted that I get a '59 Chevy that Unc had spotted. This generosity made college possible. Without wheels, we could not have afforded to attend U of L and live cheaply in Indiana. She knew that. I will be grateful forever.

Later, after my sister, Lila, died suddenly at age 28 and left two children, Mil understood immediately when this 25 year-old Lieutenant Junior Grade went to court to gain custody. Home ownership was needed to win custody. Sitting at her modest kitchen table, she produced 15 crisp $100 bills, a fortune to me, for a down payment. We paid her back, but she did not ask us to.

Miss Alma

"I call a spade a spade, unless I step on one in the garden"
Miss Alma Orme

Next door to Unc and Aunt Mil on Lake Street was Miss Alma Orme, an Old Maid right out of the stereotypes of Old Maids. Miss Alma had moved to her tiny house after her mother, with whom she had lived her entire life, died. She moved the remains of her dog, Brownie, with her and placed him in the back yard. Miss Alma knew exactly what she wanted and what she believed. No compromises. One thing she wanted was a perfect yard, and she wanted it cheap. I was a 13-year-old kid who worked cheap. Unfortunately, her yard was full of the toughest crabgrass in Indiana, and power mowers were expensive. Her lawn was a two-day, two-dollar deal. She could not be satisfied. No amount of trimming was enough. She was the kind of demanding old lady that drove kids nuts.

Somehow, all of that did not seem to matter. She loved my dog, Rex, a free spirit with a police record. And, in spite of unrelenting criticism of my lawn work, she decided that I was worth her time. Miss Alma liked to talk, and she loved to argue. Surprisingly, she was well informed and up to date on politics and social issues. The lady had a mind like a steel trap. She knew her history, and was no slouch on physics and math.

Miss Alma would wait to eat her lunch until I showed up, put on a couple of little steaks, fix us some coffee, sit down, and start a discussion over something in the current news. She could play Devil's Advocate pretty well, but I could usually tell what she really thought. I was often startled to hear her views, being from a Roosevelt household. She thought FDR was a Communist. It must be noted that she was not alone: not all older working Americans, many of whom revered the postwar Twenties, were enamored of the socialist trends of the Thirties.

Miss Alma struggled to comprehend a world that she could see changing before her eyes. Elvis was evil. Short shorts were an abomination.

21

Forced busing for racial integration was evil. Welfare was for deadbeats. But, believe it or not, she had a softer, more reasonable side. I came to understand that this side of her was a reflection of a Libertarian, "rugged individualism" strain in her thinking. She was bothered by arguments that America did not always live up to its philosophy. Equality and liberty meant a lot to her. She was a complicated lady.

To be around Miss Alma was to be branded with 1950s images. You could ignore them or cover them up, but they were there as reminders of where you came from. There were, to be sure, some sinister images that reflected the intolerance and narrow-minded arrogance and sanctimony of her generation, which had worked its way through wars and depression. Our conversations sometimes sounded like an early version of Archie Bunker and the Meathead. But Miss Alma also reflected images of how to behave, of right and wrong, and of common decency. She feared God but loved Perry Mason. She seemed to judge the world by the rectitude of Perry Mason, Dragnet, and Dr. Marcus Welby.

Miss Alma said she wanted to die quickly and, like with many things, God saw it her way. She dropped dead of a heart attack in 1967 when I was in the Atlantic serving as Senior Watch Officer and Navigator in a submarine. I missed her funeral and I had trouble finding her grave. She was buried with her mother and her name had been graved on the back of the stone. It saved her some money.

Miss Alma had been proud of me, though she balked at some of my choices in life. I was serious about a girl too early, but she pried a small diamond from a golden pendant that she treasured for a willful teenager to use in an engagement ring. (Her own one true love had jilted her at about the same age.) I committed to adopting kids at age 25, too early and unwise in her view, but she left her best furniture, china and silverware for my family to enjoy.

Miss Alma was bereft of motherly instincts so I was not like a son to her. I was her student, and she was grateful to an extent that only dog lovers can comprehend for the company of Rex, who lies next to Brownie in her back yard.

Lessons Learned

I learned some important All-American lessons in junior high school. Mr. Willman, about whom there is more in this book, introduced me to science and made me care about it. I liked shop class, and I thought history was interesting. I can still recite Lincoln's Gettysburg Address.

I learned that you couldn't just blurt out the truth. I failed music in the seventh grade, not because I have never understood music, but because I called the 24-year-old teacher an old bitch. (She slept around, unforgivable then, and it was not a secret.) The Principal gave me a good chewing out. She was soon fired for getting pregnant out of wedlock, which was frowned upon in those days. At 8th grade graduation, the principal pulled me aside and said: "She *was* an old bitch!"

A math teacher, Mr. Milo Eiche, was the faculty member responsible for the Patrol Boys, who were student street-crossing guards before it was decided, probably by lawyers, that this awesome responsibility had to be in the hands of adults. He had selected me as Captain, and I got to wear a gold badge. I was responsible for "deploying" my troops each morning to their respective corners.

One morning Mr. Eiche, a 300-pound fellow who had little trouble with control of his class, had his long paddle lying on his desk. It had three holes drilled in it for special effect. The other boys were admiring it and, in one of those teenage moments when the mouth is engaged before the brain, I said it did not scare me. Mr. Eiche said: "OK, I'll trade you swats." There was no place to hide. He bent over, exposing an enormous expanse of rear end. I hit him as hard as I could. He grinned. I bent over and I think my feet left the ground. Tears welled up, so I turned away from the other boys as I declared that it did not hurt at all.

Mr. Eiche became assistant principal and school disciplinarian. We had some 16-year-old thugs in junior high school who were a head taller and 70 pounds heavier than I was, but Milo Eiche had to use the paddle infrequently. The word was out.

I thought about Mr. Eiche later as I studied game strategy in military policy, especially the concept of deterrence. It did not matter how powerful you were if the other guy could end the game and looked like he was willing to do it.

It was a good life, and a good time to be growing up. We did not know what "helicopter parents" were. Kids walked a mile to school across busy streets. We played in creeks, ponds and even swamps. We divided up into teams and had wars where the weapons were cattails used to hit our enemies. No one supervised fireworks on the 4th of July. We made carbide "bombs." BB guns and pellet guns were everywhere. My brothers and I took turns shooting each other with BB rifles in the back, moving ever closer until it hurt too much to continue. (The ear and the back of the neck were favorite targets.) I was thrown out of the local theater for having a BB pistol. No one even thought about calling the cops.

Of course, it is a different America today where criminals outgun the police and where victimhood has been extended to violators of the law, especially if they are in a "protected class." The nature of big cities, coupled with this dubious twist based on celebration of "diversity," makes it sensible to consider control of guns in large population centers. We probably need to consider what can be done to control criminals with guns without violating the essence of the Founding Fathers' concern that non-criminals have the ability to confront tyranny. I wish I knew the answer.

In any case, I accept the fact that a boy cannot carry a BB pistol around these days. There are other such things that no longer will fly, like carbide bombs and cattail fights, but this admission of reasonable limitations on kids' behavior does not apply to the range of spying and control now exercised by helicopter parents.

The world was not totally different when I was a kid. We dealt with the dark side of society without 24-hour news coverage and without making the lunatics look like they were in the mainstream of life. We did not allow the media to legitimize sociopaths, make a meal out of every incident, and blow any incident out of proportion if race or gender can be said to be a factor. There were sexual predators and all kinds of criminals in our days, too. Cavemen had to deal with deviants from social norms.

Homosexuality was no more or less present then than now, but we dealt with it differently. I recall a number of situations where boys exposed themselves and invited younger boys to "play." One kid who put needles in his penis joined the Air Force and made Sergeant! One big, fat, sad boy in the neighborhood tried at every opportunity to cop a feel of other guys, including me. It was weird, but kids learned to deal with such situations. I do not remember a specific lecture to watch out for predatory sexual behavior, but we all knew what was normal and what was not. Remember, this was in a world where we celebrated social norms and not deviations from those norms. So, we were wary of those who deviated from the norms. By the way, though some were abused, I do not think they were as much abused as they were tolerated as part of reality.

In today's America of a third of a billion souls harbors greater risk to children from social misfits than when I was growing up. Modern communications magnifies that danger because children are more accessible and vulnerable. It is necessary to be more vigilant than we were. It is also true that society has grown more tolerant of deviations from social norms than in decades past.

The problem is that many now celebrate rather than tolerate deviations. A lecture to children about avoiding precisely what the ACLU celebrates and defends is necessary. Good luck at making the lecture stick! It must be repeated over and over again because avoiding the deviants does not jibe with the TV, the movies, and the video games. No wonder kids get lured in by freaks on the internet. They have been told that social misfits are OK, and that to say they are not OK is to be homophobic, intolerant, or just plain stupid.

In the 1950s, we were expected to be knowledgeable of right and wrong based on clearly understood, and reasonably unambiguous, social norms. You were expected to be wary of deviations from acceptable behavior and from right and wrong. You were expected to be independent in

Steve Kime

handling yourself at fairly young age without constant supervision. What was considered normal, unsupervised time on your own recognizance might be considered child neglect today in the face of the tolerance we have for social deviance. You were supposed to be able to walk around in town and make the right judgments about the behaviors you encountered. Rules, guided by accepted mainstream thinking, were followed. It was probably true that deviations from mainstream thinking got suppressed, but it worked reasonably well and neighborhoods were safe. Deviants from social norms, we are now told, got their feelings hurt.

Families supported the rules. If Dad, and there were lots of Dads in those days, had to go to school or to the police station, it was to support the rules and get *you* straightened out, not the cops or the teachers. For kids raised with these expectations and in these circumstances, it made perfect sense to say that, if you were old enough to fight for your country, you were old enough to vote.

No one thought that you would be living at home after you were able to vote.

Chapter III
Sputnik and School Days

While coping with childhood, the Berlin Airlift was barely noticed. We were, after all, just kids doing the things kids do. Still, it was impossible even for children to be insulated from a new, global awareness and some high international drama. Mainstream America is more insular in outlook than much of humanity, but American horizons did get wider after the war.

Global issues were very much on the public mind when the Cold War began, mass communications were dawning, and a new global order was evolving. My generation, at a very young age, was immersed in the news. We may have been the first "global" generation that went through childhood, puberty, and early adulthood conversant with history as it took place. We all noticed that old Harry Truman was no pushover and his "buck stops here" talk changed minds about him.

The Korean War made a big impression. General MacArthur's arrogance and firing, and the danger of more A-bombs in Asia, were big news. We knew about the Rosenbergs and their execution for treason for passing nuclear secrets.

America in the late 1950s began to be challenged by unrest at home and got a comeuppance from abroad. The Soviet Union shook the confidence of an America that was beginning to feel omnipotent. Sputnik changed the emerging Cold War from an old-fashioned ideological dispute into a struggle between intercontinental nuclear superpowers. It was seen as a dead serious, zero-sum game. We had an enemy. America, historically safe between two oceans, was feeling vulnerable.

"Duck and Cover" messages had kids crawling under their desks. Wags of our generation had a more graphic message: "assume the fetal position, put your head between your legs, and kiss your ass good-bye!"

High school students had a mission. The whole country had a mission. We needed to pull up our socks and quit studying basket weaving! Engineering was the rage. For all the colossal industrial strength that America had come to represent, we were about to be overtaken! A Soviet hydrogen bomb was added to the Russian Bear's rocket capability. These were intense concerns for my generation, at a time when our only major concern should have been the Prom.

My own high school career was mixed. In their wisdom, school bureaucrats vectored me to general math and vocational studies. In spite of the national attention to Sputnik, there was a strong social element in "counseling" in those days: lots of poor kids filled the general math, "truckers' English" and shop classes. I aced the math course, which had more future felons than mathematicians in it. I was sloppy in the drafting course but excelled in woodshop. I did not take books home until my senior year when I met Wilma, valedictorian of the class behind mine, and felt I needed to do it. We were in chemistry class together. She got an "A" and I squeaked out a "B."

I was no standout in extracurricular activities either. In our yearbook under "activities," it says "none." So, it is was no surprise to me that high school counselors did not push me to try to go to college. Remember, in those days there was no illusion that every kid should go to college. There was recognition of the reality that college is not for everyone and that somebody had to actually work. I looked like a worker.

It did not occur to me that I was wasting my time, but it did occur to

Mr. Willman, who had been my science teacher in eighth grade and was now at New Albany High School. Robert Willman had been an Army Captain during the war, and was a charter member of The Greatest Generation. He had gone to college on the GI Bill, become a teacher, and was a patriot.

By the way, he, and especially his wife, Dixie, were unapologetic, active Liberals and Democrats. Dixie bordered on being a radical Progressive in a decidedly less than radical environment. I genuinely liked and respected both of them for their convictions. Dixie and I had a heated political discussion that began in the Fifties when I was a teenager, and ran until both she and Bob died in 2010. I never got the best of her, and I learned something very important: you can disagree with someone and still like them.

Mr. Willman was a less vociferous liberal than Dixie,

but definitely a person of liberal leaning. Interestingly, this did not show in his U. S. Government course in which I learned more about the American Presidency than anywhere else. The man showed that the color of one's politics did not have to get in the way of the truth. He was a patriot.

Captain and Dixie Willman
of The Greatest Generation

Author's photo

Bob Willman was one of the first of a very few teachers inducted into the New Albany High School Hall of Fame, which included only a handful of honorees in over a hundred years of history.

Mr. Willman had seen several children of my family go through school, get married before age 18, and get a job. He pulled me aside and read me the riot act in my sophomore year. He was harsh with the counselors and forced a change in my curriculum. I refused to give up woodshop (Unc approved), but Mr. Willman insisted that I cram in all the math, English and science the school offered in my remaining two and one-half years. I did, and he checked to be sure that I did.

In those years, resume padding for children was not as common as it is now. I had to work, and there was no one to goad me into frivolous extracurricular "activities" in order to make me appear well rounded. The real world prevailed for young men of my station in life. Mr. Willman saw to it that I was hired by the Parks Department for summer jobs and after-school work. I had maintained a lawn cutting business of several dozen households since before junior high school, so I earned a respectable amount of money in my teens.

In the future, it became painfully obvious that my military bearing was unimpressive and my marching was awful. This ineptitude was matched by a total inability to dance. Deep down, I just could not see the point of either marching or dancing, and still don't. You don't get anywhere. This probably indicates some important character flaw, but I can't figure out what it is. In any case, this flaw put an end to an early infatuation with a pretty girl who lived in a mansion in Silver Hills.

Silver Hills was an area atop little hills overlooking New Albany. It was a prestigious place to live and some mansions were built there for captains of local industry who did not choose to live in the stately mansions below on Main Street. Inevitably, as the boom times passed, parts of Silver Hills were developed in the twentieth century for those who were not the barons of the 19th Century, but were still plenty rich by working folks' standards. In my day, the "mansions" were modern four- and five-bedroom ranch houses. (They look smaller now.) White-collar people with well-paying jobs in Louisville dwelt there. This was Shangri-La to the blue-collar folks who labored below. Nancy lived there.

She asked me if I wanted to go to one of the after-school "sock-hops" with her. I said I would, but had never danced. To the girl's credit, she offered to give me a dancing lesson. I drove a borrowed clunker up the hill. Her father met me and looked as skeptical of me as he was about my brother's 1936 Oldsmobile parked in his driveway. Maybe it was feeling as self-conscious as I was. I was sure that Nancy's father bought her sweaters for Christmas that cost more than all the clothes I owned plus the car I drove up in. "Dancing" was a disaster. Nancy was courteous and sweet about it, but there was just no way that I could do anything but the most rudimentary waltz steps. We were "friends" afterward. Her dad must have breathed a huge sigh of relief. The '36 Olds may have deposited a little pool of oil in the driveway.

The coaches did not bother with poorer kids unless they had serious athletic talent, but they had to tolerate us in gym. Once, when playing basketball in gym, I was reintroduced to health care for blue-collar families. We were playing basketball, which is a blood sport in Indiana even in gym class. I was at the top of the key guarding a kid with my arm stretched out and was not looking when

the ball was hurled at about the speed of sound toward me. The ball caught the four fingers on my left hand extended outward and drove bones through the back of my hand.

In shock, it did not hurt as much as it sounds like it should, but it was a terrible sight. The coach, with a laconic "Son, I think it is broken," had someone take me to the tender mercies of the Catholic hospital nearby – the home of the nuns that had removed my blisters a few years ago. There was no discussion of tendons, future mobility, or the other details that would be routine today when the bill can be sent to health plans or the taxpayers. The bones were pulled back into place, a compress taped there for a while, and a tight cast applied. Six weeks later, it was removed.

I would wear a scar for the rest of my life where the bones had protruded, and I would never be able to completely close that hand. The Navy never detected the injury, and I never talked about it with anyone until after I was retired. At Navy physical exams, it was not my hand that got probed and squeezed. I could handle tools and equipment, rig a submarine for dive, play Ping-Pong well enough to win a tournament at Harvard's NROTC Unit, and played tennis, badly, at The National War College. After retirement, I discovered that, because the condition had worsened with age, I had to play golf one-handed.

Work

In high school I learned how to work, and not just for myself. Jack Seville, a shop teacher whose leadership skills quickly made him principal of a big middle school, patiently taught me, at 16, to tackle hard jobs and finish them. As a summer job, Jack supervised construction at the Department of Parks. He built roads and bridges with high school kids like me as minimum wage (90 cents and hour) laborers. We were not a bright or disciplined labor force, but he was a leader of the kind I would later learn to appreciate in military service. We dug bridge abutments in what was an open sewer. We applied creosote in blazing sun. We learned to look at plans on paper and execute them in wood and concrete. I never heard Jack Seville raise his voice. He jumped into the mud where a footing would be dug and showed us what to do. Jack led by example.

During the winter, Mr. Willman saw to it that I got some odd jobs. One of his duties was to manage the high school's audio-visual program and radio station, at the time the most powerful student-operated FM station in the country. He helped me prepare for the test to earn the license of a 3rd Class Radiotelephone Operator, and I knew how to operate the radio station. I was dispatched to other classrooms to show films. Bob Willman was a dedicated Rotary member and he got me the gig as projector operator when Rotary had films to show. I got $10, a nice sum for easy work, and I met the movers and shakers of our little town. Mr. Willman almost burst with pride years later when he introduced me as Rotary's speaker for a meeting.

I worked some summer months for Mr. Franks, the maintenance boss of county parks who had been a truck driver and operator of a grading machine for highway construction. His first name to a boy like me was "Mister." This unassuming man in his sixties taught me to get things done on a shoestring. He, like my brother Junior, could fix anything, or make something if it did not exist. These were essential skills for future submariner.

There are too many stories about Mr. Franks to tell them all. I will never forget his telling me to be very careful with the vicious Gravely mowing machine that tended to run away from skinny kids and even turn around and come after them. I lit the monster off and promptly hit a stump, saw it turn around, and abandoned the area while it ran into the sewer-fed creek. It did not stop running but just sat there churning up turds and God knows what else. Mr. Franks, who was eating a sandwich, did not look surprised. He just told me to wade in when it ran out of gas and finish the job. To my surprise, he did not hang around to supervise. He figured I had learned the lesson. He was right.

Mr. Franks had me construct horseshoe courts. He left it to me to get the dimensions right. When I was done, he told me to go to the local foundry and get some clay that had been used in pouring molds. By the way, Mr. Franks never asked if you knew how to drive a dump truck, tractor, or anything else. He just assumed that you could do it or would figure it out. He did tell me not to put too much clay in the old truck because the tires were paper-thin. Being 16, I did not ask how much was too much, and when I was at the foundry it seemed to make sense to get it all in one trip. The back bumper of the old Ford truck dragged the ground as I pulled away, and the hood thrust ominously up in front of me.

I got about six blocks and a tire blew. As I got out of the truck, two of the three remaining tires blew. Cell phones, like Dick Tracy's wrist radio, did not exist, so I hoofed it the mile to Mr. Frank's office. He did not bat an eye. He armed me with a jack and one good tire and told me to fix it. I rolled the tire and carried the jack back to the truck. I unloaded all the clay in a pile, rolled two of the tires to a gas station for repair, and hand-shoveled the clay back into the truck. It took two truckloads and hours that were never reflected in my paycheck. No matter how quietly Mr. Franks gave instructions after that, I listened carefully.

I was responsible one summer to get to the tennis courts early in the morning and wet them down and roll them before other kids got there to play. Some of these tennis players were acquaintances and classmates. I did not resent this. I reflect on it now as a product of the time when the Working Man knew his place. This unpleasant observation is perhaps a key to understanding the time. Everyone was supposed to know his place. This is, of course, contrary to absolutist images of democracy, and it does not comport with militant notions of social equality that came into vogue later in our history, but it was what it was in my day in the Fifties. A half-century later, in 2007, New Albany High School, after

150 years of graduates, inducted the inaugural class of the NAHS Hall of Fame. One of the young men who played tennis on those courts was among the seven graduates inducted, but so was I.

One other work experience taught me a lot. Since I had mangled my hand in a basketball game, the local Goodwill Store manager, who had met me at Rotary, declared me as handicapped and hired me to drive the collections truck. He said this exaggeration enabled him to have someone who understood his directions, and that was probably true. The folks he had were all willing, good-natured, and

even sweet, but were mostly retarded citizens who needed a paycheck. I am glad I knew them, and I learned much from working with them. I also got to meet quite a few old people who had lost spouses or parents and who were cleaning out attics, garages and houses. I learned how to move heavy furniture and pianos but I learned some things about people, too. There were some great stories in that job, and a terrific look at the past as represented by the stuff that is left when people die. I still have old tools given to me by survivors of past times.

In this day of computer games, smart phones, and Facebook, I am sad for young people who do not get to do something like dig a bridge footing in a sewer-fed creek or clean out an attic. Believe it or not, you learn something when you get into the mess, you learn something while you are in the mess, and you learn something when you wash it off. It is reasonable to worry that future decision makers could be computer-literate, intellectual and physical softies who have never worked alongside people that were actually *doing* something.

New Family

> *Happy families are all alike.*
> *Leo Tolstoy*

The most important thing that happened to me in High School happened in Doc Rose's chemistry class. It was powerful chemistry. I was 16 and a senior when Wilma Snook, a junior and valedictorian of her class, strolled into class with her ponytail. I was a kid who rolled the tennis courts so the popular, rich kids could play tennis. I could not believe my luck when she accepted a date to go to the old Grand Theater in New Albany for a movie. It turned out that she was not rich either, but everybody knew her.

We borrowed old cars from family and changed flat tires and ran out of gas like youngsters all over America. We walked a lot. We shared a 26-cent butterscotch sundae because we could not afford two of them. In other words, we were blessed with the kind of innocent, small town romance that, sadly, kids do not enjoy these days. Remarkably, she is still here over 50 years later. Like many high school kids in Indiana in the Fifties, we considered marriage in the near future, but events intervened.

Wilma Snook came with family. This was Middle America in the Fifties, and family was the anchor of American culture. I disdain those that treat this fact with contempt today. They are fools who do not recognize in the attack on the American Family the seeds of their own culture's destruction.

My generation came to accept tolerance of many deviations from the mainstream of American culture that is steeped in the family and family values. We have accepted those who think, look, and act differently from us. Most of us, however, never succumbed to the bizarre notion that deviations from the mainstream of American culture can be allowed to *replace* mainstream core values, like the centrality of family, in some misguided Progressive idea of social evolution. We have had to endure charges of misogyny, homophobia, and racism for insisting that the centrality of family values is crucial to maintaining our great country. If this is merely old fashioned, and the family is to be dumped in the ashcan of history to satisfy those at the fringes of our society, then I am grateful that I grew up in America when I did.

Wilma's mother and father were special embodiments of family. Carl Thomas Snook was a wiry little guy who carried one of those wooden toolboxes around looking for work in the Depression. I still have that toolbox. He had been a bellhop at the old Brown Hotel in Louisville as a boy. School was not for all the children in his family, just as it was not for all the children in my father's family. My first real encounter with him was when I was walking to Wilma's house and found Mr. Snook in his side yard. He was digging up and clearing the sewer pipe that ran from his basement, under a walk, and into the main line at the street. It was a dirty, sweaty job. He could not move one big piece of sidewalk. Both Dad and Unc had taught me never to stand and watch another man, especially an older man, work, so I stripped off my T-shirt and grabbed one side of the chunk of concrete. We finished the job a couple of hours later. He became a lifelong friend who really did mean *mi casa es su casa.* He did not have much, but it was mine if I wanted it. It went both ways. Carl Snook was a terrific grandfather to our kids and a model of decent, honest America. He was Salt of the Earth.

Alberta Snook adopted me as a son. She never said so, but she did. During my long engagement to Wilma and during my college years, she was a mother to both of us. The lady worked until 9 PM at a clothing and fabric store. We would pick her up after school and work, and she would make a hot supper. Alberta never missed a grandchild's birthday. She gave of the most important thing of all: her time. Her presence exuded family, and we were blessed to have her with us until age 92.

Opportunity Knocks

Mr. Willman discovered in my senior year that I had not taken the College Boards, the SATs of that time, because there was a $25 fee. He was furious that counselors had let this happen. Students who played tennis tended to get the college counseling in those days. Mr. Willman insisted that I take the NROTC test, the only option still available. It was free. I took the test and did fine. There were interviews scheduled with Naval Officers.

Mr. Willman asked me if I knew what to expect. I had no clue what an officer was. He told me to appear the next day for an "interview" in the counselor's office. I sauntered in the next day in jeans and tennis shoes with holes in them. Mr. Willman stood up from behind a desk and said, "Get out! Come back tomorrow like a gentleman and be prepared to act like one." I was shocked and embarrassed. Aunt Mil knew what to do.

The next day I showed up in borrowed shoes and clean pants. I knocked at the door and he waved me to sit down. He asked me my name and I screwed up again. He was nicer this time and instructed me that he would be addressed as "Sir." I said, "OK" and he glared at me. I said,

"Yes Sir," and he nodded. It took about an hour, but he got the job done. So did I. In a couple of weeks, a Navy Lieutenant interviewed me, and so did an older man who I think was a retired officer. I wore the suit that Aunt Mil had tailored to fit me.

I had never seen a body of water bigger than the Ohio River and had no clue what I was getting into. I had not even thought about college or a professional career. I had been raised to expect a life of work somewhere nearby. But something very important was happening to me. The Navy, in spite of the "none" under "activities," offered me a full NROTC scholarship.

Wilma Snook and I got serious about one another and talk of the future was in order. This was not unusual for a senior in high school in those days. Wilma had a year left in high school. Some sort of direction needed to be set. College at the University of Louisville (U of L) made sense. The NROTC Scholarship would not cover everything, but books, tuition and the munificent sum of $50 a month made it possible, with jobs, for Wilma and me to go to college. U of L accepted me with advanced standing in some classes, including Biology and Chemistry, vindicating me for the "B" I got in Doc Rose's high school class.

Wilma Snook and I announced that we were engaged and would be married after I graduated from U of L. Skeptics abounded. We would prove them wrong.

Wilma Snook and Steve Kime in 1958
author's photo

Chapter IV
Worldviews:
Perspectives rooted in boyhood

"May you live in interesting times"
Chinese Curse

Americanism and modern political philosophy

Looking back over the decades, it is clear to me that the things I learned in boyhood and the perspectives taken to college were at least as important to my education as the things learned and the perspectives developed in higher education. This includes college at The University of Louisville and at Harvard, Submarine School, the Foreign Service Institute and The National War College. This is not to diminish those superb institutions where I was exposed to incredible teachers and mountains of information. It is, rather, to emphasize the powerful influence that full immersion in Americana had on me. It is why this chapter of this book, which reflects perspectives gained before higher education, was written.

Later in this Story I will write about my good fortune to attend Harvard University as a junior officer. At this point it is worthwhile to note the enormous influence of Professor Louis Hartz, my Harvard mentor in the study of modern political philosophy, on me and many other scholars of American thought and history. This great teacher and scholar wrote the classical study of American political thought: *The Liberal Tradition in America* (1955).

Professor Hartz attributed American political views to the way the country was settled and to the nature of the people who settled it. He emphasized the liberal orientation of the original settlers escaping from Europe and their general acceptance of the leading Enlightenment philosopher, John Locke (1632-1704). Hartz noted that Americanism lacked the feudal, conservative history that Europeans had to overcome,

38

and was practically devoid of ideology. The American pioneers' efforts to settle a vast frontier was the primary factor in forming the American worldview and its liberal focus on the individual.

Of course, I had no clue about Hartz or Locke as a boy in Indiana. I mention them here because, when I heard the lectures of Louis Hartz, they sounded like intellectual versions of ideas that I had heard all my life. Hartz was a product of Ohio and Nebraska before attending Harvard and being recognized for his genius. Indeed, the Founding Fathers were deeply steeped in the thinking of the Enlightenment philosophers, and the founding documents of America reflect that. The boy who learned to recite the Gettysburg Address in seventh grade and studied the Constitution and all the presidencies in high school was a rapt student of the gifted philosopher and lecturer, Louis Hartz.

The term "liberal" has been distorted by contemporary politics, which juxtaposes leftist ("liberal") politics and rightist ("conservative") politics. To worsen the distortion, the media, and many politicians and demagogues, do their best to confuse the meaning of both terms!

Liberalism is in fact a doctrine that emphasizes individual rights and freedoms. Liberalism emerged in the Enlightenment as a reaction to the notion of sovereignty based on religion and to the war and chaos wrought by God-ordained kings and queens. Government in democracy -- sovereign power -- comes only from the consent of the governed. Democrats, Republicans and Libertarians are all "liberals," who base their thinking on individual liberty and limited representative government. (Progressives and leftists will hate this statement, which attests to its validity.)

Philosophy of the Working Man

As the war drew to a close, we learned that President Roosevelt died and a fellow named Harry Truman, who we thought could not possibly be up to the job, took over. The war had masked the pro-union, near-Socialist proclivities that had been common in the Thirties and thrived among the unions, including The Brotherhood of Railroad Trainmen.

Martin Anthony Kime, my dad, was one of these, and so were a lot of
Working Men.

Some aspects of this homespun philosophy were a strange amalgam of
Trade Unionism, Socialism and Nationalism that appeared in Europe and
America in several forms in the Thirties and Forties. Hitler, Stalin, and
FDR all had varying mixtures of this amalgam in their political makeup!
The Molotov-Ribbentrop Pact in 1939 and the odd bedfellows who met at
Yalta in 1943 partially reflected this.

There has been reluctance to recognize the cross-connecting strains of
Trade Unionism, Socialism and Nationalism in the history of the period,
and this has been part of the American failure to understand its own
politics, and the Russians' politics, for decades.

Roosevelt was a God to the working class. There could be no polite
discussion in my neighborhood with anyone who did not know
that. A huge segment of middle-America was made up of lifelong
FDR Democrats, and some of them, and their offspring, are still out
there. Truman, viewed as a pathetic shadow of the Great Man but
still a Democrat, beat Governor Dewey in 1948 because of these
underestimated folks.

These were not the same as the Democrats in the South who were, at
bottom, American conservatives (and, sadly, some racists.) The middle-
American Democrats I am talking about were honest-to-God Socialist-
leaning Democrats. The educated elite who led the FDR Democrats, who
were different from the working class that they wanted to lead, called
themselves "Progressives" and had arisen from the days of Woodrow
Wilson when Socialism and "Internationalism" were in the air. Members
of this intellectual elite were dissatisfied with a strict interpretation of
our Constitution and launched discussion of the need for "flexibility" and
substantial changes to it.

Eugene Debs, a unionizing hero of railroaders, had written in 1900:
"Promising indeed is the outlook for Socialism in the United States." He
was premature, because prosperity and World War I retarded Socialism
in America until the Great Depression in 1929 when, once again,
allegiance to American capitalism declined. Leftists and Progressives

were divided into too many competing schools of thought for any of them to dominate politics, but together they achieved tremendous growth in unionism.

Leftist and "Progressive" leaders wanted to create a different America, but the common working folks among them, including my family, were not revolutionaries. They simply felt that the Working Man was not getting a fair shake, and they turned to the unions and a New Deal in the 1930s. Working people credited the government with busting the Trusts decades ago and with pulling the country through a terrible Depression. Many thought that government, with the unions, might provide a more just society.

The mobilization of the Working Class by an intellectual elite bent on moving society toward Socialism was a familiar refrain in Western Societies in the first four decades of the Twentieth Century. Individualism, these elites thought, must be submerged in the power of government. Lenin was frank about it: he called it "The Dictatorship of the Proletariat." The German Socialist, Edward Bernstein called it "Evolutionary Socialism." FDR sought "A New Deal" to modify Capitalistic America that was more evolutionary than it was revolutionary.

It took a World War and a Cold War to slow down the elitist, leftist political currents of the Thirties. Those currents were based less on individualism than on the power of government. They remain deep and strong today in the Progressive movement.

These currents affected my generation but did not persuade it. We loved Kennedy's very non-Socialistic exhortation: "Ask NOT what your country can do for you; ask what you can do for your country." But, there are times when we respond to the siren song of Socialism, seeing in it, as in The Great Society, some social justice that compensates for flaws in the American Way.

We were attracted to the sound of a "living Constitution" that could change with the times. We wanted to embrace the change that came with accelerating technology and communications, but the dangers of a flexible approach to the Constitution would become apparent over the next half-century. We would not let The Great Society become just another welfare state. We were taught in middle school that our Constitution was strong because it was flexible. We accepted flexibility as strength, but we have so far not allowed the term "living Constitution" to mean that judges can make it up as they go along.

We embraced change. Perspectives rooted in childhood partially shaped the ways that we dealt with the changes that America absorbed over the last 70 years of her history. We did not, however, continue to carry all the baggage from America's past.

The generations that influenced us, and the ancestors of that generation, carried some unpleasant baggage. Slavery had left large and ugly scars on the national psyche. Racism was deeply embedded in the culture. The pioneer spirit, a crucial part of American social development, came with the murderous and unjust history of Manifest Destiny. The entrepreneurial spirit, equally crucial to Americanism, came with the ugly spectacle of runaway capitalism in the nineteenth and early twentieth centuries, which left lingering tension between the Working Man and the Businessman. Women had been exploited and suppressed for two hundred years, an injustice that had begun to come to a head early in the Twentieth Century. Fixing all of this would have huge implications for the culture, the workplace and the family.

The Greatest Generation harbored views based upon this unpleasant baggage from the past. We were influenced by these views, but we have not absolutely adhered to them as challenges and changes have occurred. The perspectives presented in this chapter, projected into the future, are the perspectives developed while growing to manhood in small-town America with all its scars and warts.

My cohort had heard and seen Archie Bunker up close long before he appeared on TV in the Seventies. His caricature was hilarious to us precisely because he was not our role model.

Our model family in the Eighties was neither the Bunkers nor the Cleavers. It was the Huxtables, a black family that exuded family values and participated in the American Dream that captivated the nation.

Widening Horizons

Global issues were very much on the public mind when the Cold War began, mass communications were dawning, and a new Global Order was evolving. My generation was immersed in the news at a very young age. We may have been the first "global" generation that went through childhood, puberty, and early adulthood conversant with history as it took place. We all noticed that old Harry Truman was no pushover and his "buck stops here" talk changed minds about

him. The founding of Israel and The Korean War made big impressions. General MacArthur's arrogance and firing, and the testing of Russian A-bombs were big news. We knew about the Rosenbergs and their execution. The rise of Khrushchev in the years after Stalin died in 1953 was watched closely.

Domestic horizons were also widening. We formulated our own worldview in a time of general prosperity and a national coming of age. Postwar America was becoming an economic juggernaut and international strongman. There were

jobs, and people worked hard and made some money. Homes and cars were bought. Suburbs appeared. The middle class grew.

The domestic environment was orderly and disciplined. The law was the law, and bad guys got caught and jailed. Hippies and drugs were not tolerated. Families were responsible for discipline and good manners. Teachers were role models and authority figures. Mr. Eiche kept his paddle in plain sight. Helicopter parents did not exist to disapprove of school discipline or to keep their children indoors. A few complainers could not even think of getting rid of the Manger or the Ten Commandments in front of City Hall. Kate Smith boomed out "God Bless America" and thrilled Americans. The Pledge of Allegiance was taken seriously. Everyone stood respectfully for The Star Spangled Banner. The anthem was not butchered at ball games. The media were in tune with the culture. Americans would and did die for their country. Americans were charged with being citizens, not encouraged to be victims. The majority did not hide behind a minority that populated an "all-volunteer" military.

It was also a time of creativity and muscular growth in America. There had been others, of course: the brief American romance with canals, the burgeoning mills of New England that dwarfed Marx's hated Manchester in England, the romance of settling a seemingly endless frontier, the burst of railroad expansion, and the initial love affair with the horseless carriage. All of these left permanent imprints on the American psyche, but the Fifties were special to the politics and economics of the late twentieth and early twenty-first centuries.

Every child could identify every new car, and impressive cars they were! At twelve, I drove Unc's 1947 Cadillac, which was as big as a Sherman Tank. The T-Bird and the Corvette made a statement. Four-barrel carburetors ruled the road. The '55 Chevy and '57 Ford with their big engines and startling simple beauty and the Chrysler with its fins and in-your-face gas mileage became icons in a parade of icons. More important, they joined television, mass-produced and cheap appliances, nuclear-powered submarines and the other revolutionary changes that would make the 1950s a game-changer for American society.

Beaver Cleaver and American Exceptionalism

The concept of American Exceptionalism is rooted in these material things as well as in American philosophical and moral underpinnings. Americans *produce*! We invent things and then we mass-produce them. Then we buy them and encourage invention of still newer things. When America began to turn into a "service economy" at the same time that "international interdependence" came into vogue, the American Idea began to weaken.

It was empowering to grow up when the country could decide to build 4-lane highways that would crisscross the continent, and then actually *do* it! Superman and Wonder Woman wore red, white and blue. Today, at the "All-America Barber Shop" in Centreville, Virginia, all the pictures are from the Fifties.

Beaver Cleaver and Ozzie and Harriet seemed rich to families like mine and, even then, represented ideals rather than realities. Still, many Americans shared the strong social, philosophical, economic and political benchmarks that guided the

Cleavers and America in the Fifties. These values were woven into the national fabric, and they will impact America well into the third millennium. Dragnet's Jack Webb always got the bad guy with his "just the facts, ma'am" approach. Gunsmoke and I Love Lucy arrived at the right conclusions and The Mickey Mouse Club presented mainstream social concepts and values to children. Dr. Huxtable confirmed that American core values were neither white nor black. They were American values.

Even Hollywood had it right. Today, misguided and ill-educated commentators and entertainers ridicule those values and sneer at the mention of "Happy Days." Shame on them. They are so fixated on Socialist-inspired Progressivism that they cannot understand that belief in old-fashioned decency and rectitude does not automatically come with the racial prejudice and injustice of that era.

Progressives say that the Fifties raised expectations of perpetual American greatness steeped in social injustice that could not be sustained. They suggest that unrealistic expectations keep America from gently going into the inevitable Good Night that European nations accepted. They are correct to point out the injustices that existed in those days but they are far too pessimistic about our ability to correct them without destroying The American Way. Those injustices were vestiges of history that were doomed to be eradicated with time. There were clear signs of steady progress at eradicating them. They were not integral to the essence of Americanism, but antithetical to it. They could not last. How odd it is that Progressives think history progresses downhill and only by accepting decline will mankind advance. I did not understand this as a young man, and I still do not get it.

Racism: a legacy to overcome

Americans should always pause when they address racism to acknowledge the tragic, unjust fate of Native Americans. To grasp and settle our frontier we engaged in brutal ethnic cleansing. History, of course, is replete with cases of one race brutally displacing another. We still see it happening in both primitive and so-called "civilized" settings. We have not dealt with our own case very well, and our preaching to the rest of the world on this and other issues must seem strange to thoughtful international observers. America's guilt trip over slavery and its aftermath overshadows the unfortunate history of American "Indians" and the need to correct the mess we have made of their lives.

New Albany was active in the Underground Railroad during the Civil War, and Indiana had, in 1869, passed a law insuring "the education of Colored People." My high school was integrated in 1951, and I had a close friend in the eighth grade who was black, but my Dad did not know. In spite of these positive signs, progress at racial integration was difficult, painful, and far too slow. Racism was strong in the 1940s and 1950s, even in an area like southern Indiana that had made modest progress. Racist jokes were rampant. I remember being told not to pick up a penny because "a nigger might have touched it." My friend could not swim in the local swimming pool.

To defend the Beaver Cleaver ideal types of the Fifties is not to deny the emerging political and social crosscurrents of the time. In a moment of remarkable national prescience, former 5-star General and President Eisenhower tipped us off about the dangers of the Military-Industrial Complex. He was right: the war business was profitable and alluring to Capitalists. It was, and still is, tempting to make money on defense while neglecting the domestic infrastructure. Plowshares, and roads and sewers, fit The American Way better than swords. Ike hit the nail on the head. We must not forget it.

After the rise of Mao Tse Tung in 1949, the Chinese were the Asiatic Bogeyman, and they were behind the Korean mess. It had been easy to lock up American Japs and call it a fancy name like "internment," and it was easy to hate Chinese, even though they had built our railroads. We had South Korean allies who fought hard, but Koreans were still called "gooks," a pejorative corruption of the Korean pronunciation of the country's name, "*Hangook*." It would be easy to hate other "gooks" and "slopes" a little later in Vietnam. This ugly current of racism, a strong vestige of the Pacific War, ran deep in American society for decades. It probably helped to suck America into Vietnam.

It was quite a revelation later when Asian children clobbered Caucasians on the SATs! There is a lesson here that Americans are beginning to understand in the early 21st Century. America enjoyed single-superpower status for a brief period and some became abused of the notion that our superiority was racial as well as military and economic. It is amazing that polyglot, Melting-Pot America would harbor notions of racial superiority, but we did. We were slow to understand that the junky Japanese cars of the 50s were merely a prelude to superior vehicles that would challenge and nearly topple General Motors. Korean cars followed Japanese ones. As noted later in this Story, Asians led by the Chinese may make capitalism work better than we do in this century, unless we return to the work ethic, personal productivity, and educational excellence that built America in the first place.

Korea was not complicated at first. Americans could stop this Communist plot, and there was no reason to believe we would not kick some butt, again. Soon this simplicity waned and there were a lot of people wondering why we were losing so many men in such a useless place. The flash of jingoism that followed the first blush of victory in the late Forties was dampened considerably by the Korean intervention in 1950. What was revealed in the American popular mindset was a core principle that lingers today: we need to take care of our knitting at home and we do not need to be meddling abroad. The notion that America should "never fight a land war in Asia," still great advice, is rooted here. If asked, ordinary Americans would extend that thought to the rest of the world.

These things were important in the formative years of my generation. Slavery was beaten, but racist attitudes, which existed across the political spectrum, were rampant. This fact became very important in the 1960s and 1970s when there was slow, grudging acceptance of serious racial reform, especially in the lower classes. Members of my father's generation, in spite of the fact that they were born nearly half a century after the Emancipation Proclamation, had grown up with institutionalized segregation. That generation had the assets and positions of influence in the Sixties, and progress at racial integration was bound to be slow.

Progress was far too slow to gain acceptance of what Americans should have seen as a matter of right and wrong. Radical Blacks and Whites, and revolutionary leftists who wanted revolution more than equality for colored people, took advantage of the fact that progress was too slow. They invigorated and aggravated racism that was abating with time. Of course, those pushing for immediate racial equality would say that correction of injustice should not wait, and that they were on the correct side of history, which they were.

They were right in theory but wrong in practice. The racial progress that took us fifty years might have been done in less time with a little more patience, and without the riots of the Sixties. This assertion can easily be misunderstood and those who, unlike Reverend Martin Luther King, will always choose disruption and violence will refuse to understand it. Let me try to explain anyway.

My generation was entering adulthood as the Great Society was introduced. We were well acquainted with the attitudes of the wartime and depression generation that preceded us, but we were disposed to social change. In fact, change of all kinds was in the air. There had been nuclear bombs, Sputnik, television, jet airplanes and interstate highways. We had absorbed the lessons of the Holocaust and read <u>To Kill a Mockingbird</u>, and we accepted <u>Brown v. Board of Education of Topeka</u> in 1954, which overturned the terrible decision in 1896 that allowed state-supported public education. We had enthusiastically voted for the Kennedy/Johnson ticket, though we were surprised that it was Johnson and not Kennedy that worked hardest for racial justice. Reverend King was right and he appeared at the right time.

From deep in the roots of American philosophy there grew increasing discontent with the racially limited concepts of American equality that had evolved during the previous 17 decades. "Separate but equal" was fundamentally un-American. In a resurgent, massively endowed America, it was rapidly becoming unacceptable to tolerate injustice and inequality. There had been earlier attempts in American history to challenge race and gender inequality, and those attempts had left their marks, but the movements that began to gain steam in the Fifties were not destined to accept a Two-Steps-Forward-and-One-Step-Back approach. My generation would prove to be a critical medium in which these movements would be tested. To be sure, we were creatures of a resurgent economy preoccupied with our flattop haircuts, blue suede shoes and Rock & Roll, but we were destined to be the adults to judge the Sixties, hold on during the Seventies, and power the Eighties and Nineties, and we were disposed to correct injustice and inequality.

Norman Rockwell's, "The Problems We All Share," on the cover of LOOK Magazine, January 14, 1964, showed a black child trying to attend school accompanied by federal marshals. It reflected the change underway and the sadness of most Americans.

We were the generation with one foot in the past and the other in the future just as Brown vs. Board of Education of Topeka was being decided. We grew up among old racist ideas and racist jokes. At the same time, we were imbued with a new American optimism and a sense of opportunity to build, like the Interstate Highway System, an America worthy of its founding philosophy and the documents that embodied that philosophy. Beaver Cleaver was white, and he may have been oblivious to poverty and injustice, but he was not a racist.

This may sound like highfalutin philosophizing for a railroader's boy, but it is not. There were seeds of change deeply imbedded in my generation, and we felt it. Perhaps those seeds came from parents of the Depression and Progressive politics nourished in War and its remarkable economic and social aftermath. I do not know. I know that our worldview was profoundly impacted. We did not see cries for social equality and justice as a threat. The racist, backward-looking supporters of Alabama's George Wallace who were so vocal in the Sixties did not represent the mainstream. They were "dead men walking" in American politics. We knew we could do better and we earnestly wanted to do better. We would be the young adults of The Great Society.

While we were ready and eager to deal with social injustice, we were skeptical of the politics of Progressivism, which aimed at rapid and radical structural and conceptual change in American governance. Like the 19th Century Lord Mayor of London, Edmund Burke, we believed in preservation of the essential elements of society and governance as we adapted to change that our own philosophy required and time imposed. This brand of moderate conservatism has characterized the mainstream of American politics for decades -- not the more conservative and radical Tea Party conservatives who emerged in the early Twentieth First Century. This is why that movement was and will remain a minority movement.

Demanding equality for blacks was right and obvious, but "Ebonics" was quickly rejected as ridiculous by thoughtful people both black and white. Like most good ideas, someone always pushes the logical to the extreme. My generation could agree that "nigger" was hateful speech, but speech codes on college campuses are wrong. All crimes against persons of any color are hate crimes. Politically Correct definitions and creation of special protected categories of people is a move exactly in the wrong direction. The behavior of authorities should be color- blind, but criminals that fit a profile should be "profiled." If criminals walk like ducks, you should search for ducks. Such notions are common-sense extensions of thinking of the America I grew up in. They are not foot dragging about correct and badly needed social progress.

We celebrated the contributions that diversity made to American culture and were ready and willing to accept new spices in the American stew, but we rejected the idea that The American Melting Pot should give way to a polyglot of separate, racial identities. Kwanzaa, like Ebonics, was a step backward. "Black Studies" is no more a viable intellectual area of inquiry than "White Studies" would be. Affirmative Action, careful and deliberate discrimination in reverse, was viewed as reasonable until it was abused and even Black leaders started to see its flaws and reject it. It is a tragedy that "diversity" has become a basic principle of the

Politically Correct. It promotes division and retards real equality. It is no more American than "Separate but Equal" was.

My generation has not fought reasonable attempts to lift up the less fortunate. But, when social programs get out of hand and exceed their public mandate, we object. Generally, the folks I grew up with would not reverse "The Great Society" or end Welfare. Welfare is needed, but "Workfare" makes more sense. Smart Democrats grasped this in the Nineties, but the Progressives demurred. My generation readily accepted Social Security and Medicare as parts of the fabric of our culture, but they must change to meet the times. We would fix all of these when they become broken. They must be workable in the kind of modified Capitalistic system that has evolved and which we generally support. When it comes to such social programs, we might be dubbed the "mend it but don't end it" generation.

The tension between Progressives who would change the fundamentals of society and government and moderates who want to promote equal justice and opportunity while preserving the best of America should be familiar to the reader today. That tension, aggravated by radicals at both the left and right political extremes, is at the root of political stalemate in the second decade of the Twenty First Century. That tension will probably generate more serious political and social battles in the future. It is questionable whether Progressives goals to fundamentally change America and the "mend it don't end it" views of what is still a majority of Americans can be easily and peacefully resolved.

It is a shame that the movement toward racial equality could not, and cannot to this day, accept and credit the white majority that has supported it. Instead most black spokesmen focused on the white racist minority and the Ku Klux Klan. It is hard to criticize them for this. Sadly, the worst kind of demagogues and black racist thugs, and some with political agendas that were more about Progressivism and radical Socialism than about racial justice, rose to prolong and aggravate the struggle and to advocate violence. King was murdered, and there were not enough heroes and visionaries like Congressman John Lewis. The 2015 movie Selma is instructive. The movement could not be celebrated without distorting the supportive role of Lyndon Johnson.

Sadly, despite very substantial progress, my generation and our children and grandchildren have not eradicated racism in America. There are plenty of reasons for black and brown Americans to be unhappy with an imperfect society. But we have made enormous progress that most of those who are dissatisfied should acknowledge and build upon. Some do, but unfortunately there are those who cannot deal constructively with a glass half full. The struggle is the life's blood of radical minorities like Al Sharpton who, like vultures, descend whenever they can fan the flames of racism. John Lewis lives, and we have a black President, Attorney General and other Cabinet members, but Al Sharpton and his ilk still thrive.

They are egged on by leftist media, which see both a story that attracts viewers and a chance to further Progressive and Socialist goals.

Enter Mass Media

> *"We are dominated by Journalism."*
> Oscar Wilde

At the prompting of his new wife, Dad bought a black and white TV in about 1952. The news in those days mercifully came in 15-minute doses, often with the deep voice of Edward R. Murrow who had earned credibility in WWII. Children, in playground disputes, would say "I know it's true—they can't say it on TV if it ain't true!" The First Amendment and The Fourth Estate had an awesome tool in television— mass media with pictures.

Murrow taught America, and the media, an important lesson. He started a trend that is underappreciated by historians. A democrat, he used his influence, and public airwaves, to bring down conservative "Red Scare" Senator Joe McCarthy. Regardless of how one judges McCarthy, who saw a Communist conspiracy everywhere, Murrow demonstrated that the media could and happily would destroy a politician. The Media could push an agenda. Further, he showed that the vast current of social, "progressive" thinking in America, which was shared by many in the Heartland who revered FDR, could be energized and tapped by a concerted media effort.

Great Society legislation also tapped an American left-leaning undercurrent. So did Watergate reporting, with the help of an inept Nixon Administration. At CBS, Murrow successor Walter Cronkite, another sonorous voice, would become "the most trusted man in America." He was an opinion leader and not just a reporter. CBS was a steady voice for change in America. Walter Cronkite openly supported the Environmentalist agenda with an alarmist segment called "Can the World be Saved?" He would harness the great Progressive undercurrent against the Vietnam War when, somewhat late, he saw clearly that it was a stupid, unwinnable misadventure. Cronkite was correct on this issue, but he addressed it as a politician rather than as the fine newsman he had been since WWII.

The Watergate scandal was a watershed event for the Left and the media. The Nixon administration had begun to revive pride in an America that had been to the Moon. Nixon opened talks with China, and Kissinger was clearly trying to stop the Vietnam debacle. I had been a student of Kissinger and I saw these things from Moscow, where the strength and prestige of Nixon's America was on the rise. Nixon's first term showed promise of stabilizing the American social and political environment where most Americans were comfortable.

Nixon could have presided over the kind of orderly change that would have worked for a long time. The left and the media hated this and salivated when a third-rate burglary at the Watergate, amazingly, brought Nixon down. Nixon's paranoia and ineptitude were matched by incredible tenacity in the media. The story festered into a huge scandal. The left and the media still feed off of their success at turning a time of pride into a time of shame in America.

Dan Rather followed Cronkite at CBS and helped marshal left-oriented thinking during the post-Watergate funk that American politics suffered. It turned into a Progressive heyday. The "news" became like the scolding of a child: America was bad and we should be ashamed of ourselves. Rather carried the banner for this strain of thought until the public grew weary of it during a resurgence of pride in America in the Eighties. Before this resurgence, Carter rode the undercurrent of shame and confusion to the White House. This undercurrent of "shame on America" lingers in the media to this day.

The media had evolved to see its role as more than reporting the news. "Reporters" claimed star status and immunity from responsibility for objectivity as an entitlement of the First Amendment. Every reporter, and anyone with a pencil can claim to be a reporter, assume a natural right to lead public opinion,

"report" ideology as reality, and be immune from responsibility. The bond between the media and the left-leaning, "Progressive" social undercurrent faded somewhat after the Carter Administration. Then, CNN arrived in 1990, funded by the spouse of "Hanoi Jane" Fonda. Media scolding got a new voice and reemerged as a major force in the early twenty-first century.

America is based on absolute ideals that are not achievable in an imperfect world. The fact that America was destined always to be striving for perfection is intuitively accepted and understood by ordinary people, but intellectual elites try to exploit this fact as a weakness. When America is not perfect, as she inevitably is often not, it is the duty of the Fourth Estate to hold our feet to the fire and point out our flaws. This is why freedom of the press is included in the First Amendment. The problem is that the media and so-called "educated" elites are quick to strike and suggest that another "America," a socialistic one with its wealth distributed much differently, is needed.

Mainstream American thought, though it embraces constructive change, would preserve American cultural, political and economic practices and values. The struggle between media attempts to promote more radical change in America and the mainstream of American thought has been going on for decades. It has waxed and waned during my lifetime, but it has always been there.

It is arguable that the media, heavily influenced by American left-leaning elites, has led the Democratic Party to commit political suicide several times. A party that boasted majority status could not win a majority in several presidential elections because the media's favorite was ushered into the nomination as the Democratic Party's candidate. Their favorite is often a candidate far out of tune with mainstream thought. Many Democrats that I grew up with would have voted for a "Scoop" Jackson or other moderate Democrat, but their party would not put moderate people forward.

Conservative Media are a 21st Century phenomenon. It is not clear yet whether this will simply offset clearly left-oriented "news" sources, or if these conservative media will only serve to polarize communications into two camps. With this polarization, discerning people can hear both sides, and it is possible that they will hear more of the news, but there is a huge risk that listeners will stay with the side that is congenial to their thinking. "Spin" will prevail. Gridlock will be the result. Natural change, adjustment to reality, is retarded.

It is sad to think that polarization of national news into Right- and Left-Wing camps, which brings distortion instead of clarity to reporting the news, is the only alternative. Since the constitutional guarantee of freedom of the press says nothing about objectivity, honestly, etc., polarized "news" may be here to stay.

Polarized government is not a surprising result.

The American Way of War

America was built and defended by families like my Uncle John's in Sunfish, Kentucky. One of his boys was a priest. Several boys worked the factories of Louisville. Some kept the farm. Three of them joined the Army when underage, and John, Jr. lost his life helping to destroy a critical bridge in Germany. Four of Uncle Joe's sons, along with two of my brothers, served. Kime served in the Army in WWI and the Navy in WWII. He was a founder of The American Legion.

It is sad to mention just a few of them because there were hundreds among and close to my relatives and quite a few did not come home. These men belonged to the Greatest Generation and fought in just wars. As I grew up, it was difficult not to think of these men when politicians sent American boys to die in places like Vietnam, Bosnia, Afghanistan and Iraq.

I had absorbed much of Middle America's attitudes about war as a boy and carried those impressions with me throughout a long career, including a tour of duty at The National War College where an understanding of the role of force in U.S. national security policy is crucial. It seemed to me as I grew up, served in the Navy and went on to serve in higher education, that ordinary Americans' core attitudes on war, as I had understood those attitudes since childhood, were repeatedly ignored by the national leadership.

Politicians, many of whom never serve in the military, are quick to sacrifice our children out of hubris and a twisted interpretation of what the Founding Fathers thought was proper for national defense, or much more importantly, what most Americans think or what the Civil War and the two World Wars should have taught us. The "national interest" has been grotesquely distorted since WWII to justify the ideological adventurism and posturing of politicians. Still, the children of working class America, following the example of The Greatest Generation, continue to answer the call to arms.

This absurdity came to a head in the Vietnam debacle and eventually resulted in the all-volunteer military. But this meant that a minority of kids with lesser opportunity but more guts would "defend" the country from threats to The American Way of Life that politicians conjured up. The reader might be shocked, even annoyed, by this perspective, and some, even in the heart of working America, who see themselves as more sophisticated in the workings of international affairs, would disagree; but the fact is that Americans did not universally accept the extension of Manifest Destiny to the entire globe after the World Wars and our emergence as a Superpower. Most rejected muscle-flexing by a Superpower America and World Policeman. The almost universally accepted American way of war is straightforward: if there is a clear and real threat to the nation, mobilize resources and crush it without mercy or regret. Speak softly but carry a very big stick. Use it if you must.

It is strange that politicians in America, settled in large part by working folks leaving the incessant wars of Europe for a rich continent protected by two oceans, would make political points by saying that the rest of the world should follow the historically unique and geographically blessed American model.

Advocates of "One World" fed Americans a steady diet. Many accepted this because it only seemed right to try to export something so good to parts of the world that seemed so deprived. Of course, "Global Village" and "Interdependence" propaganda masked the fact that true international equality meant a common denominator outcome for America. This reality began to be felt in the 1980s and is coming home to roost today as Americans realize that exported jobs will never return

It took Ronald Reagan and his "Shining City on a Hill" image of the American role in international affairs to begin to dispel the Global Village nonsense but such notions are powerful things. Very wealthy and successful business leaders shamelessly joined the Internationalists and Progressives and profited greatly from selling America out overseas. Wars and nation-building are big money-makers. A lot of money and careers were made fighting wars and vainly attempting to build little Americas in sand and jungles.

All this happened and still happens, but it is very American, at least in the America where this officer was raised, to tend to your knitting at home. Charity also begins at home. Loyalty and duty is to country first.

These attitudes are described as Isolationism by the political and social "betters' of the Working Man, or Working Woman. It is an attitude hated by leftist political elites who are certain that they know best what is good for lesser citizens. Thankfully, Americans are not stupid. They know the difference between ankle-biters and real threats to the nation's security. Moreover, they understand that not every society thinks or acts the way that Americans, unique in their location and evolution, do. Americans understand that it is folly to insist that our model be transplanted everywhere.

Most Americans can live with the incredible diversity in the world and certainly do not want their children sent to fight about it in the sand or some jungle. If radicals in Afghanistan (or Pakistan) attack us, blow them back to the Stone Age immediately without apology. We knew where they were in 2001, but even if we had not known, a good guess and a really big stick would have served. It would have been over quickly, the message would have been quite clear to friends and foes everywhere, and if necessary we could send it again.

Most Americans, though imbued with what their elitist "betters" would tag as simplistic, insular Working Man's philosophy, ask pretty straightforward questions. Why send our young people to die in some fine-tuned effort at military punishment for acts of terrorism, or for some feckless attempt at social engineering or "nation-building?" Does punishment in the 21st Century require thousands of boots on the ground? For ten years? Why destroy a country's electrical grid and then spend billions to fix it? Why remove a Devil we know and can deal with to enthrone a Devil we do not know and probably cannot control? Why dump billions of dollars into the sand or a jungle to see it diverted into the Swiss bank accounts of dictators? This is not rocket science; it is good old American common sense.

I may be wrong about the views of some in my cohort, but I'm convinced that the views presented in this chapter, which evolved from the wellspring of the Forties and Fifties, reside in the hearts and minds of a majority of my generation. Toward the end of this book, the implications of these views for US military doctrine will be explored.

Chapter V
College Horizons

I matriculated at The University of Louisville in September of 1958. The University of Louisville at the turn of the Sixties was a good place to grow up and learn. Public universities are the laboratories of America, good places to begin academic studies, especially for students who have not had access and exposure to the intellectual richness that America offers. Prestige schools benefit greatly in their graduate programs by students who have sharpened their minds at the nation's public universities. So does the military.

Our military is also greatly enriched by students from the nation's social and cultural mainstream who attend public colleges and universities. The officer gene pool is strengthened and inoculated against elitism. There has long been discussion about the existence of both NROTC and the Naval Academy, and about the differences and tension between the graduates the two approaches to training officers. The Navy knew what it was doing. I know; I served in both programs.

Of course, I did not understand any of this in 1958. I was amazed to be at college and not working on the railroad.

The Navy was a mystery to me. I knew boats and canoes and had built a 16-foot rowboat from scratch in woodshop, but I had never seen a body of water larger than the Ohio River. A former enlisted sailor who had won an NROTC slot saw that I was overwhelmed at the quick Navy immersion and introduced me to the crucial art of spit-polishing shoes. He was overwhelmed by the college immersion, and I helped him through remedial English. We learned to be Midshipmen together, and he would become a fine Surface Warfare Officer. He was terribly wounded in Vietnam when serving in swift boats.

Once I visited a destroyer where Commander Blakeley was in command, and we met years later in my office on the Pentagon's E-Ring as senior

Navy Captains. When he died, I was amazed at the turnout of his former shipmates at his funeral in Arlington. He could not have been admitted to the Naval Academy, but he was washed in American values and served as an American hero.

We were at U of L at a key time in history. Sputniks and nuclear submarines were launched. A U-2 was shot down. Eisenhower warned of the Military-Industrial Complex, and JFK won, or at least was declared the winner, in a squeaker of an election. The Bay of Pigs debacle tested his young Presidency. The Students for a Democratic Society (SDS) began to organize, and even at universities like U of L in the middle of God's country, we began to feel the storms of discontent that presaged the social and political storms that racial tensions and the Vietnam War would later precipitate.

A very close friend at college was active in SDS and became a lifelong leftist. It was impossible to be around him, or to be in college between 1958 and 1962, without seeing the stirring of radical thought in the intellectual community.

Many notables, including Churchill and Disraeli, have said something like: "A young man who isn't a socialist hasn't got a heart and an old man who is a socialist hasn't got a head." There is wisdom in this, but it was not just the Socialist impulses that always thrive among students *and professors* who examine political alternatives blissfully disconnected from reality.

There were serious social issues that commanded the attention of thoughtful people of a wide variety of outlooks, ages and experience. It was palpable. The American public would soon elect the veto-proof 89th Congress that would launch the Great Society.

It would soon be clear that leftward trends harbored some who were to become the radicals of the Sixties and Seventies. The currents of impending radicalism buffeted students like us, but like many in America, we were buoyed by Camelot in Washington and the freshness of the Whiz Kids in the White House.

Former Naval officer and Patrol Boat hero John Kennedy inspired a nation with his upper-class phrasing and street-level challenge: "Ask not what your country can do for you, ask what you can do for your country." No talk about entitlements in that! His charge to put a man on the moon in a decade was a challenge from the Fifties to the Sixties. Thanks, JFK. We needed that.

Midshipmen wore the uniform to class on Wednesdays. Most professors and students handled this with grace in an era of nascent radicalism. Not too many years later, as an officer-student with an office in the Harvard NROTC building, it would be different. They tried to bomb the place.

Author's photos

Ignoring warnings about basket weaving, and to the consternation of my Navy advisor, I shifted my major from Chemistry to International Studies with a focus on the Russian Language. Wilma took the same major. Sputnik had pumped new energy into the Cold War, and some of the folks in Indiana sensed a whiff of sedition. At a minimum, it seemed strange to Hoosiers for nice clean kids from Indiana to be interested in such sordid stuff as Russian.

Attendance at U of L was expensive and required that Wilma and I work to cover costs. The Chair of the Language Department and senior professor in the International Studies major was Dr. John Broderius, a great bear of a man who spoke several languages and was an etymologist of note. He intimidated faculty and students alike with his formidable stature and stern demeanor. But, for reasons I never completely understood, the Big Guy loved Wilma and me. We studied hard, came to class prepared, and took college seriously, but we were not the only students who did. It may have been Dr. Broderius' understanding of our roots in Middle America and our hopes to make a mark somewhere that he liked. He was from South Dakota and had struggled mightily to become the impressive character he was. Whatever his reasons, he adopted us.

I had operated my high school's FM radio station and audio-visual equipment and Dr. Broderius, who had found the funds to establish a Language Laboratory at the University, asked me if I would help set it up and run it. He sat down with me and we selected the equipment, which was quite rudimentary by today's standards. He asked me to oversee the installation and operation and to hire students to run it 13 hours a day. Wilma became one of the operators. We got 90 cents an hour, enough to get us both through college and afford lunch most of the time.

A prominent U of L graduate contributed some money to the International Studies Program to fund research paper contests. We were encouraged to compete each year and submitted research papers written for courses in the major. Either Wilma or I won each year, and the other often got second place. It usually meant several hundred dollars for tuition and expenses. This opportunity prepared both of us for future requirements, like honors theses and dissertations that both of us had to write. U of L was a good school, and its liberal arts program was certainly not basket weaving. Academics in those days were not for sissies. Academics since then have been eroded as American colleges have descended into the Politically Correct and into the ether and anonymity of the Internet.

U of L grew to be the largest university in Kentucky and I cannot vouch for it today, but it was a great school when Wilma and I attended it and it had only about 5,000 students. Its engineering school was renowned and its liberal arts college had a demanding and dedicated faculty. It took untold hours of study to earn an "A" in Dr. Sutton's Russian History class, which was superior to my Russian history class at Harvard.

One professor, who was born in Central Asia, warned half a century ago of the mess we see today in the Muslim world. U of L was a solid undergraduate institution. H. Grant Hicks was a professor who had flown with the Flying Tigers in WWII and who lived on a farm in Indiana like many of our ancestors. He had no PhD, just a mountain of first hand knowledge about Asia. There were no easy marks in his classes! I will never forget my pride when Mr. Hicks wrote a letter of recommendation for me and credited his 19 year old student with "maturity of insight." Wilma and I still laugh about the exaggeration.

College summers were vital parts of my education. The Navy gets credit for half of this. I worked for the Park Department half the summer. The Navy required that midshipmen go on 6-week summer "cruises" to learn about Navy careers. These were not just rites of passage for me; they were openings to other worlds. For a boy who had not been out of Kentuckiana, it was a big deal to go aboard an aircraft carrier at age 18, sail around the Atlantic, visit Bermuda and Nova Scotia, and paint a massive reduction gear in the carrier's engine room in 110-degree heat. Fourth Class Middies were "lower than whale shit," but it was a life-changing cruise for this Midshipman. I was a sailor.

My sophomore summer was spent with the Marines and Naval Aviators. I got to be yelled at by a diminutive Gunny Sergeant who looked like Napoleon and acted like Hitler. I corrected him once for mispronouncing my name and quickly learned that his way of saying it was just going to have to do. We made an amphibious landing like in WWII. The Marines had not yet learned that counterinsurgency was on the horizon.

Naval Aviators did not impress me much, but the Grumman F9F fighter did. Going downhill, we broke the speed of sound on a training flight. At 19, I was hooked. The Navy paid for flight lessons at a Louisville airport. I did the ground school and soloed in a Tri-Champion. Roaming over Kentuckiana at several thousand feet, one could see how small, but beautiful, my part of the planet was.

Russian summer

The summer after my junior year was special. Dr. Broderius insisted that I compete in a new program called IREX that would exchange student groups from Russia and the US. The Soviet Union was in an interesting decompression after two decades of Stalinist terror.

Khrushchev, once he succeeded in executing the Secret Police murderer Beria and shoving others aside, had initiated a policy called an *"ottepl,"* or "Thaw." There was a general loosening of dictatorial control over cultural, economic and political matters. This period would come to an end in the mid-1960s when it became obvious that the Soviet system could not survive an extended Thaw but, for a short period, we had glimpses into the Russia that lay just beneath the surface. The IREX exchange students would see this.

Full-immersion Russian was taught at Indiana University before the journey. It was to be 20 students, each with a different level of Russian. I had only had classroom instruction and a few semesters of grammar, so it was good luck to win the twentieth, least capable, slot. The student in the first slot grew up with Russian-speaking grandparents and had nearly fluent Russian. I was paired with her when had free time to wander around. We were tested before and after six weeks of living and travel in Russia.

1961 was a great time for a student of Russia to be there. The Thaw was in the air, and so were new attempts to express Soviet power. The Berlin Wall was built that summer. The Minister of Defense had begun to talk about a new nuclear-based military strategy in January of 1960, and in September of 1961 they would explode a 100-megaton device in the atmosphere. Nikita Khrushchev banged his shoe at the UN. Stalin's corpse was still in the Mausoleum that summer, looking "a little green around the gills." A girl in our group fainted at the sight of him and I had to carry her out. Khrushchev, to emphasize the end of the Stalin Era, unceremoniously removed Stalin from the tomb soon afterward.

Our delegation was able to talk to people on the streets. We stayed several days at a sports camp in the Ukraine with several Soviet athletes where we lived in tents so deep in the woods that the buses got mired in the mud on the way.

They had to string a wire from a telephone pole to power the TV set that would bring us Khrushchev's speech to the UN and to hear Soviet excuses for building the Berlin Wall and see the burly boss of the Politburo bang his shoe on the table.

The Russian youngsters turned out to be pretty down to earth. I was struck by the fact that they understood that they were living, technologically, in the 1930s. Some accepted the all-purpose Russian excuse that The Great Patriotic War was to blame, but many did not really buy it. The shoe-banging and nuclear saber rattling just did not square with the way they lived. They seemed to be wondering, "If we are an equal nuclear superpower, why is it that we have no refrigerators or food to put in them, and why do Americans all drive cars?"

They had, as most Russians do, a quite non-ideological sense of humor. Once, in my fledgling Russian, I was in an earnest discussion about how much one man could dictate to such a huge country. I asserted that Khrushchev was no longer just another Politburo member or part of a Ruling Triumvirate, but indisputably "the most powerful member of the Communist Party." Unfortunately, "*chlen*," or "member" has the same dual meaning in Russian as it does in English. I had earnestly and spontaneously said that Khrushchev was the biggest prick in the Communist Party! The Russian youngsters rolled on the tent floor and laughed and waved assent until they had tears in their eyes.

When I returned from this first trip to the Soviet Union, Wilma and her parents met me in New York. They had driven straight from New Albany, waited while I endured the tough Russian examination required (8 hours of graduate credit were involved), and planned a quick trip to Coney Island before driving back. I had never seen New York, and the culture shock was acute. Years later, as my 12-year-old daughter looked lingeringly at a display of fruits and vegetables in Vienna after spending a year in Moscow, I would understand. Wilma talked me into riding the roller coaster at Coney Island. I did, but I swore to never ride another one. I haven't.

I wrote my senior honors thesis about press coverage of the period before and after the explosion of a 100-megaton Soviet hydrogen bomb in the atmosphere in 1961. The thesis showed how Pravda had decried such testing right up to the event and turned on a dime to justify it hours after it happened. Not a burble in Russian "public opinion."

In my senior year at Louisville, something useful about the military, and about myself, became apparent. I was not very good at military things. My attempts to march were pathetic, and my posture was often corrected during uniform inspections. Thank goodness, this deficiency was not a big deal at Louisville where the officers running the NROTC Unit were mostly concerned with getting midshipmen through the academic program. But my miserable performance on the drill field became an issue in my senior year.

Rank among midshipmen was determined by a formula weighted to recognize academic performance more than military "aptitude." This meant a student on top of the Class had to be slated for the stripes of the Battalion Commander. This was awkward. There were three periods where ranks in the Battalion were granted: a fall period where there was parading and marching, a winter period where nothing really happened, and a spring period where there was a lot of parading and marching.

Another Midshipman, a future Marine who starched his underwear, could march and call cadence like a Nazi. He was a solid "B" student and slated to be my Battalion XO. The Senior Marine officer at the NROTC Unit, a war hero who had lost an arm in Korea, called me in. "There is a delicate situation," he began. I interrupted him and said matter-of-factly, "It looks like another Midshipman should be the Battalion Commander for the fall drills. Do you want me to be the XO?" He smiled and said: "I know you will do a great job. You are slated to be Battalion Commander for the winter." The pressure was off of both of us.

Batallion Commander's stripes
author's photo

Setting Course

My senior midshipman cruise was more prosaic, but just as illuminating to a budding young naval officer. Since I had skipped the cruise after my junior year to go to Russia, I had to take the senior cruise after graduation in 1962 and before commissioning. For makeup, I was sent for a summer on a destroyer doing training and visiting ports in the Mediterranean Sea. Liberty was awesome and revealing. Picture a motorcycle ride from Nice to Monte Carlo. I was like Br'er Rabbit being thrown into his Briar Patch.

My erstwhile senior officers on this cruise were Ensigns already commissioned from the class of 1962 like me. They were the same as I was, only commissioned a few weeks earlier. The skipper decided that this was ridiculous and put me on the training schedule with them to learn how to be a Division Officer and Officer of the Deck. I had to do celestial navigation, try to "supervise" deck hands, who were just kids in their teens and early 20s who had guys like me for lunch. It was a kind of free ride into the world of junior officers, which, like many things, I did not have the maturity to appreciate until sometime later.

The skipper of the Louisville NROTC Unit, Captain Schumacher, determined the course of my early naval career. He was from Naval Academy Class of 1938 and was a submarine Captain who had survived the War. Though a Naval Academy graduate, he was convinced the Navy needed citizens who were educated in the civilian world. I learned years later at the Naval Academy as he celebrated his 50th year since graduation that this enlightened gentleman dearly wanted to see "his" NROTC officers in the submarine force. I was the only Louisville graduate that was likely to be accepted into that program, and he was not happy that I wanted to be a Naval Aviator.

When I unexpectedly flunked the visual part of the physical that would let me fly jet aircraft, Captain Schumacher pounced. I was called before this formidable officer and asked if I really wanted to fly school buses, helicopters, or blimps. Hearing "no," he said I should go to Submarine School, which was accepting a few newly commissioned officers. I said "yes, Sir." I got orders in days. I had never seen a submarine.

I was commissioned on September 6th and Wilma and I were married on the 8th at the Church of God in New Albany, Indiana, located between the houses were we were born. It was a typical, wonderful, Middle-American spectacle that did not cost much but was priceless. We had to be in New London soon because Submarine School started on September 22nd.

We took a 3-day honeymoon trip to Kentucky Lake and still had over $100, enough money to drive to Connecticut. Everything we owned fit in the back seat of the '59 Chevy. It did not block the view out the rear window. We stayed in a $10 motel until we found a furnished basement apartment in New London on the Thames River for $85 rent.

Chapter VI
Junior Officer
Life in Submarines

I reported in to the Submarine Base at Groton, Connecticut, but it would be a week before the Navy would pay me. Wilma made a big pot of Cincinnati Chile, which lasted to payday. Life got more interesting, but it was never better.

A local service station owner in Groton, Connecticut was surprised to see a Navy Ensign, since such junior officers rarely appeared in submarine country. Officers had always had to go to sea in surface ships (surface ships are called "Targets" by submariners) and qualify as deck officers before being admitted to Sub School. But, since the US was building submarines at a fast clip, a shortage of officers was felt. Novices like me were grudgingly admitted to Submarine School.

Ensigns joined our Navy in1862 as a rank for graduates of the Naval Academy, and to have an equivalent rank to the Army Second Lieutenant. Ensigns wore a sleeve stripe of one -half-inch wide lace beginning in 1881. Ensign got a gold bar insignia in 1922.

Half of the officers in my class at Submarine School were officers experienced at sea. Many of those officers who had not gone to sea had graduated from the Navy's rigorous Nuclear Power School and had a year in Navy uniform under their belt. In this first class to admit newly commissioned officers, I was the only one who was not a graduate of an engineering school. Submarine School was a difficult and uncompromising place and I was in over my head. Several submarines were moored at the piers, but I had not been aboard one.

Dive! Dive!

It was humiliating to find myself at the Diving Trainer, where officers learned the drill to submerge, operate, and surface a submarine. I did not even know what was supposed to happen there. Fortunately, more experienced officers, several who were qualified as enlisted submariners before they were commissioned, went first. I was not called upon until the second day, so I had an evening to memorize the drill, even if I was clueless about what some of it meant. I nearly broke the trainer when a sadistic instructor introduced casualties that paralyzed the planes that controlled depth. The Diving Trainer nearly stood on end, and we "sank." The good news was that other officers performed as badly, and I learned something wonderful about submariners: they have a fantastic sense of humor.

I discovered that most of the curriculum was more practical than theoretical. If one understood the basics of plumbing, ventilation, electricity, etc., the systems could all be figured out. The common sense that Unc and my shop teachers preached was just what a submariner needs. We had flush toilets back in Indiana. Water flows downhill in submarines, too. Things generally move from higher to lower pressure. Of course, it was necessary to learn every knob, valve and switch, but I could do that by working harder than the Academy graduates and the Engineers. I did.

Tactics and Navigation were a different matter. Engineers did not have an insurmountable advantage over me in those realms. I had taken a tough navigation course at Louisville, and learning how and when to fire torpedoes was interesting and fun. It was basic geometry and common sense in action.

I was no better than average at the diving drills we had at sea in submarines. I was adjusting to an environment the other students were familiar with, and I am sure I looked confused. I was, but I survived. I owe my survival, at least in part, to the patience and the sense of humor of the submarine instructors who could see something in me that I certainly could not see. In the end I graduated from Submarine School in the middle of the class. It was six months of Hell Week, and I felt years older.

Some officers did not make it through Sub School and the rigorous training required to earn the coveted gold dolphins of a qualified submariner. A few could not deal with the intense pressure, especially in the trainers and at sea when every conceivable casualty was visited upon harried students. But some young officers had the opposite problem. They had not learned how to take anything seriously. One hapless young man clearly was not studying enough. He got a girl, and her mother, pregnant at the same time. He spent the rest of his Navy time on a Target somewhere.

The Cuban Missile Crisis happened during Sub School. I was glued to our old black and white TV at night while struggling with the details of submarine systems. I could feel in my bones that something was happening that we would study for years, but I missed most of the subtleties during the event. I wondered what the young Russians I had met a year earlier were thinking. They probably thought Nikita Khrushchev was going to get them incinerated. In two years he would be deposed for "hare-brained schemes."

Khrushchev was a country bumpkin with a big farmer's heart and a gambler's brain. Later, I would be reminded of what Stalin said about Molotov, a member of the Triumvirate who eventually took power after Stalin died in 1953. After sending Mrs. Molotov to the Gulag, Stalin said, "Molotov has brains, but his brains are stupid." Stalin, a brutal but wily and cautious man, might have said the same about Kennedy's Whiz Kids, who did not have the sense to stay out of Southeast Asia.

My glancing view of the Cuban Missile Crisis taught me something important about Naval Officers and world events. In spite of the fact that we can be players in a drama, or have a ringside seat, we are sometimes out of the loop and don't even get the news. This applies fairly often to domestic politics. It is not just that we live in an apolitical military culture. Sometimes we are simply immersed in other things, literally in the case of submariners.

USS SARDA (SS 488)

I got what most of the other Submarine School graduates considered to
be terrible orders. Because of their backgrounds, virtually every other
member of my Submarine School Class appeared to be, and probably
was, a more promising career officer than I was. I was ordered to USS
SARDA (SS-488), a "school boat," one of the older fleet submarines
that were often tasked to take enlisted and officer students on training
cruises. This duty was sometimes hair-raising but not glamorous.
SARDA was an old warhorse that still carried the mount for a gun
forward of her bridge. I was lucky. SARDA would dive more, face more
casualties real and simulated for students, and require more imagination
to keep running, than other submarines.

USS SARDA (SS 488) Official Navy photo

Ed Wood

SARDA had a skipper who was a legend on the Thames River in New
London. A Lieutenant Commander who had been repeatedly passed over
for promotion, Ed Wood was in his third command at sea, an unusual
thing. This was because no one would dispute that he was the best ship
handler around and the skipper anyone would choose if he had to take
one of these boats to war. But Ed was a peacetime disaster. He drank a
lot and cursed more. A taskmaster at sea, he was known to kick officers
off the bridge, sometimes physically. He was rude to his seniors, many
who had been junior to him at the Academy. He despised "politicians"
in uniform and Naval Reservists whom he regarded as uniformed
imposters. He told the Commodore that the latter were like seagulls:
"they ate shit and were protected by the government."

When I reported aboard, I found that the Gunnery Officer, a full Lieutenant with Gold Dolphins, had slipped and fallen on the tank tops, breaking a leg. Captain Wood was unconcerned. "He was a f---king idiot," Ed summarized and gave me, a raw ensign, his job as a Department Head. He said I could not do worse. I saw a bit of Unc in Captain Wood.

Our first cruise came quickly. I was on the bridge to learn how to be an Officer of the Deck at sea when Captain Wood pushed and kicked a Limited Duty Officer, a former enlisted man who had earned an officer's commission and who was trying hard to qualify as an Officer of the Deck, off the bridge. He looked at me as if to ask, "so what?" I carefully eased him away from where the enlisted lookouts could hear and said, "You are the Captain, and I understand that, Sir, but if you kick me, I will kick you back." He did not say a word, and went below to send up a qualified Officer of the Deck who arrived with a quizzical look. Captain Wood qualified me as a Deck Officer very soon after that.

Ed Wood arrived at the boat one day to find a sleek, long car parked in the Commanding Officer's space at the end of the pier. He roared down the ladder into the boat and found me, the assistant duty officer, first. He had nearly choked on the pipe that he kept perpetually lit. He yelled and literally jumped up and down. With his signature four-letter invective, he instructed me to remove the offending vehicle.

I ran up the ladder, across the brow, and found a Military Police vehicle at the end of the pier. As if it were a National Security Emergency, I told them to tow the car, which had no base decal on it, IMMEDIATELY. In two minutes it was hooked up and gone. It was towed unceremoniously off the base and left by the side of the road. The new Commander of our Submarine Squadron, who was reporting aboard and had not yet registered his car, was, to put it mildly, displeased.

The skipper was summoned to headquarters to have his first "interview" with his new boss. He returned to SARDA walking quite erect, as if he had a rod implanted where the sun does not shine. He confronted me in the wardroom passageway and yelled: "What the f---- were you thinking?" I looked him in the eye and answered: "You said to take care

of it. Don't tell me to do something if you don't want it done!" I think
I saw a little trace of a smile and heard nothing. He stormed into the
Captain's "stateroom," a tiny closet with a bunk and a desk. He qualified
me to stand in-port duty independently a few days later.

I was not a Navy "lifer," an officer committed to a full career in the
Navy. So, I feel the responsibility to say that junior officers, mostly
from the Naval Academy, who might read this, will think I was crazy to
address my Commanding Officer so frankly. Actually, I am not sure that
I believe that, but I do understand it.

I admit that what looks like insubordination on my part is at least partly
a product of the fact that I was paying the Navy back for my college
education and was not yet committed to a lifetime career. (It was also a
pretty accurate reflection of my upbringing!) This is important, so let me
explain.

I love the Navy, appreciate stern discipline and firm rules, and respect
the people who make them. I know that such institutions like the Navy
need "lifers." God bless them. But those institutions also need strong
people who stay only as long as it works for them – that is, as long as
the institution and they are working well together. Otherwise, I think,
the institution fails to hear and see the results when it is *not* working
well with the human capital that is its lifeblood. Further, the military
desperately needs to stay plugged into the civilian world that it serves
and they get that from citizen-soldiers, some who stay for successful and
productive careers.

Gold Dolphins

author's photo

I could handle the job of Gun Boss on the old boat because we had
an old fire control system and the same torpedoes and engines I had
studied in Sub School. The Chief of the Boat (COB), the senior enlisted

man aboard, made sure I stayed the Hell out of his way. The COB, the last Gunners Mate in submarines, was five feet four, 300 pounds of mostly muscle, and his knuckles almost touched the ground. I was also responsible for the Deck operation, which basically involved everything external on the boat and what could be included under "seamanship." This sounds like more work than it is. Enlisted men, under COB's supervision, were very good at all these things, did all the work, and delighted in teaching me how they did it.

My real job was to earn the designation "qualified in submarines" and win the coveted gold dolphins. This meant completing a notebook of two or three hundred pages that comprehensively covered every system in the boat along with the details of tactics and operations. Each chapter of the notebook had to be signed by a senior, qualified officer after he administered an oral examination. The skipper had the final word and decided when an officer could stand for the final examination.

There are two types of people on submarines. There are qualified submariners and a lower order of the human species called NQPs. Non-Qualified Pukes could not carry their weight. They are given the most menial, dirty jobs and hounded every spare minute of their lives to work on getting qualified. Failure to qualify meant being "surfaced." This is a fate worse than death. It meant that you were doomed to ride around forever in a Target, and you would forever be an NQP.

Wilma had returned to U of L while I completed Sub School and began my first sea tour in SARDA and the qualification ordeal. This meant I had nothing to do but get on with it, so I did. Ed Wood approved my candidacy and I underwent the required final examinations by two other skippers at the Sub Base: one an oral exam by a skipper and members of his wardroom, and the other by a skipper whose boat I had to take to sea, fire a torpedo, and return to port. I passed, and was promoted to Lieutenant, Junior Grade at about the same time. I took great satisfaction that no one else in my Sub School class was yet wearing gold dolphins.

In the meantime, Kennedy was assassinated. Watching this national trauma was dramatic. The promise of Camelot, given the challenges to American social order and Superpower identity at the time, was probably naive and doomed to fall prey to reality sooner or later, but the abrupt end of Kennedy's Thousand Days on November 22, 1963 really shocked us. We thought the handsome young President might actually handle the challenges to our Fifties-era worldview. We thought, like we erroneously thought about the feckless-looking Harry Truman, that LBJ could not possibly cope.

The good news was that Wilma was back! A new U of L graduate With High Honors, she had returned to Connecticut and was quickly recruited to teach at Mary Morrisson Elementary School outside the Submarine Base in Groton. She jumped right into a third grade class with none of the "how to" education courses under her belt. Of course, she was a smashing success at this, too. She enrolled at Willimantic State Teachers' College and proceeded directly to a Master's Degree while I was on sea duty. We moved into a tiny house near the school, a move that broke our bank, so once again we lived on a pot of Cincinnati chili, our favorite made with lots of spaghetti, until we had a payday.

Disarming Story

Often life at home for sailors is Hell, and it makes a Navy career almost impossible. In those days, pay was terrible. My base pay as a new officer was $212.11 a month. It was very difficult for enlisted sailors and their families to make it. Tension at home resulted from poor pay and deployment at sea. Sometimes sailors, like people everywhere, just make terrible choices.

A very competent Chief Petty Officer was not paying attention to his job. He began to arrive late. I confronted him, and he claimed that he had married a crazy woman. (Not his exact words!) She had spent him into deep debt, drank too much, and hated the Navy. He said he thought the only way out was to kill her. I explained to him that this was not a good idea and insisted that he stay aboard for a day or two. He did, and seemed to calm down. He headed home a day before we were to get underway for a week.

I got a phone call in the afternoon. It was the Chief. "I'm going to kill her," he said matter-of-factly. I told him that I was on the way and to wait to talk to me. He agreed. I raced over to his house to find him sitting on the steps outside his house with a .32 caliber revolver in his lap. Drunk as a skunk, his wife was screaming at the top of her lungs about what a useless human being he was. (Not her exact words either.) It occurred to me that he was not wrong about her being crazy. Killing her was illegal but not totally irrational.

He did not object when I took the revolver, unloaded it, and threw it into the back seat of my car. Fortunately I did this before the police arrived. He went quietly with them. I did not mention the gun, and the policemen did not ask about it. I still have it. The Chief was charged with disturbing the peace, which was unfair but not surprising given that it was not the first time he had been warned. It was a lot better than if he had still held the gun.

He did not return to the boat and he eventually left both the crazy woman and the Navy. Nowadays she would claim part of his meager 20-year retirement pay. I don't think she did at that time. I generally agree that a Navy Wife earns part of her husband's retirement pay. Mine absolutely did earn that. But that nutty woman did not.

Racing Home

Once, we were heading home from operating in Long Island Sound in company with another boat that had undergone upgrades. She had newer GE engines and a sleeker profile. Ed Wood was not going to let that boat get into port ahead of SARDA. It turned into a race. After passing "Point Alpha," a marker two miles ahead at the entrance to the Thames River, one boat would have to fall in behind the other in the channel of the River.

SARDA kept adding "turns," or shaft turns, beyond the normal full speed load. No one on the bridge asked if any red lines were passed, and no one reported that they were. It looked like the two boats were making the same speed, but the challenger was a nose ahead. We had the inside track, so when we made the turn westward into the Thames, it would be very close. A final buoy before reaching the River loomed dead ahead.

It was supposed to be left to port and a slight turn eastward to leave it to port would slow us a tiny bit.

The skipper changed course a couple of degrees to the west and the buoy slid about three meters down the Starboard side while our challenger, following the rules, left it a respectful distance to port. Now, with a slightly wider inside track, SARDA came left and led up the River. We were so close I could hear the orders on the other bridge. To the credit of the sailors of both boats, no one squealed.

This incident reminded a senior officer of another incident when the boat was in the Mediterranean in a naval exercise. SARDA was supposed to be the bait for an aircraft carrier task group that would search her out and kill her if they could. I think the skipper of the carrier was from Ed's Naval Academy days and two ranks senior to him, a Navy Captain. SARDA slipped out of the exercise area and hid on the bottom so close to shallower water that rocks stirred up and hit the hull. As soon as the exercise began, Ed Wood charged directly at the carrier and "sunk" her with a barrage of pretend torpedoes. He surfaced and sent a message equivalent to "Bang, Bang, You're Dead" to the carrier. There was outrage. Ed had not followed the rules! It was unfair, etc.

The skipper ignored complaints about fair play and knew he would take his lumps later. He mumbled something to the effect of "in war there are only winners." If you are going to pretend to be in war, games and rules were silly. This made no sense to planners and trainers, but it made perfect sense to Ed Wood who was a warfighter, not a game player. In a peacetime Navy, he would never be promoted. In war, he would have been decorated.

I am not certain how Ed Wood's behavior fit the Honor Code at the Academy, but I would have gone to war with him. So would every man in that crew.

A Ship Dies

SARDA was worked like a rented mule. Every one of her officers had more diving experience and more ship handling practice than officers on other boats. The old girl was not selected for the major improvements and updates that her sister ships got, so she was scheduled to retire in 1964. I was kept aboard to prepare her for decommissioning and did the task with some sadness.

Ed Wood retired at the mandatory retirement date. There was a sad ceremony where senior officers said a lot of things they did not mean. I will never forget Lieutenant Commander Wood's final words in uniform. The officer who had been rejected by his beloved Navy said he would gladly stay if the Navy would let him. Then he was piped across the brow by a boatswain mate's whistle.

A ship is a living thing. A man can love a ship and be indebted to her, and seeing her die is not a pleasant task. In my case, I had benefitted enormously from her final year. I had become a seagoing officer in SARDA and had learned more in her than I would ever learn at any school.

SARDA Claims to Fame

SARDA had more dives than any submarine in history. I was the Diving Officer for her 10,000[th] dive and for the last of over 13,000 dives. She was the last submarine hull to sport a 5-inch gun on her forward deck, an anachronism that was removed before I came on board.

SARDA was also known in the submarine force for a unique painting in the officers' wardroom. Tell someone you were serving in SARDA and they would reply: "Oh, the boat with The Painting." While undergoing shipyard overhaul in the 1950s, the ship's officers commissioned a beatnik painter in Philadelphia to do a painting to mount on the bulkhead opposite the wardroom table.

The story is that he had his mistress, apparently a comely and well-endowed lass, "sit" for the painting in a bathtub. The result was a long green figure in a tropical island setting with waterfalls and dancing figures around it. Timothy O'Leary-like, it was somewhat ambiguous and fuzzy, but sailors would immediately see a shapely nude dominating the piece.

It was a part of submarine history that belonged to the SARDA
Wardroom and not to the government. As the last officers in her crew,
the Skipper, the Limited Duty Officer who had been kicked off the
bridge by Ed Wood, and I drew straws. I won. The picture still hangs on
a Kime wall.

USS SARDA's wardroom painting
photo by the author

USS IREX (SS 482)

I was transferred to USS IREX (SS 482) in 1964. IREX was deployed
frequently but sometimes was assigned local school boat duty. Like
SARDA, IREX was a hard worker, like a utility infielder on a baseball
team who gets a lot of playing time. The new nukes got all the priority
and were better equipped for the glamorous assignments, but in the early
Sixties boats like IREX were old workhorses that picked up the slack
when there were problems.

Diesel sailors got to be real sailors and do the fun things that sailors do.
We visited ports. We saw sunsets and sunrises. We lived with the sea and
not just under it. We drove our boats like men-o-war had been driven for
centuries: tugboats did not take us in and out of port. We navigated by
the stars. THEY, the nukes, were engineers and technicians. WE were
sailors.

During the next three years, I would hold every Department Head job
in IREX, serve as Senior Watch Officer, and work on the practical
factors for command qualification. I wish that every young man in his
mid-twenties could have an experience like I had in those three years.
I learned more about ships, machinery and people in those three years
than at any other time in my life.

USS IREX (SS 482)
Official Navy photo

As a 23-year-old officer I carried quite a bit of responsibility aboard IREX as we prepared for a deployment to the Mediterranean and through the Suez Canal to Pakistan. Our mission was to deliver an accompanying submarine, the old USS DIABLO, to Pakistan. We had trained the Pakistani officers who, by the way, were to lose their lives on December 2, 1971 when their boat, renamed the GHAZI, was sunk by the Indian Carrier VIKRANT.

IREX was blessed with a fine skipper, Lieutenant Commander Douglas Murray, a Naval Academy graduate and solid submariner. Not only did he possess the legendary submariner's sense of humor and gift for the profane, he was the kind of leader that younger men looked up to. He exuded competence, having been a successful Engineer and Executive Officer. His greatest flaw was a tendency to declare every problem a "ten minute job." IREX probably got tougher and more interesting assignments because Murray was in command. He had that kind of reputation. Doug Murray, and his successor, Robert Denbigh, taught me what being an officer is all about. Every young man should have role models like these talented leaders. To the Navy's great credit, both were eventually promoted to the rank of Captain.

The 1964 – 1965 cruise to the Mediterranean, Red and Arabian Seas in IREX was an incredible learning experience. It began in Rota, Spain, where we loaded Löwenbräu Light into one torpedo tube and Löwenbräu

Dark into another. Apparently some things specifically forbidden could be done anyway. Swim call in the heat of the Arabian Sea was greatly enhanced.

We visited Malta, and Beirut, which was the Pearl of the Mediterranean before the rabble destroyed it. I led a tour to the Holy Land, then in the hands of people who insisted that Jews in my group of sailors be identified. I refused and, after a standoff, was permitted to travel on. Catholic nuns escorted us to all of the famous biblical sites in the area without incident.

Before heading to Suez, the Red Sea and on to Karachi, we had scheduled a quick painting of IREX. The appropriate grey toned paint was stored in pressure-proof cans in the "paint locker" topside. Unfortunately, the paint did not survive the trip. IREX looked a little the worse for wear and really needed to be spruced up. A British warship was willing to help but had only black paint to spare. The skipper, to his credit, did not bat an eye. All hands fell out on deck and IREX became solid black. Black was beautiful, and IREX finished the cruise looking different, but good.

IREX spent my 24th birthday in December anchored in Egypt's Lake Tisma, and visited Aden in what would become the Republic of Yemen. Aden was a dangerous place, full of whacky radicals where liberty rules required going ashore in pairs. British soldiers were killed the week that we were there. The suicide attack against the United States Navy destroyer USS COLE (DDG 67) on October 12, 2000, was no surprise to anyone who had made a ship visit to that port. Similarly, it was no surprise that terrorists would find congenial hideouts there in this century.

It was hot as Hades in the Arabian Sea, though the glass-smooth sea and our wake, lit up by millions of luminous sea creatures, was beautiful. It was so hot that it was nearly impossible to make water in the old stills that we had on board. You need a temperature differential between the intake water and the stills to precipitate a meaningful amount of water. Showers were very strictly limited. So, we had swim call, a much-enjoyed event. A fifty-gallon drum, cut in half, made a grill and steaks were broiled. Beer that had been stowed and locked in torpedo tubes in Rota, Spain was broken out. The crew stood "Port and Starboard," meaning that they were divided into two sections and one enjoyed the picnic while the other minded the store.

There were lots of sharks and dolphins. During swim call we posted our best sharpshooter on the bridge to scare away any sharks sighted while we got everyone back on board. Some skeptics said sharks were not really a big problem, so we did an experiment on the midnight watch. Three 5-gallon milk cans served as bobbers and "21 thread," the Navy's all-purpose rope, was used as fishing line. The enginemen fashioned an enormous hook out of cold rolled steel. A huge chunk of raw pork was the bait. In those days, I am sorry to report, garbage was put over the side, so we put our makeshift fishing gear out with the garbage. We were not prepared for what happened. The milk cans disappeared and the line was pulled so hard that we were sure it would part. IREX was making about 12 knots so the beast started to wear out in a while. Several sailors pulled on the line until the shark was pulled alongside. It was enormous and scary looking. Estimates at the time were that it was about 22 feet long, but it grew considerably during the cruise. No one was anxious to go out on deck to try to release it, so the line was cut. There were fewer participants at swim call after that.

Our stop in Karachi, Pakistan was an eye-opener. I was the Officer of the Deck as we approached the city and I will never forget the blanket of haze and dirt that hung over Karachi. It was visible for miles and it accurately signaled the nature of the place. We were welcomed of course because we were delivering a submarine to Pakistan. We had trained the Pakistani crew, who were capable and grateful sailors, and they were good hosts. The U.S. was playing a balancing act with India at the time and we were treated well. None of this could mask the reality that was visible on the streets.

Pakistan was dangerous and dirty. The briefing for anyone going ashore scared even the most randy sailor. Travelling in groups was recommended. There were plenty of hand-made souvenirs to buy but no entertainment to speak of where sailors could let off steam. Instead, there was Breathless Corner, which was a kind of Hell on Earth. Mothers

should not appear

blinded and crippled their children so they would be more pitiful beggars there. Bodies were collected on the streets early each morning. Ordinary Pakistanis were not very friendly to what, even in 1963, must have been perceived as foreign infidels. Many years later, as it became apparent that Pakistan was the base of radical anti-Americanism that flourished in neighboring Afghanistan and that there was only reluctant assistance from Pakistan in fighting terrorism, I was not surprised.

After transiting the Suez back to the Mediterranean, we visited Spanish, Italian and French ports and were the first ship to visit Ibiza in the Balearic Islands, which was later spoiled as a tourist Mecca. There was one bottle of Johnny Walker Red on the island when we visited Ibiza, and we helped drink it.

In Monaco, a special treat was provided when a stretch limousine unloaded a case of champagne for the crew. I never found out who these benefactors were. (They might have been from the palace, but Princess Grace did not acknowledge that when I asked her the next day.) I was duty officer and all the other officers were ashore, so I made a command decision. Off duty men would drink half the champagne and wait eight hours to relieve the watch. Those on duty would drink the rest after they were relieved. They did.

In Beirut another officer and I had an interesting experience. The city was an open market for about anything, including jewelry. Someone provided a contact who showed up in a limousine and whisked us away. We were told to look downward and not out the windows as the machine twisted through alleys. When it stopped, we went in a door, up an elevator, and into a room that looked like a pirate's den. Open drawers revealed thousands of loose jewels and pieces of gold jewelry. My colleague was from a rich family and probably made the trip worthwhile for the sellers, but, of course, I had no money to speak of. I did buy some amethyst, Wilma's birthstone.

Also in Beirut, I attended a dinner party hosted by the Naval Attaché with the Captain because the Russian Attaché would be there. I got a one-night promotion because the only dinner-dress uniform on board besides the skipper's was that of a full Lieutenant. (He had longer arms than I did.) My modest service as an interpreter that evening, which impressed the boss, was "mentioned in dispatches," and was reflected in my fitness report. Every skipper I had mentioned my interest in Russia and politics. This made a difference in future assignments.

Sub Stories

> *A Fairy Tale begins with: "Once Upon a Time"*
> *A sea story starts with: "Now this is no shit"*
> *Bruce Schick*

The quote above is from Bruce Schick, an IREX sailor and diesel boat skipper. Materials used in this book are Reprinted from <u>Whale's Tales, Recollections of a Diesel Submariner</u>. DBF Press, 2006. Sadly he died recently and can no longer provide signed copies. His stories about life in the boats reveal much about my own coming of age in the Navy, and about the Navy itself. It deserves reading, especially by young officers.

My tour aboard IREX was a critical part of my life and education. Where else does a youngster in his mid-twenties get the kind of responsibility that the military confers on its officers? As a 24-year old liberal arts graduate, I was Chief Engineer when we underwent shipyard overhaul. We cut the pressure hull open, removed all the equipment, and overhauled it. This included engines and generators as big as a truck, a half-million pounds of lead-acid batteries, and shafts and screws. We put it all back together, with key inspection slips at every juncture signed by me. Then, with over a hundred sailor and "yard bird" souls aboard, we took her out and dived her to test depth. Shipyard overhaul is about leadership and management as much as it is about fixing machinery. For the rest of my life, on political, strategic, intelligence matters, or on how to repair, manage, operate, or build anything at all, I knew I could do it.

This kind of confidence is drummed into hundreds of young men, and today women, every year. I have often summoned it. One incident while I was aboard IREX is a an example. We were scheduled for docking and maintenance at the marine railway at the Submarine Base at Groton. This is a feat of engineering where a ship is maneuvered onto blocks that are set up to receive its hull and pull it up a set of rails by huge chains. The chains are then locked in place when the ship is high and dry. This was done to IREX. The marine railway officials signaled that all was in order, and the non-duty crew was sent on liberty. The skipper was holding Captain's Mast, a disciplinary hearing, in the officers' wardroom. I was still aboard as teams prepared to go beneath the boat to crawl into tanks and inspect the hull, screws, and sonar domes. Just as they began to to do this, a huge, metallic bang was heard inside and outside IREX.

I was in the Control Room, two ladders below the Bridge. It took only a few seconds to get to the Bridge and see a horror that I can still see to this day. The chains had let go, and IREX was slipping slowly, as if in a nightmare, backward into the Thames River. Railroad ties were flying tens of feet into the air and had clogged the steel screw guards. I sounded General Quarters. In the first split seconds I thought first about the enlisted engineers who were probably already inside the tanks and under the hull and the hopelessness of their situation. Miraculously, I saw some of them, soaking wet, scrambling up ladders and jumping to the pier as IREX was steadily sliding by.

Submariners at all ranks and ratings are conditioned to deal with casualties. Each watch section not on liberty contains personnel that can get the ship underway. In a flash, men in the maneuvering room had unlocked the shafts and piped up their readiness to "answer bells on the battery." I looked aft at the railroad ties in the screws and decided to risk wrecking one of them, at least. I ordered a back bell on the port shaft, and someone at the helm acknowledged a rudder order. A fuse that had been pulled in a maintenance procedure had to be replaced before the rudder could be used. The skipper, rushing to the Bridge, hit his head on the conning tower hatch, which someone slammed shut on hearing the collision alarm. We backed her out, fearing that we had lost some shipmates, and we got her tied up to the next pier.

It was a tense time as we tried to account for members of the crew. We weren't sure who had left on liberty and who had not. We were sure that one sonarman was inside the forward sonar dome. Incredibly, all were eventually accounted for! The sonarman had elected to go pick up guard mail before inspecting the sonar dome, a choice that most probably saved his life. A few seconds was the margin between our great good fortune and a calamity.

There are on any submarine a million lighter moments. If you perpetually smell like diesel oil, breathe the methane-supplemented air of a hundred young men, and sleep on top of a torpedo or a battery, you have to have a sense of humor. They were a saucy bunch, too. I will never forget the competition to meet Princess Grace at the bottom of the ladder when she came aboard for dinner in Monaco. To their disappointment, she wisely elected to wear slacks.

Once, a Commodore known for his uptight attitudes rode IREX to justify his submarine pay. This guy wrote the skipper's fitness report. Enough said. One of our machinists mates had a vocabulary that was, to put it kindly, full of very short words. He also had a wicked sense of humor.

In the process of snorkeling, during which the boat sucks in air to run its engines submerged and charge its batteries, the conning officer raises the snorkel mast and carefully inspects whether the Snorkel Head Valve on the mast opens and shuts properly if water inundates it. (Otherwise the flooding could sink the boat when a huge valve, the Snorkel Induction Valve, is ordered opened. It is a routine task for well-qualified crew but an inherently dangerous one.) IREX had the first snorkel in the Navy, a curiosity to visiting officers. I gave the order, "prepare to snorkel on two main engines." The snorkel mast and the periscope went up and I noticed that the Commodore had hurried to the conning tower.

I examined the Snorkel Head Valve through the periscope as usual. Written in neat block letters was Machinist Mate Second Class John Fields' favorite saying when things did not go his way: "LIFE IS A SHIT SANDWICH." I pretended not to see it and continued with the routine, shouting "Open" and "Shut" as the valve reacted properly to the sea. I pronounced it OK, and the Commodore tapped me on the arm. "Let me take a look," he said. By this time, the skipper had wedged his way into the small space alongside his boss. I pretended that I had not heard the Commodore and lowered the scope. The skipper frowned at me, raised it, and motioned the Commodore to take a look. I held my breath. The

Commodore took a long look, turned the scope to me, smiled, and said, "Looks OK to me, too" before going below. He was a submariner, too.

Commander Bruce Schick, cited above, tells a typical IREX story. The sanitary tanks, into which the toilets flushed, had to be blown to sea when full. A nonqualified mess cook, who works for the cook who has seen this go wrong a few times, does the unpleasant chore. Done properly, this is routine, but if a mess cook vents the tank improperly, he blows sewage into the crew's' compartment. The duty auxiliaryman is called to set it right. Unhappy, he heads to a nasty scene. Schick tells it this way:

> *The cook scraped a two-finger glob of peanut butter from a nearby jar and ambled back to the head. Arriving at the scene he asked the auxiliaryman what the problem was. The answer was immediate and furious. "Your #@$^%$# mess cook has blown shit all over the place."*

> *The cook reached up to the overhead (ceiling), scraped off a glob of peanut butter which he had kept concealed in his hand, tasted it, and reported, "yep, that's shit." The auxiliaryman promptly puked.*

No one messes with the cook in a submarine.

Submariners of all ranks and rates will rise to an occasion. Petty Officer Second Class Fields won a contest to lead a delegation of enlisted men from IREX invited to a dinner with Princess Grace and Prince Rainier at the palace in Monaco. The Wardroom was worried, and this was made worse by Fields' assurance, "Don't worry! I won't f—- up."

,Fields, resplendent in his dress blue sailor's uniform, was a model of tact and diplomacy by all accounts, including that of the Princess herself, who raved about the debonair young man who presented a bouquet of orchids! That day, at least, life for Fields was a cucumber sandwich.

When IREX was in the shipyard in Philadelphia, the Captain wanted to refurbish the officers' and crew's quarters. The estimate for doing this was astronomical, and the Navy rejected the work requests. Every submariner on the planet has to become a "cumshaw artist," or wheeler-dealer, who could get things done by bartering. Shipyard workers would kill for a leather Navy foul weather jacket, and a pair of boots would get some valve handles chromed. We left Philadelphia with beautiful officers' and crew's quarters. "Don't ask, don't tell" meant something else before it was applied to sexual orientation.

Submarines can be peculiar little communities. A crew can take pride in something that seems ridiculous, like the painting in SARDA's wardroom. Once my Chief Engineman and I came up with a crazy idea. The engine rooms, where four Fairbanks-Morse 38D8&1/8 engines rumbled, were difficult to keep clean. The engines and all their associated machinery always leaked some oil in the bilges, condensation was an issue, and foot traffic fore and aft constantly traversed the engine rooms. We decided to paint the engine rooms white, including engines, generators, bilges, and bulkheads! This sounded crazy, but it turned out that it was easier to keep the engine rooms clean once the ordeal of scrubbing and painting them was over. The engines were beautiful with white enamel on them. They could be hosed down with hot water and soap. It became a "signature" trait of IREX on the river and a source of pride. Sailors in port from other boats would come over for a look.

Having noted the famous painting of the USS SARDA, I would be remiss not to mention that the IREX wardroom once had a famous painting too. Unlike SARDA's painting, IREX's art was not just suggestive. The masterpiece disappeared years before I ever saw IREX but that painting is still part of submarine lore. There are theories ranging from accusing a "yardbird" in the Philadelphia shipyard to a dastardly theft by the wardroom of another boat, but its fate remains a mystery.

"Polaris for Peace"

During the early 1960s it became almost impossible for old diesel boats to get repair parts in a hurry. A "priority #2" supply chit was required to get immediate treatment and such requisitions had to be signed by an officer with the rank of Full Commander. Only half the skippers of the diesel boats were Full Commanders. A "Polaris for Peace Stamp" on the chit helped. Every officer had to do a stint as supply officer, and I had a 2nd Class Storekeeper to help. He was a stud.

We managed to get crucial parts, as for the "stills," temperamental equipment that condensed fresh water from salt water. When we were going to be deployed, we managed to get crucial parts by "accidentally" putting a "2" in the priority box, making my rank illegible, and stamping over it with a "borrowed" Polaris for Peace Stamp. The young lady who received supply chits was a well-endowed brunette whose First Class Electrician husband was deployed in a Boomer, or Polaris sub. My Storekeeper had a cozy arrangement with this comely lass. When the Boomer was deployed, we could get almost anything we needed. "Needs of the Service" took on a new meaning.

SPRINGBOARD

IREX was in St. Thomas of the Virgin Islands fairly often. Every January, at the first sign of snow in Connecticut, we would leave for an operation called SPRINGBOARD. While spouses shoveled snow, we Saved The World For Democracy by honing our skills in Caribbean waters for six weeks. The operations tempo was very high. Targets (destroyers and other surface-skimming craft) and antisubmarine aircraft needed to try to find us for practice. This was tiring, so we spent a little time in all the ports. St. Thomas had a large drawback: there was a federal judge there who had no patience with sailors who misbehaved. He had kept one locked up for months, and the Navy was having a difficult time getting him out. We were cautioned that it was an unsympathetic Federal Jurisdiction, and we warned each member of the liberty party to be on his best behavior.

The best behavior of my 1/C Torpedoman was not very good when he had a few drinks in him. He was a solid 220 pounds and about 6'3" tall. He put two fellows in Sick Bay, tore up a bar, and got thrown in jail. He was a bad actor, so neither the Chief of the Boat nor I really cared if he rotted there, but there was real danger of it becoming a highly visible Navy incident, embarrassing the skipper and IREX. The COB and I went to arraignment the next morning. We sat in the back row.

The Judge went through a number of whores and bums before our Petty Officer was brought up. The Judge pointed to our uniforms and asked, "Is there anyone here with a good word for this sailor?" I checked the Chief of the Boat who prepared to stand. We did not move or speak. The judge pointed at me directly and said, "Sir, aren't you going to speak for this man?" I stood and said: "Judge, I have nothing good to say. If you will turn him over to me, the Chief will administer appropriate punishment." The judge released him for the cost of repairs to the bar, which the COB paid in cash from a huge wad in his pocket. I explained my deal aboard the boat and the Chief took care of it. We made a long deployment and visited many exotic places, and I'm not sure the Torpedoman ever crossed the brow. The torpedo tubes glistened. God knows how COB got his money back.

Family

In January of 1965, on the way back across the Atlantic in a fearful storm in the Bermuda Triangle, I got the news that my father had died. Dad was not yet 62 years old, but he died an old man. The railroad had used him up. He was from a time when not all of the boys, and none of the girls in many families, got to go far in school. The eldest, Uncle Edwin, became a medical doctor but the other boys went to work. My aunts, like my mom, were to be mothers. Period. Dad was very bright, so bright that there was a brief time when he began studies that would have made him a priest. He did not get far, and, by 16, he was married and working on the railroad. As he put it, he "pounded cinders" all of his life. Like almost all his peers, and most of his children, he shortened his life by smoking. The Railroad retired him at age 60 because of heart issues. He drew his railroad retirement check for only a few months before he was gone.

We got the message on IREX several hours late due to the storm. I had completed a midnight watch strapped to the bridge by lifelines and had turned in when the Captain gave me the unexpected news. The skipper said we could stop in Bermuda and let me debark and head home. He stiffened a little when I immediately said no, reminding me gently that he decided such things. I explained what I knew to be true: Dad was a working man who would not want the sailors aboard, who had not seen their families for months, to be delayed a day because of him. I stood the midnight watch. IREX proceeded directly home.

My family would have to wait for the funeral. Wilma met me at the pier, and we drove directly to Indiana. In a little anteroom at the funeral home, I got to say good-bye. This was important to me, a son whose father was a roughhewn man of few words whose emotions were not easily shared. He had not communicated very well. I think Dad had been pleased with my hard work as a kid, and I was touched when he gave me a little suitcase when I went off to college. He wondered about the value of college and said outright that it was a waste of time for girls like Wilma, so the gift was symbolic. After we were married, his most remembered comment was a question: "Are you kids ever going to have anything but dogs?" One of my greatest regrets is that he could not be there the following year when Carl Martin Kime, a future Marine Colonel named for both his grandfathers, was born.

In January of 1966, my sister Lila died at age 28. She was a bit older than I, but I considered her my little sister. She had quit high school and left home at 15 to marry. It was partly a rebellion against a turbulent home situation caused by the early death of our Mom, the remarriage of Dad, and the inability of some of my siblings to deal with it. Lila was the kind of beauty who could stop traffic, and she was infatuated with a 16-year-old boy who was every bit as attractive.

It was America in the Fifties, and getting married at 15 was tragic but not unusual. Neither was it unusual when the marriage, funded by menial jobs and suffering from the narcissism of an uneducated boy, failed. A son had been born in 1956 and a daughter on JFK's Election Day in 1960.

At the funeral, it became clear that the future of Lila's two children, Barrett and Lauren, was murky. The father had not paid child support, was remarried and living elsewhere, and it was an open

question whether he wanted them. His parents, decent hardworking people, had taken the children for the funeral, but that did not seem to be a viable permanent option. Very importantly, the authorities at the county childcare authority were concerned about the welfare of the children. A warrant for nonsupport had been issued for the father before Lila had died. The lady in charge of county childcare support insisted on a court hearing to smoke out the capability, attitude and intentions of the father and his current family. She asked me where I stood on all this, and I said we would find a way to deal with this if the father and his family would not or could not. She asked me to attend the hearing.

In court, the father was mostly concerned with getting back the $1,300 support money he had to put up to stay out of jail and with getting any new warrant from being issued. His wife was clearly unenthusiastic about ending up with two new kids. The judge asked me what I thought, and I told him. This was a family responsibility. He gave me temporary custody of the children pending a review by the court in several weeks.

I called Wilma after the hearing. It was a short but life-changing phone call. "You are bringing the kids home, aren't you?" The magnificence of those few words from a 24-year-old straight from the heart, and from the American Heartland, cannot be measured. She had just learned that she was pregnant with her first baby, was teaching full time and working on her Master's Degree, and was often stuck at home while I was at sea. We were in a tiny house with three dogs, were keeping a horse, and we were not making much money. Even now, half a century later, I marvel at the plain down-to-earth spontaneous goodness in her. Every single thing she has done since that day confirms it.

I first took the two children to Wilma's parents' house where Carl and Alberta Snook did not bat an eye. The kids were received as new grandchildren without hesitation or reservation. During the new grandparents' lifetimes, no birthday was ever missed. I flew with the children to Newark, picked up my T-Bird and drove home. They were told the first day that I was Dad and Wilma was Mom.

Our worlds were changed forever. We bought a house in Mystic, Connecticut with the loan that Aunt Mil Denny provided. The T-Bird was traded in for a used maroon 1964 six-cylinder station Chevrolet wagon. Barry, age 9, and Lauren, age 5, were enrolled in school and, bright children that they were, did fine. I went back to a busy schedule at sea and Wilma, incredibly, coped. No wonder that my children to this day consider the lady a Saint.

Dodging a bullet

After two years in IREX the Navy wanted to move me to another submarine in Key West. I wanted to stay in the Navy one more year to see if I got selected for postgraduate school, and going to Key West meant a two-year commitment. But the whole truth was about something else. Wilma had wanted a horse since childhood, and I had bought her one. Prince, a big white gelding, was the fulfillment of a promise I had made to her as a teenager.

I checked with the officer in Key West whom I was slated to relieve. He was being moved to New London under a Navy policy that held that officers needed to be moved around for the good of their careers. He wanted to stay in Key West. I had never been to Washington, D.C., and I had no idea how to get my orders changed, but I resolved to give it a try.

I flew to Washington and went to beard the submarine "detailer" in his cage. This powerful Captain's cage was in the dilapidated Navy Annex to the Pentagon. He controlled the destinies of junior officers like me.

I stood before a full Commander outside the Detailer's office and stated my case: it made little sense to move, at considerable expense, two officers who were content to serve where they were. The Commander began to tell me the Navy Facts of Life. Finally, I interrupted him and said "Sir, the truth is we just bought a horse, and there is no way I can keep him in Key West."

Immediately, like in the Wizard of Oz, a disembodied voice came from inside the Captain's office: "He told you the truth. Change his orders!" He did.

I never met the Wizard.

The Road Not Taken

The dramatic changes in my family in the mid-60s noted earlier came as big decisions had to be made both by me and by the Navy. Two issues were key: nuclear power and higher education.

Hyman Rickover, the Godfather of nuclear submarines, lacked the broad perspective of a good Naval officer, but he was a national treasure and all of us knew it. He presided over a technological revolution at a key time in history about as effectively as could have been done.

Rickover was a cultural revolutionary, at least in the Navy; he changed Navy cultural patterns. Because his mission was to effect radical change, the Navy would never have promoted him. As I will discuss later, "pattern maintenance," sticking to established pathways, is required for success in the Navy, so Rickover's career had come to a dead stop. It took Congress to impose Admiral Rickover on the Navy.

He understood that the maxim, "perfect is the enemy of good enough," which had to guide submariners trying to keep the old boats together, simply could not be applied to nuclear reactors underwater. Perfect had to be the standard. His obsession with quality and safety of propulsion systems made sense.

History justified Hyman Rickover, but the price was extremely high. It is not proven that he had to be a jerk to do his job. Rickover's personnel process wasted promising Navy human capital, and it blatantly abused decent human beings and dedicated Naval Officers. My skippers, solid role models and leaders, were not to be nuclear submariners. Rickover discounted many of the things that make a Navy great and that make going to sea a fabulous profession.

It became clear to young seagoing officers that he was narrow-mindedly selecting engineers and yes-men. I do not mean to suggest that only losers were selected to operate nuclear submarines: history proves otherwise. But Rickover was brow beating outstanding officers who had proven themselves at sea and who would have been just as able to run a nuclear teapot or anything else.

He threw them out of his office because of math grades they made as teenagers or young men, or because they just might disagree with him. Those who valued the things that make a seagoing profession attractive saw Rickover making terrible personnel decisions.

Once, as Engineer Officer, I was given a math quiz along with other officers at Groton. I apparently did OK for a lowly liberal arts type and was told that I would be summoned to see the Great Man. I did not go. I wrote, in hand, a resignation. I did not want to serve as an engineer for the rest of my career. Even commanding officers in nukes were engineers first, foremost, and always. But there was more than that.

I had discovered that Rickover blocked officers that he might want to recruit from being put on the selection list for Postgraduate school! Rickover made a Naval career a Hobson's choice. In his view, it was nuclear teapot school or nothing. This institutional myopia made me angry with the Navy for the first time in my life.

I wanted to be selected for what was called the Navy's #671 Program in International Studies. I had applied for it and, since I was better qualified than those selected and had done everything possible on sea duty, could not figure out why I was not on the list. I applied for admission to Harvard's John F. Kennedy School on my own. I had no clue how I was going to do it, having just adopted two kids and with a new baby and no Navy paycheck. But I was going to graduate school. Damn the Nuclear Teapots—Full Speed Ahead!

Surface! Surface! Surface!

I loved submarines and submariners and still do. But there is a time for all things and in 1967 I sensed that my time in submarines was coming to an end. It was clear to me that there was no way to speed up a system that would require me to spend the next decade doing the same things that I had already done before it was possible to get a command in submarines, if in fact there were any non-nuclear submarine commands left. And yet, graduate school did not seem to be a Navy option, or even a hope, for me. There seemed to be no Navy future for an officer like me.

I was just 26 years old, so some Navy readers will recognize in this the immature perspective of a junior officer on policy matters far out of his pay grade. Some will see arrogance. Both are at least partly correct, but I know that now only in retrospect. This is very important for military leaders to understand: not every officer is a "lifer" dedicated to marching lock-step through a rigidly predetermined career. A personnel system that relies too heavily on Naval Academy graduates for the long haul, while simply exploiting other officers in the junior ranks, risks losing an enormous amount of talented human capital -- and flexibility -- as those junior officers leave the service to seek their opportunities elsewhere.

The Navy was certainly correct to require 15 years of experience to attain command at sea, and it was correct to place its eggs in the nuclear basket; but it did not place as much emphasis on higher education as it should have, and it was shortsighted to deny graduate school to proven officers.

Much later in my Navy career, it occurred to me that some of the best nuclear submariners probably agreed with my view of Rickover and the way that he selected officers. Many of us who wore dolphins, had good reputations as seagoing officers, and either chose a different pathway or were forced into one, were highly valued and promoted by Navy leaders, including nuclear submarine admirals.

And that has made all the difference.

Chapter VII
Dolphins Speak
And a Door Opens

For the record, I understand that the
Navy is not about, and must not be about,
individual officers and what they want.
Some would say that good officers suck it
up and bow to the "needs of the Service."
Some of the best officers I know adhered
to this concept, and I have always been
acutely aware of the fact that I did not.

An institution like the Navy could not tolerate a personnel system full
of people like me. I sometimes regretted being part of a Navy that I
loved and respected but did not fit very well. I convinced myself that the
honorable thing was probably to leave the Navy.

My intention to tell Rickover to take his job and stuff it made its way
up the chain of command to the Staff of the Deputy Commander of
Submarines, Atlantic, a few hundred yards away from the submarine
piers. It is important to understand that *all* submariners are members of
a large extended family. The many submariners who stayed in the Navy
but did not choose to become nuclear reactor operators, or simply were
rejected by Rickover, were still members of a powerful and supportive
Navy submarine family. There were very senior submarine officers,
including those Rickover could not avoid, who continued to value the
seagoing attitude and culture of officers from the old diesel boats.

Many of these officers, and some who endured and survived Rickover and became nuclear submariners, had earned their Gold Dolphins helping to hold the old boats together with baling wire and duct tape. They must have missed the camaraderie and "damn the torpedoes" attitudes of their diesel-electric brethren as they dealt with Rickover's anal-retentive nuclear submarine force.

Directors of Naval Intelligence wore dolphins. Chiefs of Naval Operations, Fleet Commanders, and Chiefs of Naval Personnel often wore dolphins. Some of these, including war heroes, a couple of whom wore The Medal of Honor, served tours as senior officers in Groton.

I was questioned by one of these heroes, a Captain on the Staff of the Deputy Commander of Submarines in the Atlantic. Maurice "Mike" Rindskopf had been the youngest skipper of a submarine in WWII, the USS DRUM, and had won a Navy Cross and a Silver Star for his heroism. He was a rare high-ranking Jewish officer in the Navy of the time, was destined to be Director of Naval Intelligence, and was not your average career officer. He listened to the opinions and views related above, nodded, and asked what I wanted to happen.

I said I wanted to be accepted into the Navy's Graduate Program in International Affairs and I wanted orders to fulfill that program at Harvard. He did not reject this audacious youthful arrogance but did not commit to do anything in particular. He just told me to hang in there. I had not yet even been admitted to Harvard, by the way, so I was far out on a limb.

I got orders to Harvard in a couple of weeks and managed to get admitted to the Masters in Public Administration Program at the JFK School of Government. I called Admiral Mike Rindskopf over half a century later to thank him. In his 90s he was grateful to be thanked for his good deed but did not remember it. He died shortly after we talked in 2011 at age 93.

My submarine family weighed in and prevailed, but I never learned the details of what must have been some very interesting messages and phone calls. I am sure that some Navy china got broken. There were some big-picture officers out there to whom I am in debt, but I will never know who they were. It is one of many reasons that I love the Navy. The only paperwork I ever saw was a one-paragraph Navy set of orders.

Massachusetts

Families of Naval Officers are used to adjusting to change, but my growing family saw dramatic changes in 1966 and 1967. We had two new children in grade school and a new baby. We were trying to find furniture, mostly used, for a house. Now we were going to Massachusetts and changing the whole direction of our lives. I was going to lose submarine pay. Wilma was going to have to give up tenure in Connecticut and she had no job yet in Massachusetts. We did not have a prayer of selling the place in Mystic for enough to get a house near Cambridge. Sadly, we would have to find another home for Prince, Wilma's big white horse.

Ma and Pa Kettle would have loved the family that set out for Massachusetts in 1967 to find a place to live. There were three dogs and three kids in the tired 1964 Chevy wagon that pulled up to a real estate office in Winchester, a prosperous old town dominated by a magnificent Congregational Church on a hill. We had no idea that we were out of our element and miles out of our pay grade. Outside the office, I ran into an old fellow in overalls who might have been a janitor. I asked him about the availability of rental properties in the area. He asked who I was and what I was looking for. A real estate agent rushed from inside and started tugging at his arm, but the old guy shook him off.

I explained that I was a Naval officer going to Harvard and needed a place to live, but I couldn't afford much. Raising an eyebrow, he mused, "The only person that ever rented my house and cut my grass was a Naval Officer." He shook off

another frantic tug at his sleeve. "I am Marshall Symmes," he announced. "How much can you pay?" I offered that I could handle $250 a month, a pittance in Winchester. He did not seem to mind this ridiculously low offer, but his agent almost broke out in hives. Mr. Symmes said to follow him up the street, leaving the frustrated agent standing on the sidewalk. I fired up the Chevy and followed him up Main Street.

We stopped at Marshall Road and Symmes Corner, an area landmark. An old three-story Victorian house stood there across from the elementary school. It was the house where he was born. He wanted it cared for, and he knew that a Naval officer would keep his word to do that. There were tears close to the surface, and I could easily see that this was not about money.

I stuck out my hand, and he shook it. There was no lease. He came every month to sit in the parlor, talk a bit, and get a $250 check. I refinished an old hat rack and umbrella stand that I found in the attic, and he sighed every time he hung up his hat and coat. We stayed there over three years, and the rent was never raised or even discussed.

photo by the author

Furniture and paintings from that house are in our home today. Mr. Symmes said that I could have anything in the attic that I would refurbish and take care of. The dust up there was several inches thick. Still life paintings of fruit and flowers had to be placed in the bathtub for soaking before they could be cleaned. They were fine. A beautiful Victorian love seat and rocker again brought tears to the old guy when he saw them restored. My woodshop teacher and Unc would have been proud. I still have them.

I scrubbed out the old unheated attic, painted it, and installed a desk, chair, and lamp next to the old woodstove that was still there. In the next 38 months, this would be where I would read hundreds of books and write hundreds of pages.

I cut the grass regularly.

Chapter VIII
HARVARD

Harvard was a life-changer. The JFK School of Government, surprising to me in a decade when most college faculties and students hated the military, was glad to have military students in the classroom. Students had to apply for admission to Henry Kissinger's two-semester seminar on National Security Policy and I am convinced that military experience helped in that process. I got in.

I stacked up the books on Kissinger's reading list, and the stack was taller than I was! Along with tough essay questions, his tests would include items from the indexes of those books to be identified. Midnight oil was burned. He also required a seminar paper. My paper, "The role of the Soviet Military as a Socio-Political Institution," has influenced my thinking ever since.

The draw of Kissinger's course was not the Professor. It was the fact that every week he invited a well-known guest to attend the seminar of 35 students. We heard from the horses' mouths. Secretaries of State and Defense, National Security Advisors, and four-star officers happily trekked to Harvard Square for an afternoon. It was heady stuff. When we studied a topic, the policymaker and the authors of our books were there to discuss it.

The 1967 Arab-Israeli War, the third in a series of ugly, hate-filled conflicts, happened as my family was headed to Harvard. It was a lightning-fast affair of 6 days in June during which the Israelis cleaned the Arabs' clocks. It shook the world and surprised pundits and politicians. The lessons were important for hardware analysts but, in my view, crucial for national security planners and high-level strategists.

The Israelis had revealed in 1967 how Israel was going to react when Israel was attacked. In war, they would gather their forces and strike decisively. It was a tutorial in national and cultural character more than it was a fight. Kissinger's class in National Security Policy was a perfect place for an academic autopsy. The '67 War did get some attention, but we never really came to grips with the central lesson: that the usual notions about the elements of national power were beginning not to apply, and clearly did not apply, to the Israelis or the Middle East. Everyone had cut their teeth on Hans Morganthau's 1948 landmark book Politics Among Nations, and we needed new, nuclear age, international political models. We fell short on this in the Sixties.

Similarly, guerilla warfare, which was certainly not new but was coming of age in the era of superpowers, was beginning to throw a monkey wrench into the thinking of "classical" military strategists. Kissinger, to his credit, was quite aware of this ongoing change and required his students to study the writings of Vietnam War Historian Douglas Pike. We talked in his Seminar about the Tet Offensive as it happened in early 1968 and had the benefit of hearing from officers who had been there.

Sadly, it was clear that at high levels in the military and the government the Vietnam War was a strategic and tactical morass and was growing into a political Tar Baby. Thousands of young men, drafted to serve their country, were mere pawns in a game that the political and military leadership did not know how to play. Poor and patriotic boys answered the call. Influential families could get their sons exempted. College campuses and Canada became refuges. In a year, Kissinger, who wanted to end this craziness, would get a lot of tar on him. It would take another half a decade to end the madness.

Henry Kissinger's course was not the best one I attended in my first year at Harvard. Merle Fainsod, the leading national expert on the Soviet Union of his time and the most gifted scholarly lecturer I have ever heard, mesmerized an auditorium full of students once a week. He met with the graduate students himself in seminar. He would appear five seconds early, open his notes, lecture for exactly forty-five minutes, close his book, and leave to applause, a rare thing at Harvard. I wanted to be like him and know at least some of what he knew.

Professor Fainsod liked people who worked. I am sure he was just as demanding of faculty as he was of students. As a collateral duty, this amazing man was the Director of the huge Widener Library at Harvard. He worked hard, and he saw which students camped out at the library. I did not get to see him one-on-one until after midterm exams. Graduate students did not have to take that exam if they wrote a paper, but I chose to do both because this was my first semester and I wanted the experience of a midterm exam rather than gambling that I could handle the final exam, which was a scary prospect. We met to discuss the midterm exam and my plans for the paper.

Fainsod's office in Weidner Library looked bigger than the Oval Office. I was intimidated, but was soon at ease with a man who genuinely loved the study of Government and Politics and cared about students who really wanted to learn something. (He was incapable of the bluntness that would take note of the number of graduate students at Harvard who were merely smart draft dodgers and academic vagabonds.) He asked what my goals were at Harvard and I replied that I would like eventually to earn a PhD there. I got an A on the test, enjoyed the counseling session, and only found out after the fact that the Professor informed the Navy that he would support me as a PhD candidate.

Harvard gets a bum rap. It is not merely a bastion of flaky, "liberal" thought. It is true that some left-wing thinking, even quite a bit of it, is ever-present at Harvard, but I saw plenty of intellectual counterbalance to it. When the noise level seemed to suggest that only anarchists and traitors existed at Harvard in the late 1960s, serious students at Harvard knew that courageous, objective faculty

would hold that great institution together. One academic hero, my dissertation advisor Professor Adam Ulam, took a lot of heat for his stand against radical thugs. (If we had more professors like the three noted below as my Harvard Mentors, there would not be speech codes on college campuses today.)

I had one other first-hand experience with Harvard's ability to self-correct academic imbalance. One visiting professor offered a course in Russian History that I had to have. He was an avowed Socialist who announced at the outset of the course that students unsympathetic to the Bolshevik Revolution would not do well in his course! My questions during the sessions clearly placed me in the category of "unsympathetic." I was not alone in this, and the word got out, not from me, about the disturbing intellectual atmosphere in this class. I learned a great deal in this course from the readings, and that fact was reflected on the exams, but it was clear that two or three graduate students would not be objectively treated no matter how well they did. The grades for that course did not impact any of those students and the "professor" was not retained for a second semester. (By the way, two or three of us would have gladly taken competitive exams on Russian History with this "Professor." I still would.)

It was not just radical students and faculty who were disappointed with the American intervention in Vietnam. A handful of years after the French endured the 1954 debacle at *Diên Biên Phu*, the Kennedy Administration was dabbling in Viet Nam. Anyone who thought Mao Tse Tung or Ho Chi Minh gave a damn about Karl Marx, a discontented German Jew who suffered boils and carbuncles, was out of his mind. What on earth were they thinking? The wisdom of this would have been questionable to a cab driver, but the highly educated and politically "connected" players in Washington, some of whom talked to Kissinger's class at Harvard, failed to understand the terrible danger of getting mired down in a land war in Asia. Too bad they did not consult my Marine hero brother or any of the folks back home.

I resented the draft-dodging radicals on campus who were far more concerned with their own safety than with international politics, and behaved radically to soothe their consciences. But I thought that Vietnam was a terrible mistake that was allowed by US policymakers to grow and fester.

The My Lai Incident in March of 1968, in which an Army Company raped and murdered over 300 unarmed civilians, had great impact on people who usually gave the military every benefit of the doubt. To be sure, the anti-war media and radicals on campuses did their best to feed the disgust that the incident evoked. Indeed, it was disgusting, and the country was not prepared to try to understand the circumstances that caused such incidents in the midst of war. America was certainly not used to the circumstances of an ugly guerilla war like that in the jungles of Vietnam. In any case, it was impossible to justify My Lai in terms remotely close to American values. It did not fit at all with what has been described here earlier as the American Way of War.

I had a tense discussion with the Marine Executive Officer of the Harvard NROTC Unit. This gentleman, Colonel and combat veteran of Korea explained, without a hint of anger or impatience, some facts of life to me about how and why such atrocities happen. He did not justify. He explained, and I learned something that rang true with what most Americans already knew. Americans have no business taking American values and American soldiers into messes like Vietnam.

So, I cannot say that those who opposed the Vietnam War were wrong, but it is a shame that the nation's colleges became a refuge for the worst of those opposing that War. For some reason, students who live in an environment conducive to contemplative and thorough thinking turn into thugs. They ruin their own intellectual growth but there is something much worse than wasting their own lives: they polluted the academic community. (There is more on the decline of higher education that began in the 1960s later.)

I had one direct experience with the radicals at Harvard in October of 1970 when I was working on my dissertation. The skipper at the NROTC Unit had provided me with an office so I could hide away a block or two from the Russian Research Center and work. I could keep all my original research materials spread out there in a jumbled mess that helped me a lot. When a bomb exploded in Harvard's Center for International Affairs in the office of a U.S. Army officer who was a fellow there, the NROTC building was at risk. There had been an anonymous tip. I was able to gather all the materials together before being ordered to evacuate. A bomb never was placed there, but I had to quit using the office. I have heard several stories about campus radicals from officers at civilian colleges who were graduate students and NROTC instructors in those days. Stanford was apparently a more dangerous place than Harvard.

I approached the Navy in January of 1968 after getting first semester grades to see if there was any chance that I could stay at Harvard at least for an additional year to complete minimum on-campus requirements and qualify as a PhD candidate. Once again, I would love to have seen the correspondence and heard the phone calls at Navy headquarters. Some fixed images probably got shaken. And, again, some good officers I will never know, stood up.

I got a phone call from a senior Naval Intelligence Captain with a question. Would I be interested in shifting my career field to Naval Intelligence and accepting a tour of duty in the Soviet Union along with approval of an extension of duty? I had never met a Naval Intelligence Officer, and did not know what it meant to be one, but I immediately said yes. He went on to say that, after two years at Harvard, I would have to pass a Russian exam and that would probably require a year at the Postgraduate School at Monterey. I suggested that it might save the Navy money if I could pass the language exam in Cambridge and was surprised that the idea was not rejected out of hand.

I did not get a written response, and it was clear that I should not expect one: I simply stayed put and studied. Apparently it was just too hard to put an answer on paper, a policy process requiring many signatures from the uptight guardians of many special interests. I learned that it is sometimes better not to ask a question of a bureaucracy if the answer might be the wrong one. This lesson was useful later in life.

I was awarded the Master of Public Administration degree from Harvard's JFK School in 1968 and was admitted to the Department of Government at Harvard as a PhD Candidate. This meant I had to present four major and two minor fields of study, complete four successful "seminar length" papers for four professors, pass statistics and a language, and survive a General Examination by four professors in the majors. I had a year. If I could do it, I could propose a dissertation plan that might take years. It was daunting.

For major fields, I chose Soviet Domestic Politics, Soviet Foreign Policy, Modern Political Philosophy, and International Politics. I chose Chinese Politics and Soviet Foreign Policy as minors. My paper for Kissinger counted, and I wrote papers for the famous liberal Stanley Hoffman who taught the Harvard course "War," for political philosopher Michael

Walzer, who was a full professor 5 years older than I, and for a visiting professor on Soviet Foreign Policy.

I took two risks, one a serious gamble. Professor Walzer, a professor of political theory who focused on political obligation, did not agree with Professor Louis Hartz, the philosophy prodigy and spellbinding lecturer mentioned earlier. I considered myself a student of Louis Hartz and I heard every lecture he gave while I was at Harvard.

Walzer served on my General Examination Board. He frowned as I addressed his questions, and complained that I was apparently a complete Louis Hartz convert. I was, and I said so, but I knew my Louis Hartz cold and also had a good handle on 19th Century political thought. Professor Fainsod, who headed the Board, was probably a Hartz fan. I had done well in Professor Walzer's course. He apparently did not flunk me on the General Examination.

I could not accept the waste of time that Karl Deutsch's course on quantitative international politics would demand. Graduate students in Government, and Professor Deutsch considered the course a rite of passage for Harvard PhD candidates if they took International Politics as a major field. He had parlayed his Political "Science" thinking into national prominence. In my opinion, he and other "quantifiers" ruined the study of Government. They diminished it, and threatened to turn the field over to bean counters. While I believe that systematic thinking and scientific inquiry should always inform social and political thought, policies and strategies are, at bottom, subjective.

I read the Professor's book and listened to his first lecture and decided he could waste his time pretending to quantify subjective human behavior, but I could not let him waste mine. Time was too short. When I dropped his course this Full Professor was angry. Senior students said that I had better hope he was not on my General Examination Board. Thank Heavens, he wasn't. I did not tear up the General Exams, but I passed them.

To meet the requirement to read and speak Russian at a suitable level for diplomatic assignment, I followed a rigorous language study program while preparing for the general PhD examination. Since written Russian is somewhat different from spoken Russian, I underlined every word not familiar to me in a couple of volumes of _Kommunist_, the so-called theoretical journal of the Communist Party. _Kommunist_ was replete with nonsense written at the graduate level. I hired a graduate student in Slavic languages to pronounce each word in all its variations on tape and define it.

Hedrick Smith, the Pulitzer Prize winning New York Times correspondent who would be in Russia with me and would later write the best-seller _The Russians_, and I hired a Russian immigrant lady to meet with us once a week and discuss any topic she chose. I took a copy of _Smirnitsky_, the huge Russian-English Dictionary that was the standard in teaching the language, and made a flash card of every word that I thought I wanted to know. There were many boxes of flash cards. Each word was placed on tape, pronounced twice in Russian and, after a pause, identified in English. I went over these materials until I was reasonably familiar with them. (I have reviewed these materials every time I travelled to Russia.) I took the test of the Defense Language Institute and passed it.

My dissertation topic was easy to identify. The Soviet Navy was getting quite a bit of international attention and Soviet Military Policy in the increasingly complex and dangerous nuclear era was considered a very important area of study. I was interested in the role of the Soviet Navy in Soviet strategic thinking. So was Adam Ulam, who was a Full Professor and the preeminent American writer and thinker on Socialism and Soviet Foreign Policy.

I did not need to take Ulam's famous course on Socialism for

credit, but I attended every lecture. Once he stopped me after class and asked why I was always there. I told him I wanted to know about Socialism. He smiled. A lot of students were not always there, and the reason they were in school was to avoid Vietnam, not to learn about Socialism, which they probably thought they already understood. Ulam was also the head of Harvard's Russian Research Center and he recognized me as a student often in the library there.

Adam Bruno Ulam, like his famous brother, a mathematical wizard who worked on the Manhattan Project, was a genius. This man wrote huge, seminal studies on Soviet Foreign Policy and Bolshevism, including the footnotes, from memory. Students were in awe of him. He had a reputation for being very demanding, not suffering fools, and I dreaded the process of writing a dissertation under his direction. It was a Harvard legend that some students had spent several frustrating years doing that.

Just getting dissertation topics approved can take forever. Ulam glanced at my outline for 30 seconds in the hallway outside his office. A few days later, without the outline anywhere in sight, he told me to go ahead with research but not to spend too much effort on the chapter about civilian maritime power.

Two months later, after he had seen me buried in newspapers and magazines at all hours in the Russian Research Center, I talked to Professor Ulam in his office, the only time I ever did. He remembered every detail of my earlier outline, and was excited about my preliminary conclusion that the Soviet Navy in the nuclear age was an instrument subject to the politics, and the realities, of nuclear conflict escalation. He was intrigued that I had integrated current game strategy and escalation thinking with history and current Soviet military pronouncements into my emerging image of Soviet Naval Power.

Professor Ulam said to strike most of the verbiage about civil maritime matters and to concentrate on the strategic policy matters that we had discussed. "Write it," he said. I did. On my 30th birthday in December 1970, I delivered a draft of <u>The Rise of the Soviet Navy in the Nuclear Age</u> to Professor Ulam. Intended as a first draft, it was hurriedly typed from handwritten pages, without

spellcheck or a good grammar scrub, by a Navy yeoman. It was not pretty, but it was complete. The key chapter described the Soviet Navy in terms of an escalation ladder. Ulam called me before Christmas. He said he liked it and wanted to talk about it on January 5th of 1971.

I had passed the Russian Exam using tutors, so I had been allowed to stay at Harvard through 1970. The Navy had promoted me to Lieutenant Commander in September1969 after seven years of service. I learned of this when I got a bigger paycheck. I was ordered to report to Attaché School in Washington in mid-January of 1971, with further orders to report to the Embassy in Moscow by July.

I thought that at our January 1971 meeting I would get instructions from Professor Ulam on the draft and, after a rewrite, return to Harvard on my own time at a later date, probably after the Moscow tour, for further guidance.

I was flabbergasted at Professor Ulam's office on January 5, 1971. He, and a second reader who taught the Soviet Foreign Policy Course, were there and they were prepared for a final defense if I was! I said I was.

It took a couple of hours, about as long as it took for an amazed Dr. Kime, as Ulam addressed me for the first time, to get the thing, misspellings and all, bound and deposited in Widener Library.

First I called Wilma. Then I called Aunt Mil Denny.

Chapter IX
Retrospect: the Sixties

It is impossible to reflect back on the Sixties without at least noting the tumultuous events of the decade and how those events struck me and struck most of the people I knew. I have already been clear about Vietnam, which hovered over everything else, providing a steady negative context. I will always regret the failure of my generation to sound the alarm about Vietnam before the country was fully involved there. We were just too young, uninformed and inexperienced. The generation before us was too immersed in the earlier wars and the prejudices and perspectives that came with those wars. America desperately needed intelligent leadership. We did not get it.

In addition to Vietnam, Beatniks, draft-dodgers, Timothy O'Leary, Woodstock, Charles Manson, riots in Watts and Washington, and the murders of MLK and JFK were a lot for Middle America to process.

But the defining struggle of the decade was the Civil Rights Movement. The price of the hate and misbehavior by extremists on the race question had been, and still was, a long delay in progress toward the freedom and equal opportunity that the vast majority of Americans agreed everyone should have. Americans of my generation, who were assuming responsibility and raising families, were on board for real change. We had seen the abuses, and understood the injustices. Martin Luther King inspired us. We heard, and understood, when Dr. King said that his Dream was "deeply rooted in the American Dream."

> **"I still have a dream. It is a dream deeply rooted in the American dream.**
> **I have a dream that one day this nation will rise up and live out the true meaning of its creed: "We hold the truths to be self-evident, that all men are created equal."**

Unlike Dr. King, the radicals, black and white, were loudmouths and troublemakers with little real interest in progress. Many of these people reveled in violence, and many were criminals. Some were simply traitors and revolutionaries intent on making America falter.

The tactics and slogans of the Radical Left were transparent: they came straight out of familiar Socialist and Communist playbooks. I did not study race relations at Harvard but I did spend a lot of time on Revolutionary Movements, Socialism and Communism. I saw a lot that was familiar in the slogans of the rabble-rousers of the 1960s and early 1970s, and it was anathema to the generation I had grown up in.

Policemen were not pigs. Good men went when they were called, even to a miserable war, and did not cower in Canada or on campuses. Many of us did not think Americans belonged in Vietnam, but most of us will never forget and never forgive the treason of Jane Fonda and the dishonor of John Kerry.

My generation was swaddled in the FDR era. We were not predisposed to resist change or belong to *either* Party. We were a confident and independent generation, full of voters not likely to blindly follow the political leadership of either Party, and ready and willing to embrace positive change. But we saw far too many "Reverend" Al Sharptons and Jesse Jacksons, and far too Few Martin Luther Kings. We rejected extremists who saw more to hate than to love in America.

In fact, toward the end of the decade, the reaction to the extremists of the 1960s ushered in a prolonged era of skepticism and rejection of left-of-center politics, interrupted only by the Carter interlude in the aftermath of Watergate craziness.

The Democratic Party began to lose its grip on the "lifelong" Democrats that emerged after FDR. Those not enamored of FDR, who had remained Democrats, had little reason to support the increasingly leftist politics of the time. The beginnings of a fairly coherent Independent bloc of voters that would later be known as Reagan Democrats emerged from alienated democrats who were unrepresented by an increasingly leftist Party.

Steve Kime

1960s and the Decline of Higher Education

It is very important to understand that leftist radicals whose political and social agendas were about destroying the American form of government, and not primarily about Vietnam at all, were in the "vanguard" of campus radicalism in the late 1960s and early 1970s. The pollution of the academic community was not primarily about opposition to a war so stupid that it would fall of its own weight. The Vietnam War was just a foil for Socialists, Progressives, and Revolutionaries. Some were all of these.

American universities have suffered mightily for over half a century from the presence of the rabble that infested academe in the 1960s and 1970s. Some of these "scholars" hid on campuses for years to avoid military service. Colleges and universities collaborated in this. They tolerated hate and discontent at the expense of academic inquiry and analysis. Worse, they turned out a generation of academic ne'er-do-wells to spread their hate and discontent to our children for decades, and they perpetuated themselves by spawning yet another faculty generation in their own image. I suppose I should hasten to acknowledge that this blanket indictment obviously has exceptions, but the sad truth is that it generally applies.

Academe paid a terrible price for its failures during the Vietnam War era. In many cases, tenured professors were mere clones in the mold of John Kerry or Jane Fonda. For thirty years, our children were exposed to the perspectives of people who could not support a country that they would not serve. "Students" who hid on college campuses were unlikely to be intellectual or scientific standouts, so our universities became havens for second-class radicals.

The irony is that opposition to the war was not what marked these people. They were correct about the war. What marked them for life was the underlying cowardice and lack of character that traitors, draft-dodgers and lawbreakers must carry with themselves for life. Many carried their guilt into America's classrooms, and spent lifetimes interpreting everything in terms of a world and a country that they could not love and obviously did not comprehend.

Academe produced a generation of poorly educated graduates able only to languish in a Service Economy. Fortunately, a few college dropouts created a technological and communications revolution that forestalled the American decline in individual creativity and productivity that they would cause.

One result of the Vietnam-era infestation of academe was increased separation of higher education from the development of future officers. ROTC was banished on many campuses. Academe chose to "cut off its nose to spite its face." America needs its officers to be educated in the mainstream of its educational system, even a flawed system, but much of academe refused to take this responsibility. Thucydides said it best: "The Nation that makes a great distinction between its scholars and its warriors will have its thinking done by cowards and its fighting done by fools."

The Vietnam Era professoriate has about passed into retirement, but the damage it did will be difficult to repair. Fortunately, their exit about coincided with 9/11 and a new realism for America. Their students are professors today, but maybe there is hope.

The American Dream Begins to Decline

Pulitzer Prize winning reporter Hedrick Smith, in his 1912 book <u>Who Stole The American Dream</u> (Random House) has articulated this issue better than this author could.

Smith correctly argues that America has abandoned a vital part of our concept of capitalism: shared prosperity. We operated on the concept that a rising tide raised all boats. Greed and executive profit taking has led to economic inequality that is antithetical to American values. Rick Smith, is not just spouting left-wing gibberish here, as some conservatives, especially on Wall Street, would claim. He is a patriot who has hit the nail on the head. American capitalism worked because of Henry Ford's genius and not because of the robber barons' greed of the Nineteenth Century.

The sad truth is that Capitalism, unrestrained, does not always lift all boats. America has confronted this truth at other times and we find

ourselves today in a prolonged period of greed at the top, which began at the end of the Sixties. Ethics changed at the top of American corporations to reject completely the philosophy of great leaders like Henry Ford who understood that workers who shared in the fruits of production sparked the nation's economic engine. Ford saw that it was smart to have workers who could buy what thet built.

Instead, CEO's were seen only to serve the stockholders, and themselves. US government, both political parties, were complicit in this short sighted, unpatriotic, and just plain stupid approach. It dovetailed nicely with the love affair that the entire political spectrum had with the chimera of "global interdependence."

Over forty years of this folly has done great damage to the American Dream that fueled the political, social and economic system that prevailed during the salad days of my generation. It would be foolish not to think that mainstream values that prevailed at that time would not also take a hit.

Hopefully, this can be turned around. We have done it before, most notably at the turn of the Twentieth Century after a long period of excesses. Then it was domestic robber barons that had to be brought to heel. This time will be more difficult. The problem has grown international roots.

Over The Moon

The civil turmoil of the sixties did not flow uninterrupted into the anti-Vietnam fervor and Watergate feeding frenzy of the Seventies. The nation paused for a moment to be proud of itself.

John F. Kennedy's greatest achievement, the inspiration of his country, bore fruit. In July of 1969 when America landed men on the Moon, America was showcased at its best. It was almost, but not quite, enough to stop the onslaught of those who were, and are, intent on trading American achievement for simpleminded redistribution of her resources.

At least for a while, the cynics were silenced and the nation celebrated. The world was awed.

The Space Program gave us more than a thrill. The list of innovations that flowed from the Space Program was long. We could do anything. This was the America we knew in the Forties and loved in the Fifties. We innovated, made things, and we did things. We dared. We worked. We were not ashamed that America was smart, innovative, productive and rich. The Seventies held out great promise.

We squandered that promise. Vietnam hurt America's pride; even those who wanted to do so were unable to untangle the mess we had created in Vietnam. Traitors and cowards at home made it as difficult as possible. Paranoia, petty criminal activity, and dishonesty fed the cancer in the Nixon Administration. Self-righteous and self-serving politicians, egged on by a left-wing press, delighted in watching a presidency fail. These same people sucked the air out of the drive and creativity that took men to the moon. American Greatness became a concept of derision in the chatting class.

It became fashionable in the media to be ashamed that America was smart, innovative, productive and rich.

The generation just after mine was approaching adulthood in the poisonous domestic environment of the Seventies. Their huge numbers, and the cynicism of their formative age, would combine to create a cohort that would see things far differently than I do. Our *derring-do* was their daring not. My cohort would have bought more spaceships. These differences would not come to a head in the Seventies, a lost decade in many ways. They would come to roost later when NASA was diminished. In the 21st Century, those who dare not are in charge.

A New World

Harvard was a major transition from junior officer to the world of policy and strategy. I maintain in old age that nothing ever erases the values and perceptions absorbed in youth, but it would have been impossible to complete the PhD at Harvard without becoming a lifelong policy junkie.

At least it was impossible for me. For the rest of my life I would see the world in terms of policy and strategy.

The Navy knows how to do transitions. It orders you to go

someplace else. In my case, the graduate school jig was up and the Navy wanted me to go to work in Moscow. This was a key time in my life and Naval Career. I had to think in terms of being in the Navy for quite a while. I had never thought like that before. I still don't.

I was deeply indebted to the Navy, but I had not decided to stay there unless I had something worthwhile to do. This was heresy, and maybe shameful to boot, but in the spirit of *VERITAS*, I admit it.

The best officers are not "lifers." I think the US military is well served by officers who keep their options open and stay in the Service only if they can see that they can do their best there. This does not always put institutional loyalty first and is based in some arrogance, but I am convinced that great institutions like the Navy attract people who have options, and thrive when such people are supported and encouraged.

This view is not what the Navy seeks to inculcate in its officers, especially at the Naval Academy where career security, at least for average and better officers, is virtually guaranteed by an Old Boys Club. Today it is a Boys and Girls Club.

Persistent Roots in Indiana

Harvard had worked out well, and I owed the Navy several years of service to pay back for the incredible opportunity that it had generously provided. I was looking forward to what those years might reveal. I had no idea what I was getting into. I had been ordered to a position that required the dolphins of a submariner, not a Navy Intelligence position. Whatever the Navy had in mind, it seemed certain that I would eventually end up back in "Kentuckiana," so we had continued to pay Indiana State taxes. Indiana was still "Home."

In 1969, in partnership with Wilma's sister and her husband, we bought a farm near Georgetown, Indiana. This was folly to most of the people we knew. The 120 acres had a house in need of repair, required driving through a stream and over a railroad track, and was a forty-minute drive from New Albany or Louisville.

My Navy cumshaw experience in the shipyard came in handy. The railroad was replacing track in the area and I hailed a couple of railroaders working on it one day. They were receptive to a railroader's son. I told them that, if I had a couple of used rails, I could build a bridge over the creek. I suggested that I leave a couple of bottles of Early Times Bourbon, a local railroaders' favorite made in Louisville, under a nearby Sycamore tree. They liked this idea and, in a few days, the whiskey and the rails were exchanged. A local contractor was hired to dig and pour concrete footings and abutments, weld the rails to them, and affix a floor to the rails. The bridge, though it has been under raging water several times, stands there nearly 50 years later.

We planted a Golden Rain Tree on a future home site atop the highest hill overlooking the area. A grove of fruit trees was planted nearby, and a pond was soon built near the foot of the hill. Wilma's sister and brother-in-law fixed up the house and moved in to stay for decades. Eventually, after our trees died because we could not be there to maintain them, and we were well into a 20- year Navy tour, we gave up the idea of living on the 120 acres. We bought a nearby 27-acre parcel, a beautiful hill with a building site atop it. This, we thought, would be where we would go when the Navy was fed up with my career deviations.

These attempts to nourish Hoosier roots while the Navy was determining our fate did not totally fade away until the mid-1980s. By then, I was a senior Captain. The children considered themselves Virginians. The land investments turned out to be fortuitous. Interstate 64 passes close by, and the gravel roads have been paved, making our folly of past years look much better.

Rickover, Again!

During my preparations for service in the Soviet Union in 1971, The Navy said I had to meet Rickover whether I liked it or not. He insisted on seeing all submariners headed for diplomatic duty who may meet

Russians. The Admiral was convinced that some Naval Attaché had once told some Russian something, but he would not say who said what. At Attaché School the talk was that Rickover believed that any officer going to embassy duty was a slacker and it was reasonable to question such officers' intelligence and patriotism!

Rickover always kept a senior officer outside his office to manage the poor souls who had an audience with him. I told this fellow, as respectfully as I could, about the talk at Attaché School. I made it clear that I would not take politely any questioning of my patriotism. I noticed that he spent a second with the boss before opening the door for an audience.

The "interview" was a little insulting, but not as intolerable as I thought it would be. Rickover flashed a photo of some U.S. Naval Officer greeting and hugging the wife of some Russian at a party, and said he expected those of us who knew anything to be careful about what we said and did. He did not look me in the eye. I nodded and left. No harm, no foul.

One of my mentors liked to say: "Don't get in a pissing contest with a skunk. You will both smell bad, and the skunk does not care!" I understood this. Maybe Hyman Rickover did, too.

Chapter X
Russia: 1971-1973

Any student or professor of a foreign culture would treasure an opportunity to live in that culture and put the understanding and perspectives gained from books and classrooms to the acid test of the streets. Philosophy, literature, art and language are no substitute for going to a farmers' market or sitting on a park bench and talking with whoever shows up. To pay the Navy back for the incredible opportunity at Harvard, the Navy was throwing me, like Br'er Rabbit, into another Briar Patch!

*19th Century Russian Snow Scene
painting found in St. Petersburg in 1973
photo by the author*

Getting There

There was not much time to prepare. I had worked hard on my Russian. Several weeks of Attaché School in Washington D.C. proved useful. This was not just a "knife and fork" school for unwashed officers. There was a lot of practical information on how to be an effective observer and reporter in hostile situations. I often summoned that information in life.

I was surprised at the number of people who wanted to talk to a future attaché before and after he served in Russia. This was both humbling and informative. Some of these people knew more about Russia than a budding academic knew and they would never get to see what I would see so I paid attention. Some very smart analysts spent careers looking at parts of an elephant, and I was going to see the whole beast!

Navy families move. It's part of Navy culture. But moving to Moscow in 1971 was a logistical feat beyond the norm. Some stuff had to be stored God knows where. Some household cargo goes by ground and sea and, if you are lucky, does not get dropped on the pier in Helsinki before being given to the tender mercies of Russian railroaders. (We were not lucky.) Some had to go by air because it was almost certain that the other stuff would take forever. You carry so much that you get special chits for that purpose. Since we needed to buy all the non-perishable stuff for two years -- toilet paper, cereal, dried milk, etc. -- it had to be shipped separately.

Our family was to spend a school semester in Washington before deployment, so the children had to shift schools and Wilma had to quit her job. Paying for the food shipment meant selling a car, and another car had to be shipped. Wilma and I would be travelling a lot in Russia, so a nanny had to be hired and sent to Russia. Our dog had to be prepared for the trip, requiring more paperwork than for the kids. Barry, age 14, would have to be sent to Frankfurt to high school.

We did all of this and, after a short stop in London for briefings at the Embassy there, arrived in Moscow for duty as Assistant Naval Attaché and Assistant Naval Attaché for Air, an anachronistic title reflecting Navy's refusal since 1947 to admit that the Air Force had anything to do with flying over water.

Captain Franklin Goodspeed Babbitt, my boss, met us at Sheremetovo Airport. He had been an assistant attaché a decade earlier when I was a midshipman visiting Russia on the student exchange discussed earlier. That had been an interesting time of The Thaw in Russia when useful contacts, including that with Soviet Intelligence Colonel Oleg Penkovski, were possible. I learned that it had been a much more interesting time than a naïve 20 year old could have ever detected. I knew in 1961, for instance, that Khrushchev's "Thaw" had loosened the reins on artists and writers, but I had no idea as a young student that such a loosening would encourage some willingness to oppose the system in serious, concrete ways. Only a few years later, when we heard some of the repercussions of the "Penkovskiy Papers" incident, did the activities of those serving in the Soviet Union at that time become clearer.

Captain Babbitt had travelled extensively during this time and became an "on the ground" expert on Russia. He was a no-nonsense boss, but was equipped with the submariner's imagination and sense of humor. The Captain was a scholarly, well-read man who appreciated my academic background, but he made it a point to educate me in the realities of Russia at street level. I will never be able to repay him. (After his retirement, we became close friends.)

Moscow Duty

Since I was military, and junior military at that, we were assigned an apartment that no one else wanted. It was in a brand new apartment house quite a distance from the center of Moscow. In Russia, no one wanted to deal with shoddy Soviet construction before it had been lived in a while and Embassy maintenance people had corrected the errors.

We ended up with a huge apartment, and space counted in Moscow more than quality construction. We had a bedroom for each child and their nanny. There were bugs to be worked out, but they were manageable. We liked the place despite its flaws because it was a block from a huge peasants' market where farmers sold their food and wares, and lots of ordinary Russians were in the neighborhood. We bought a Russian *Zhiguli,* the Russian version of a Fiat, for Wilma to drive to the Anglo-American School where she would be teaching.

At 30, I was the youngest attaché in Moscow, but I had senior colleagues who knew the ropes and wanted to help me learn them. Frank Babbitt wrote travel reports so long and detailed that, on looking at his draft, I could not, for the life of me, remember half of what he saw. It was humbling not to be able to add much.

author's photos

Commander William Henry James Manthorpe, Jr. and Lieutenant Colonel Herbert Tiede, USMC, were also Assistant Attachés. Both were also super competent observers of Soviet society and the Soviet military establishment. Both would retire as senior officers. Bill Manthorpe would become a frequent commentator in the U.S. Naval Institute <u>Proceedings</u>. After Navy retirement, he occupied the most senior civilian positions in Naval Intelligence. Strangely, though my Navy career designator had been shifted to Naval Intelligence (1630), I was never to serve in a 1630 job. Bill Manthorpe was a serious, sterling, Naval Intelligence Officer.

Russia Close Up

As the junior officer in the office, I did everything, including travel to all corners of the vast empire that the Soviet Union had become. Captain Babbitt was convinced that knowing about the country on the ground, and reporting on it, was what counted, and we were the only people on the planet that were going to do it. I heard dozens of times his view that reading newspapers and relying on "the eye in the sky" was ruining the ability of analysts to figure these people out. We travelled. The boss liked to travel with me because I would go anywhere and was so junior that he knew I would suffer through his encyclopedia-like reports easier than my colleagues who were much more senior officers.

Together, we visited Arkhangelsk, Riga, Tallinn, Baku, Sochi, Odessa, Tula, Novorossiysk, Yalta, Batumi, Barnaul, Irkutsk, Nakhodka, Khabarovsk, Yaroslavl', Leningrad, and Kiev, among other places. He saw to it that I visited more cities with the other officers and with Wilma.

The Captain appreciated "book learning," and owned more books than anyone I knew, but he was hell-bent on my *really* seeing the country of my study.

Once, after an Army officer wrote a good piece on an article that appeared over the name of Marshal of the Soviet Union Grechko, I ventured that the Naval Attachés needed to pay more attention to such things. He was OK with that, and I should do it, but travel in the Soviet Union had to take priority.

I had subscriptions to *Leningradskaya Pravda*, a maritime-oriented newspaper, *Pravda*, *Izvestia*, and the major military and Naval publications in the public domain. I was not able to scour all this material carefully, of course. That was the job of analysts in the States with the time to do it. There were mountains of ideological nonsense to sift through. But I did pick up some interesting nuggets.

Even the Russian security system could not hide all the workings of a country of 150 million trying to industrialize itself. It became obvious to me that "open source" study was worthwhile. Not everything that is important is "classified." Sometimes the very act of publishing in the public domain is significant. This is particularly true in military publications. The Navy was too slow to recognize the importance of Language and Country Specialized Education in those days. Thankfully that weakness was finally understood and has since been addressed.

I soon learned how serious Captain Babbitt was about insisting that we press the Soviet authorities in our effort to get around and see the country. They put all kinds of obstacles in our way. They would claim that no facilities were available or appropriate, that hotels were full, that weather was prohibitive, etc. Often travel was denied without explanation.

Like good Naval Officers, if it was not strictly prohibited, we went. Once, in Irkutsk, the Captain and I wore every stitch we had brought to Siberia with us, and we nearly froze on a walk of several miles in temperatures well below zero. Our KGB tails were miffed. We had a similar experience in Tula, near Tolstoy's home, where the hotel bathrooms were outside.

An Adventure in Leningrad

St. Petersburg, which the Communists called Leningrad, has been the
heart of Russian maritime culture since Peter The Great and was full
of Soviet Navy personnel, Navy schools, and shipyards. Impressive
Naval parades were held on the River Neva on major Soviet holidays.
Naval Attachés travelled to Leningrad often for sightseeing. Sometimes,
presumably when there were sights the authorities thought we should not
see, we were not welcome.

Soon after my arrival, the Captain wanted to introduce me to Leningrad.
The authorities permitted the travel, but something must have come up
in the city that we were not supposed to see. It is a guess, but there may
have been a submarine launched from Sudomekh Shipyard, which was
located across the Neva River from a famous piece of Revolutionary
history called Lt. Schmidt's Embankment. Lieutenant Schmidt led
factory workers to riot and overthrow Tsar Nicholas in 1917.

There is a statue on Schmidt's Embankment in honor of Johann
Kruzenstern, the first Russian to circumnavigate the Earth. We were
devoted fans of Kruzenstern, the bakery where greasy meat pies could
be found, the smelly open *tyualet*, and the Mining Institute, which were
all on the Embankment with views of shipyards. These were must-see
sights every time a Naval Attaché went sightseeing in Leningrad.

In those days, we were customarily told to stay at the seedy old
Oktyabrskiy Hotel across from the train station in Leningrad. We would
lug our bags over there from the Moscow train station and were easy to
keep track of. On this particular trip, our familiar friends who followed
us everywhere seemed surprised to see us. We were told that there was
no room at the Inn and that we would have to get back on the train and
return to Moscow. I could feel the heels of Franklin Goodspeed Babbitt,
a gentleman of the Old Navy but one possessed of a legendary stubborn
streak, digging in. He let me do the talking.

I told the hapless ladies at the reception desk that we had the necessary
papers and that we were staying for the approved time of two days.
They walked over to the two thug-like figures trying unsuccessfully to

be inconspicuous in the corner and whispered. Consternation. We were asked to wait. We waited for almost two hours. Nothing. So, we took our bags to the ladies, left them there, said they were responsible for them, and walked out. We took the #12 bus to Schmidt's Embankment, paid our respects to Kruzenstern, and walked around for a while before spending a long day taking buses, subways and trams to other well-known sites in the city. We enjoyed it, but it was quite a workout for the KGB which apparently did not know we were coming to their fair city.

We returned to the reception desk to another standoff: still no rooms. We recovered our bags and announced that we would stay in the lobby! Consternation. I followed the Captain as he went into the bathroom, donned his pajamas, and fixed a cup of awful instant coffee with his ever-present submersible heater. We lay down to sleep on the benches in the lobby. The KGB tails would have to spend the night in the hallway. The ladies shooed out all the other people and turned down the lights. In the middle of the night, a babushka came in, covered us with a blanket and giggled when I thanked her for her kindness.

Miraculously, rooms were available for the second night. We were heroes to the hotel workers! From that day on, I rarely arrived in the city without having good tickets to the famous Kirov Ballet or some event. Dinner reservations at less seedy hotels were possible. One of the ladies at the reception desk was there a decade later when I returned as the Naval Attaché. She greeted me with a smile.

Misadventure in Leningrad

Leningrad was besieged by German troops for a horrific 900 days in WWII. Hundreds of thousands died. The city got some supplies by The Road of Life, which began as an ice road across Lake Ladoga with horse-drawn carriages. Eventually, trucks were used and a land route was opened into the city.

My colleague, Commander Manthorpe, and I took a bus to the outskirts of the city to see this historic route. There was an Ordnance Depot nearby. We looked around, found an historical marker, and looked for a bus to take us back to the city center. We accidentally got on a bus that was identical to the one we had taken to The Road of Life, but it did not feel right. It turned out to be a Ministry of Defense bus. We disembarked, but it was too late.

We were grabbed and taken to a headquarters office by a major and two armed soldiers where an Artillery Colonel acted as if he had caught enemy agents bent on national destruction. Two tall, fit soldiers were called in and told to strip search us. We resisted, pointing out that this was a violation of our diplomatic immunity, asked to see consular officers, etc. It took them only a second to take control and search us. I got a twisted arm for being uncooperative. They found nothing to hold us for, and I think they got a call within an hour or so to let us go, which they did.

Here is part of an account that adds detail and perspective by Bill Manthorpe, now a retired Navy Captain:

> Our goal was to visit all the monuments in the area around Lake Ladoga, which had served as part of the "road". If we happened to hear naval gunfire or catch a glimpse of activity at the naval weapons station on the shore of the lake that would have made our visit all the more enjoyable.
>
> It was a historically interesting but not militarily rewarding morning and, hopefully, the KGB personnel trailing us and watching us along the way also enjoyed rediscovering some of their history. Having finished our walking trip, just prior to noon, we planned to return to Leningrad for lunch. We returned to the same bus stop where earlier that morning we had gotten off the city bus from downtown Leningrad to begin our visit. We approached a standard city bus from the rear, and entered by the middle door. Immediately upon getting to the top of the two steps and looking for a seat I knew we had made a mistake. The bus was full of soldiers waiting for a driver. We very calmly walked to the front door, down the steps and out. But, as we did, coming across

the parking lot was an officer with drawn pistol and two soldiers with rifles and bayonets at the ready.

Of course, as sensible people, we stopped, got out our diplomatic passes and waited. When questioned we identified ourselves as American diplomats, apologized for our innocent mistake and made ready to leave. When our attempt to casually saunter off was blocked, we asked permission to telephone our embassy and that was refused. There was nothing to do but continue to protest and follow the Major and his armed troopers to the military hotel building nearby. There we were taken to a small room and left under guard of the two soldiers who, fortunately, remained outside. That gave me the opportunity to break the plastic bag full of water in my jacket pocket to turn into mush the water-soluble paper on which I had made a few notes and to reach inside my jacket to pull on the 35mm film canister to expose the film which was attached by a safety pin through its lead end so that, as I pulled, the film inside the canister came out into the light of day. Although this was all material from previous days of our trip, it was not appropriate for our captors to find it.

After about an hour-long wait, the Major returned with his troopers and asked us to disrobe so that he could search our clothes. With more protests of diplomatic immunity we refused, the Major left and another hour or so passed before he returned again with a Sergeant and his troopers, having obviously gotten permission to use force if necessary. Still protesting and refusing, backed up against the wall with arms crossed in front of our chests we refused to cooperate. It did not take much, however, for the two troopers to grab our feet and pull them out from under us so that we slid ungracefully down the wall and banged on our backs onto the floor. The troopers then wrenched our arms to the side, sat on our chests pinning our arms at our sides while the Sergeant went carefully through our pockets and person, finding nothing but mush in my pocket, in my companion's trouser crotch and several exposed rolls of film. The major, Sergeant and our assailants departed in frustration. We regained our composure, reordered our clothes, my trousers had been slightly ripped, stretched our twisted muscles and rubbed our minor scratches and bruises.

More Hazards of Attaché Duty

There were other incidents. Once the Canadian Naval Attaché and I were held for several hours on a ship that travelled up the Danube from the Black Sea to the Ukrainian port of Izmail. We had observed some Soviet Shmel gunboats operating on the Danube but had not done anything untoward or suspicious. Our KGB companions thought we were a serious danger to national security and agitated some locals to chime in. It was probably planned in advance.

The Ukrainian KGB goons were always nasty in Kiev and Odessa, but these guys were special! One kicked me, and I did not get the opportunity to return the favor. They wrote us up, giving us an "AKT," or citation for having violated the rules. They detained us for a while and probably checked with Moscow. There was little they could do short of creating a major incident with both Canada and the U.S., except to let us take the boat back down the Danube and across the Black Sea to Odessa, which we did. The gunboats sailed by us again as we left. It is difficult to imagine what was so important about them.

Occasionally, circumstances revealed a human side to the KGB. One trip was to Barnaul on the Ob' River in western Siberia. It was a chance to see the Russian Heartland, and a place where Russian small arms were made. A two-foot snowfall hindered our walk around the city, but we suited up to give it a try. The folks following us were uninspired. They manned three vehicles and, in patterns that were quite familiar, kept track of us in their warm vehicles. This worked fine on streets that were at least partially cleared but, when we headed toward the Ob' River the streets were nearly impassible in cars. We plugged on. Soon, one of the jeep-like surveillance vehicles was stuck up to both axels. We could hear all three vehicles blocks away because they were the only vehicles in town trying to drive. We waited politely while the other two machines were parked and their occupants trudged to the stuck vehicle to try to push it out. I think the entire KGB contingent was on that side street pushing that vehicle without success.

My travel companion and I could not resist. We offered to help, and began pushing. I offered to return to the hotel and report their plight to the Militsia, which might come to help. This was too much for one exasperated fellow who was probably the boss. He practically begged me not to do that but to quietly return to the hotel. We did, and we did not rat out the KGB. The next day we barely noticed the tails.

On one trip Wilma and I travelled to Baku in Azerbaijan via Odessa in the Ukraine. I have never understood what happened on this ill-fated journey to annoy the authorities, or if some unexpected event that we were not meant to see took place. Wilma, thank goodness, packed a lot of snacks and drinks, because we never had the opportunity to have a meal. We got to Odessa too late for a restaurant and checked out of our hotel early the next morning. Odessa was a beautiful but unfriendly city in those days. We were told bluntly that we had to take an early flight out of town. We walked several miles around every sector that was open to us, and we were very closely followed. We munched on Wilma's homemade banana bread. Finally, we took a cab to the airport to catch the flight to Baku on the Caspian Sea, another pretty and unfriendly place.

There was "no room at the inn" in Baku. We were getting tired, but we were stubborn. We hired a tour of the city, which is an interesting place. Finally, on my 32nd birthday, an official-looking thug told me it would be a good idea to catch the next flight to Moscow. We did.

There was quite a difference in those days between the Provinces and Moscow, where the authorities are tuned into political realities of handling foreign representatives. There is a discernible difference in attitude in Arkhangel'sk, Khabarovsk, or Nakhodka, for example, than one would find in cities where tourists were more common. Distance from Moscow affected attitudes, not just about security, but also about social and political issues. The Soviet East, like the American West, saw itself as different from the Capital.

Wilma Kime and the Kremlin across the Moskva River in1973
photo by the author

The Hidden Strength of Soviet Jews

The plight of Soviet Jews has been reported on extensively in the West, but the depth of their suffering is poorly understood. Pogroms, or massacres, of Jews were a common part of Russian and East European history, and anti-Semitism was endemic in Soviet Rule. (As I noted earlier, the Fascists in Germany and in Stalinist Russia had much in common.) I had two encounters with elderly Jews that made an impact on me.

In Riga, Latvia, we were having dinner at one of the old restaurants that still had some of the charm of a pretty little Baltic State. The waiter refused to speak Russian, and we were pleased to deal with his broken English.

The Communist Party had populated the Baltic States of Latvia, Lithuania and Estonia with enough Russians to dominate their politics and economics, but they never succeeded in suppressing the will of these countries which, like the Slavic Countries of Eastern Europe, had thriving, developing cultures when Russia was still a backward, feudal State.

An ancient Jew slipped into our booth in the Latvian restaurant and said that he understood that we were Americans. This 85-pound fellow and his Merlin-like wispy beard impressed me. He had the clear-eyed courage and determination of an old man who has nothing to lose. He said he just wanted to talk to an American. Did I know what they had done to his people? Did I know that Russians were no better than Germans? Did Americans know that there were no Synagogues in Latvia? They had to pray in his cellar. He thanked me for listening to him and thanked America for coming to Europe in the War. He asked for nothing. I will never forget him. He made me understand what the American Shining City on a Hill meant to this tough old man and millions more like him. Thank God, it is better for his people now that the Soviet yoke has been lifted from the Baltic States.

A few weeks later I was visiting my favorite second-hand bookstore in Leningrad. Old books, paintings, and sometimes furniture, could be found in second-hand stores, "*Komissioniye magazini*," where antique Russian things could be sold legally for cash. Russian families had squirrelled away treasured items for fifty years since the Bolsheviks took power. When times got tough and the political climate permitted it, items appeared from Russian attics. There was a lot of junk to sift through, but some of Tsarist Russia leaked out through these stores, which sold items for a commission. For a student of Russian history, it was a rare opportunity to see, and even buy, a piece of Russia.

This was sad, of course, but I learned that some Russians would rather such things be treasured by an American than confiscated by Communists.

As I was leafing through a large old book, a color lithograph that had been hidden inside it fell out. An old Jew, the spitting image of the old fellow I met in Riga, appeared at my side. He asked me if I was an American, but it was clear that he already knew the answer. He pointed to the lithograph and asked if I liked it. It was clearly quite old for a lithograph in Russia.

He smiled at this observation and asked if I would take it out of the country. Instinctively, I knew to tell him the truth. I said that I would take it back to America and treasure it. He winked and said, "buy it." It was expensive, but I bought it and kept my promise.

In Finland, where there are experts on such things, I was told that the French taught Russians the art of *gravura* and that this piece was an early,

circa 1730, Russian piece called *"Pochtal'ion e Dvornik"* or "The Census Taker and the Groundskeeper." My guess is that the old fellow had watched to be sure that part of his family heritage ended up in good hands. Later, an old lady encouraged me to buy a bronze statue signed by Lanceret, a famous Russian bronzemaster. It was a similar case of protecting family heritage, and I bought it and own it today.

Bronze Horse and Rider By Bronze master Lanceret
photo by the author

Face to Face With The Soviet Military

Much of my first tour in Russia was spent on the road, but my forte was the politics and strategy of the Soviet Military, as understood and observed through the prism that I had built at Harvard. When we attended receptions on the National Days of major countries, the Soviet High Command would have representatives there. These had become strange affairs where senior Russian civilian and military authorities would cluster in a group surrounded by a phalanx of more junior folk. Rubbing elbows with Capitalists was not what they had in mind. (Under Stalin, it was dangerous.)

At some events there was even a rope dividing the gaggle of Russians from others. This led to jokes in the diplomatic community about the way that very influential Russians would attack a buffet table when the restraining ropes were lifted. A horde of locusts would have been slower and a lot more courteous.

It seemed ridiculous that we would be in the same room with people I had carefully read and quoted and could not even shake their hands. At the first such reception where Admiral of the Fleet of the Soviet Union Sergei Georgievich Gorshkov showed up, I elbowed my way through the crowd of surprised officers directly to him. He and his deputy, Fleet Admiral V. A. Kasatonov, standing next to him, were amused at this and waved off a panicked Soviet Liaison Officer about to intercede.

I stuck out my hand and told Gorshkov what an honor it was to meet someone whom I had followed in <u>Morskoi Sbornik</u>, the Russian Naval Digest, though I noted that he hadn't written much since a major piece in 1967. He laughed at this, shook my hand, and asked me what interested me about his article. Admiral Kasatonov, his deputy and a past Commander of the Soviet Pacific Fleet, enthusiastically joined in. I had read his stuff, too. Gorshkov was flattered that I knew that his designation "Hero of The Soviet Union" was earned in Black Sea amphibious actions against the Germans.

This would not be the only time that we had the opportunity to engage members of the Soviet Navy High Command. They got somewhat used to the dialog, and I think they got a kick out of it. I sure did. Admiral N.N. Amel'ko, the more recent Pacific Commander and apparently a kind of roving Naval ambassador abroad, especially to the Middle East, became a frequent interlocutor. So did Admirals Sergievich and Alexiev.

At least part of the reason that Soviet military officers were a little more approachable in the early Seventies was that there was a modest thaw at the political level. The groundwork for Strategic Arms Limitations Talks was being laid. Also, the Soviet side was interested in talks to prevent an incident at sea between the two Navies, which had taken to bumping, thumping and playing "chicken" with each other at sea and between aircraft. This latter interest fit neatly into the proposition in my thesis that the Soviets were not actually prepared to move through the middle levels of conflict escalation as confidently or as quickly as their Naval posture sometimes seemed to suggest.

Of course, political officers were watching, and these wily Russian veterans and patriots were unlikely to spill their guts about Soviet strategic secrets, but it was possible to see and understand the kind of people that we would have to deal with in any future conflict. I think that Gorshkov liked to assert whatever independence he thought he could claim from the Army-dominated Soviet Military hierarchy and enjoyed the attention. I had thought this about Gorshkov's public writings, and this was confirmed when I met him.

The Navy in Russia was favored in the days of Peter the Great who harbored grand thoughts about extending Russian influence abroad. Such grand thoughts certainly were entertained in the Kremlin in the 1970s, but the military context was dramatically changed. The greatest change agent was intercontinental nuclear weaponry and the risk of escalation of conflict to nuclear levels. Navies were expensive and resources were scarce, even in a country willing to spend an enormous part of its budget on weaponry. Showing the Flag was nice, but ships had to be justified in terms of fighting a nuclear war. It did not help that Khrushchev had blurted out that ships were floating coffins. In Russia, the Strategic Rocket Forces (SRF) were riding high, Russian history favored a huge Army, and the Navy came last. Submarines could play a role with the SRF, but surface ships were a tough sell.

It was interesting that before long I was able to exchange a few words with Marshal of the Soviet Union Grechko, the Soviet uniformed Secretary of Defense. I think he wanted to be seen talking to Americans at this time of US-Soviet strategic talks. He did not want the Navy, which was negotiating its own US-Soviet Agreement on reducing incidents at sea, monopolizing the conversation!

Witnessing Détente

Attendance at huge military parades on Soviet national holidays was a ritual for military attachés and the press. It was an incredible display of marching men, their hardware, and massive missiles. The spectacle was billed as a demonstration of mighty Soviet power. This struck me as not entirely accurate. I was there in my Naval regalia along with all the other military representatives in Moscow, near the row of old men stomping cold feet on the top of Lenin's Tomb. They were like a row of crows lined up on a telephone wire.

These old fellows were a sad and insecure bunch. As they had moved up in the Soviet pecking order, Stalin had messed with their heads. Each of them would cheerfully stab any of the others in the back.

Since Stalin's death in 1953, they had spent two decades trying mightily to get an unworkable system to work, and the gap with the rest of the world just got bigger. The Russian people still longed for the mass murderer, Stalin! Here they were, braving the cold, making speeches no one paid any attention to, and whipping out their enormous phallic missiles to show the world that "ours is bigger than yours." This was at a time when smaller, faster, and higher-tech weaponry was beginning to dominate intercontinental nuclear equations. Their fears of being left behind were growing every year.

I thought then, and I think events proved later, that the Soviets were interested in SALT because they knew they could not keep up with U.S. production and innovation. Further, they had a morbid fear that American inventiveness, if it ever actually came up with answers on the strategic defensive side of the competition, would leave Soviet military power in the dust. The military realities that the Soviets clearly understood were accompanied by somber economic realities. The Breadbasket of Europe, thanks to the glories of Socialism, would have to buy American and Canadian wheat. Détente would be a necessity.

The U.S. Embassy became a much more interesting place than it had been earlier in the Cold War. Kissinger would appear at the Embassy virtually unannounced. We would get to deal with Naval Officers that we would not have met in more normal times.

Once, I was sitting at my desk, and a senior visiting U.S. Navy Captain pulled up a chair and sat next to me. Carl A. H. Trost, who also wore Gold Dolphins earned in the old boats, asked me if I knew anything about the officers whom he and a visiting young junior Admiral Hayward were to meet. I told them that I knew their writings and had even spoken to them. He listened as I told him what I knew and what I thought it meant. Both Trost and Hayward would become Chief of Naval Operations. The young Assistant Secretary of the Navy who attended those early sessions was John Warner, later the Secretary of the Navy and a United States Senator.

On May 26, 1972, Presidents Nixon and Brezhnev signed an Anti-Ballistic Missile Treaty and an Interim Agreement to limit Strategic Offensive Arms. The day before, Secretary Warner and Admiral Gorshkov signed the Incidents at Sea Agreement. Thirty-eight years later I pointed out a picture of the event in Senator Warner's office to my grandson who was an intern there. Admiral Hayward and I, the acting Naval US Attache, stood behind the two men signing the document.

Observing the Observers

Détente or no détente, we continued to be followed everywhere. It is unfair to blame the KGB for keeping a close eye on attachés who travelled everywhere, talked to people at random, and always tested the boundaries of what was permitted. Paranoia is a staple of the Russian personality. The relationship between the attachés who pushed the envelope in Russia and the KGB agents who followed them around ranged from merely uncongenial to downright nasty.

Most of the time the "tails" in Leningrad were tolerant, if not friendly. We would walk for miles along the back streets behind the shipyards, and they kept a reasonable distance. They did not even notice when an old truck exited the yard where nuclear submarines were built and we picked up a piece of metal that fell off the vehicle. It looked like a strip of tin from a Spam can. This turned out to be a scrap of titanium, and it confirmed an important breakthrough in the construction of Soviet submarine hulls.

Once, Commander Manthorpe and I were on a trip to Arkhangel'sk in the Soviet far north in the winter, and our Aeroflot flight was forced by a snowstorm to land in Leningrad. It was the winter after President Nixon had been in Leningrad during the SALT Treaty signing. Bill Manthorpe had been a U.S. liaison officer to the KGB, which was responsible for security during the presidential visit. He worked directly with senior KGB officers in Leningrad.

Since we were in Leningrad unannounced and without "company," we decided to take a cab into town to see what we could see. We spent a couple of hours there while, presumably, the KGB was playing catch-up. Finally, thoroughly cold and tired, we went to the Evropeiskaya Hotel to see if we could get a room, knowing of course that this was the end of our impromptu visit.

A whole flock of KGB types, led by their boss, burst into the hotel lobby where we waited. Bill Manthorpe rushed up to the agent in charge, threw an arm around his shoulder, and said as loudly as he could, "Yuri! So good to see you again. How are the wife and kids?" Poor Yuri was at a loss for words. His team looked at him like they did not know him. Finally, there were polite handshakes. The KGB kicked us out of town as gently as possible. They got us a car to the airport and kept a wary eye on us as we waited for the next flight back to Moscow.

On one trip, the "authorities" apparently were going to have a night out on the town at the expense of the State. My travelling partner and I were denied tickets to the Kirov Ballet that evening, but it was made clear that we should take dinner at the only decent restaurant in town. (Barishnikov was dancing the part of Duke Albrecht in *Gisele* at the Kirov.) When we arrived at the restaurant, we noticed that the entire KGB contingent and some ladies were at a table laden with *zakuski* and open bottles of vodka, wine and beer. They had spent two hundred rubles and had not yet ordered dinner! We were seated in their line of sight, and it soon became clear that the waiter was in no hurry. They were settled in for a fine, slow dinner.

We ordered two bowls of soup, slurped them down, and went to get our overcoats. It was bitter cold outside and snowing. There was consternation. As the tails scrambled to get their coats I whispered to one of them, "We really did want to go to the Kirov." We left the restaurant for an ambling two-hour walk back to our hotel. They tramped along behind us, hopefully reflecting on how nice it would be at the Kirov watching *Gisele*.

We learned in January of 1973 that Wilma was pregnant. Her favorite food, watermelon, like almost all fruits and vegetables in winter, was not to be had in Moscow. Since I had to be in Helsinki in February, I arranged to have a watermelon shipped by PanAm Airlines from Florida to Finland. I was taking the train from Helsinki back to Moscow and would have to undergo the usual badgering by customs officials at the border in Vyborg. The watermelon was a large one that did not fit into my suitcase very well and there were telltale bulges on both sides that made the suitcase appear more pregnant than Wilma was. Since I had a diplomatic passport, customs officials could ask questions but only search in extreme cases.

A rough looking customs lady, flanked by a uniformed guard, looked suspiciously at my pregnant suitcase and asked, "Do you have any fruits, vegetables or seeds in your luggage?" I could have said "I cannot tell a lie," but I lied. I looked her straight in the eye and said, "nyet." I heard the guard mumble "arbuz," Russian for watermelon, under his breath. They exchanged glances, smiled, and shrugged. She nodded and walked away. Wilma had watermelon on her birthday.

Cherniye Lyud'i (The "Dark Masses")

I had wondered since my first Russian history course at U of L what ordinary working people in the Soviet Union thought about the way they lived and how they were governed. I tried to find out.

I visited the *rinok*, or market, in every town. I never failed to stop at any stores where I could. Stores were pathetic. I saw many state-operated "stores" with yards of empty shelves and a dozen or so tins of canned food. There is no way that those places made enough rubles to pay the uninterested people tending them. There is more food and merchandise in any Wal-Mart today than I saw in the entire Soviet Union in state stores in 1971 and 1972. This is why, when Soviet Naval Officers were in Washington for Incidents at Sea Talks, I made sure that they visited a Safeway Store.

It was sad to see how hard it was to scratch out a living on a tiny plot of land allocated by the Party. Yet, those tiny plots yielded one-third of the food that the country produced. If the Communist system had not permitted peasants to cultivate their private plots for food and to sell at local farmers' markets, there would have been famine.

This was, of course, proof that "that which belongs to everyone belongs to no one," and it rankled the Communist purists who had eradicated the farming middle class in the late 20s and early 30s. Stalin called successful farmers "kulaks," which meant "fist," implying that they held fast to the riches they took from the land, riches that could be spread evenly to everyone if the land simply belonged to everyone. Whole Kulak families, the farming expertise and leadership that had made Europe's Breadbasket bloom for decades, were shipped in unheated boxcars to Siberia. Those who seek to redistribute other people's income should think about the results of Stalin's war on the kulaks.

I talked to anyone who would talk to me, being careful never to talk to the same person twice and to make it crystal clear that it was a spontaneous contact to the KGB goons who were never very far away. Most Russians yearned to know what Americans were really like, knowing in their gut that they would never find out from the press and Party pronouncements.

They knew a lot in their guts, those Russians. They knew that the system did not work and could not work. They knew they lived in the 1940s. They knew that a lot of their plight could be blamed on the Germans, but for how long? They knew that Americans had stood up to be counted and had come to save Europe and support a prostrate Russia, and most of them knew it was ridiculous to believe that these same people wanted to kill Russians now.

Some of the most charming Russians I met were at the *rinok*, or peasant market where ordinary people could bring foodstuffs and some crafts from the countryside to the city. They reminded me of folks who used to come to American towns with fresh food from their farms. Such hardworking people were not politicians, and generally disdained people who were. It was difficult to believe that they paid any attention whatsoever to the gobbledygook in Pravda. It was not even written in language most of them would recognize. Now, the price of potatoes and cabbages were different things.

I saw a lot of ships and tanks and military infrastructure in this tour of duty, and they helped to estimate the state of Soviet military power, but I am absolutely convinced that getting a handle on the hopes, fears, and dreams of the Russian people was the most important thing that I did.

One story is particularly telling. An Army Lieutenant Colonel assigned to the Embassy had tried to drive with his family into Moscow from Helsinki. Ignoring advice, he was driving an old 8-cylinder Ford station wagon. The water pump, with over 100,000 miles on it, let go near the famous old town of Novgorod. To the consternation of his KGB tails, he managed to get his family on a train and on to Moscow. The car was left on the side of the two-lane road. A water pump was ordered through Stockmann's Department Store in Finland, the source of anything from the developed world. It came in a couple of weeks, and the Colonel was looking for someone to go with him to rescue the car.

I was interested in seeing Novgorod, an old town established in 860 and on the road south taken by Vikings a thousand years ago as they descended the river systems to settle Kievan Rus' on the Dnieper River. Alexander Nevskiy, Prince of Novgorod, had turned back Teutonic Knights invading Russia in 1240. It sounded like an interesting adventure.

We packed up tools in an old embassy utility vehicle and set out, undaunted by the difficulty of replacing the water pump on the old Detroit behemoth. In a few hours we were treated to a wonderful sight. The car was jacked up and a couple of fifty-something peasants were trying to figure out how to fix it. They had no keys, but that was clearly not going to be an obstacle. When we showed up, there were heartfelt greetings. A crowd of ill-dressed folks, looking very much like hardworking people that knew hard times, soon formed.

Several fellows, delighted to see the new water pump, said that they could figure out how to do the job. They had learned on American Jeeps during the war, one older man said, and they were in debt to America! They took the tools and set to work. Chairs appeared and a couple of ladies produced two china cups and saucers, painted in Russian peasant style. Tea and cookies were served. We enjoyed the company of these wonderful, simple, and open people for a few hours while, with the banged knuckles and salty vocabulary that accompanies a water pump job anywhere, the task was done. The ladies insisted that we keep the cups. The men would not discuss payment, so we left some tools.

I was "at home" with those Russians that fixed the Ford. They reminded me of the kind of folks who would appear to help on an Indiana byway. These simple folks were not political people. They were no more imbued with Communism than my Dad was imbued with Capitalism. I have often thought about the notion that "they are just like us," and my experience tells me that there is a lot of truth in it. To be accurate, my experience told me that they were much like Americans in the Midwest in the late 1940s.

Moscow-St. Petersburg highway near where the Ford was repaired in 1972. Photo by the author

History is important in any society, but in the Soviet Union history sometimes seemed more important than the future. The Communist Party kept a tight rein on the past, which it could control far better than it could determine the future. It really matters where a nation has been, what lessons it has learned, and where the image of the past suggests the future might lie. So, the Communists simply rewrote the past as they saw fit. Politically astute or ambitious Russians would pay great attention to writings about the past for clues about what to think, say, and believe. A joke among common people was: "How do you identify a soothsayer in the Soviet Union? He is the one who can predict the past!"

It is an important sign of weakness and decline when a nation pays more attention to altering its past to fit the present than it pays to recognizing the truth and dealing with it. One has to worry when the U.S. Constitution is misrepresented by politicians and judges. Or when children are told to read Huckleberry Finn sanitized of the racist colloquialisms of its day. Russians would understand that, when the currently prevailing Politically Correct dominates the past, the future is in trouble.

As I prepared to leave the Soviet Union in 1973, a whiff of weakness was in the air. The Soviet Leadership was diminished by its overtures to the West, the failing harvests, and a sense that they were stuck in a Russia of Stalin's time.

Russians seemed to understand that, except for intercontinental nuclear superpower status bought at frightful expense and glorified daily in the press, Russia was going nowhere. The Communists could control the past and dominate the present, but they offered a future that could not be believed.

Russian School Children, 1972
photo by the author

Chapter XI
Career Purgatory

"May you come to the attention of those in authority"
Chinese Curse

It was time for us to go home in 1973, and time for the Navy to decide what to do with me. Wilma was pregnant, and we were anxiously waiting for Navy orders.

For the second time in my career, I got orders that did not jibe with my family's hang-ups over pets. The Navy wanted to send me to a plum Navy job in London operating a key part of its system of surveillance of the Soviet Navy. Highly classified then, but common knowledge now, was the system of listening devices that covered, among other things, the Greenland/Iceland/UK gap in the Atlantic Ocean. It was important data collection or "bean counting" that directly affected Navy policy. It was a promising opportunity at the leading edge of technology for a Lieutenant Commander. It was not very good use of the education and experience the Navy had paid for.

Wilma cried. Our old dog, a Brittany spaniel, would not survive the 6-month quarantine that the British required. I sent a message to the Detailer responsible for assignment of officers like me. This fellow, I would learn, already thought that I had enjoyed preferential treatment by officers wearing dolphins and by Naval Intelligence Officers who overvalued my academic credentials and political orientation. Orders to a plum job were clearly not his idea.

His response to me was less than understanding and may have reflected annoyance by others in the system besides him. I got the chance to shut up and do as I was told or take what could be found in the Washington area. I replied that it would help to know the alternative. Was there a better use of my education and experience?

Instead of a reply, I got orders to Joint Duty in Washington, a potential career-ender.

Joint Duty: a Career Death Threat

Joint Duty is not about smoking pot. It can be worse for your health.

It is about adjusting to other cultures. Army and Air Force Officers, who do not come of age at sea, are from cultures alien to Naval Officers.

You could exhume the bones of any Naval Officer worth his salt and you would find an operating philosophy that had turned into fiber: "That which is not specifically forbidden is permitted." The other Services have the opposite philosophy.

The United States did not develop a European-style General Staff Structure atop its separate Military Services. Instead, we evolved a Joint Services structure under a powerful civilian Department of Defense after 1947. An Air Force was created from the Army's stepchild, the Army Air Force. These were mostly Army ideas, launched by the powerful and influential Army officers who emerged from the war and whom the new President held, rightly, in high esteem. Officers like Secretary of State George Marshall were broad-gage thinkers at political and social levels well above the areas of expertise of the senior Naval Officers of WWII. Generals Douglas MacArthur and Dwight Eisenhower, each in his own way, would reflect Army influence in the politics of postwar America.

So, guided mostly by an Army worldview, the future of the American military would, though inter service rivalries remained important and loud, essentially be "Joint." Alfred Thayer Mahan, the oracle of a maritime view of strategy and world politics, was definitely not dead, but his teachings would be expressed more and more in a Joint context that was uncongenial for Naval Officers.

"Joint duty" was the buzz phrase for orders to the Joint Staff, which would become a fairly effective organization by the 21st Century, but served for years as a pale copy of a German General Staff resisted by the U.S. Navy. This is not just the myopic perspective of a clearly biased old retired Naval Officer. It is a fact that for years the Navy did not send its most promising officers into the "joint environment" lest their "real" careers be interrupted and their worldviews be corrupted by the influences of officers wearing different-colored uniforms.

This is actually an understatement. Naval Officers sent to joint duty were passed over for promotion in droves. This phenomenon fed upon itself: since the Navy treated joint duty with disdain, the Army, and an opportunistic and savvy Air Force, grabbed all the important and almost all of the senior jobs. Naval Officers not at the top of their year-groups were sent to the worst jobs where people who did not much appreciate an attitude of "that which is not specifically forbidden is permitted" would write their fitness reports. Even if they did, a Naval Officer's fitness report written by an Air Force officer who said you walked on water did not float in the Navy.

Over twenty years later I would be the lone Naval Officer on a Commission aimed at improving joint service education and training. I was destined to have more joint duty than any Naval Officer I know, but as a young officer, I had been sheltered from the career politics of joint duty until I left Moscow in 1973. I had to be told that a career death knell had sounded.

My orders in 1973 were to report to the Estimates Directorate of the Defense Intelligence Agency. This was Joint Duty. There were two other Lieutenant Commanders already there, and one was senior to me and had already been passed over for promotion. No one in my chain of command was a Naval officer. I was doomed. There may have been officers in that circumstance who got promoted, but no one I knew had ever seen one. I took my medicine, reported to my new duty, and resolved to start looking for an academic opening somewhere after the family got settled.

New Roots: Virginia

Wilma, in her ninth month of pregnancy, was back in Indiana preparing to move to Washington. My Indiana childhood friend, Denny Cox, and I looked for a house and settled on a place in Fairfax, Virginia that the family would grow to love. We had saved some money while in Moscow, and had made some money selling our Ford businessman's sedan for the price of a Cadillac, and could muster a down payment if the owner would accept a lot less than he asked. He did. I drove over to Indiana and brought the family back in a Ford station wagon that Carl Snook, now in the car sales business, had arranged.

On September 8th 1973, Wilma, who had been standing in the commissary line at Cameron Station, Virginia, had to go to Fort Belvoir to the Army hospital to have the baby. Wilma's parents, who were there in 1966 when our first baby was born and I was at sea, were waiting outside the commissary. Her dad had to return to get the groceries, and I raced from the Pentagon, a typical Navy family tale.

Z-Grams

At this point the Story is in the Seventies. Any Naval officer commenting on the early 1970s must address the Zumwalt era and the Z-Grams he issued when he got a Wild Hair. Admiral Elmo Zumwalt was CNO from 1970 to 1974. He had been promoted ahead of many other, more senior, contemporaries by politicians. Thank God, I was out of the country most of this time.

If you believe that the world was going to Hell in a handbag, Zumwalt was ahead of his time. He embraced the Politically Correct before most other craven social engineers got around to it.

Social change must preserve what is worth keeping. This is particularly true of traditional cultures like that of the Navy. Change that is too fast to be absorbed without attacking the core of a culture is not helpful. It can be destructive. Zumwalt sought to cram social change down the throat of a squared away, venerable, institution. He tried to impose frivolous notions while sacrificing core values. Length of hair, type of clothing, or vocabulary was more important than good order and discipline. It is too silly to recount instances of Commanders feeling a vegetable to improve their "sensitivity," and I refuse to do it here. Neither will I try to explain black enlisted men, because they were black, yelling at white officers, because they were white.

The Navy needed, and always needs, to adapt to change in society, and some Zumwalt-era ideas had merit. I have spoken of the problems of forcing qualified officers to wait too long for command, and Zumwalt had a point on this issue. He was not dead wrong on some loosening of appearance standards, but he ran roughshod over the institution in implementing these kinds of peripheral changes. Of course, race relations required thoughtful command attention and better awareness of racial sensitivities, but it was stupid to diminish traditional order and discipline as a means to achieve these things.

I was not a traditional Naval Officer in some important ways myself, but the Zumwalt era was a net loss in my view. Zumwalt's tenure was the Silly Season in our Navy's history. Obviously, people with power disagree with me. The next Navy destroyer class, at this writing, will be the Zumwalt Class.

Washington Distractions and Learning Experiences

Besides Watergate, other distractions and amusements were part of my introduction to Washington duty. Once, while I was walking down the E-Ring in the Pentagon near the office of the Secretary of Defense, a bizarre thing happened. I was wearing my best blue-striped suit because of business in those hallowed realms. I shared with Secretary of Defense Melvin Laird baldness,

height and periodic setbacks in the ever-present struggle with weight gain. In my civilian suit, we looked somewhat alike.

As I approached a corner where the E-Ring met a large transverse corridor, I was reading a document. Coming up the corridor was a four-star Air Force General straight out of the cookie cutter that turns out Air Force Generals: he was tall, handsome, skinny, bore more ribbons than he had years of service, sported flashy footgear, and was in a hurry. We collided, and he landed unceremoniously on his behind. I was still standing and about to offer apologies when the startled officer, still on the ground, blubbered in mortification: "I'm so sorry, Mr. Secretary!" I gave him a withering glance and said, "Carry on General!" I hurried on my way and did not look back.

I also got an introduction to the complexities of what would become "Don't ask, don't tell." As I was growing up in New Albany, a girl about four years older lived across the alley. A tomboy, she was a buddy of my older brother. This was a nice kid who was a straight "A" student. Soon, as with a boy a block away who became a Major in the Army, the word was out: she was a "queer" as they said in those days. She was ostracized. She finished high school but left town and was not heard from in those parts again. The rumor was that she was in Washington. I always felt bad about this because she was nice to me and her mother, a widow who paid me to rake leaves and cut her grass, was devastated by the situation.

When I came to Washington in 1973, I decided to look her up. Her last name was unusual and I found it in the telephone book. She had taken a masculine first name. I called her and she seemed friendly, but wary. We had lunch. She was a sharp, confident person. It started out well enough, catching up on the neighborhood. Then she probed to find out something about me that was important to her. Basically, she was asking, "What do you think about people like me?" Not expecting such directness, I fumbled a bit but finally got it out, sort of. "I think that we should be tolerant of people who are different from us," I babbled inarticulately. She scowled. "Tolerant?" This, she said gently but firmly, was the problem with people like me: that we could not accept people like her as just the same as us, with the same rules, the same opportunities, and the same respect. She was courteous about it, quickly finished lunch, and I never saw or heard from her again.

Societies grow and change and, slowly but surely, some of the values and mores at the edge of mainstream thought get absorbed and integrated, at least to some extent. The process begins with understanding and tolerance. Because society's core institutions, like the family, are steeped in its values and mores, a society cannot absorb deviations from norms too quickly, or completely in some cases.

This is so in spite of the fact that those who deviate from the norms will demand mainstream status and, in our country with our founding documents, insist it is unfair not to be treated like everyone else. They are wrong.

"Fair" is determined in the mainstream, not at the fringe. Gay people should be tolerated as all human beings at the fringes of a culture should be tolerated, but they have no claim to represent the mainstream or core of society, which sets norms and establishes mores. Changing the way the society operates to force acceptance into the mainstream of the culture weakens the fabric of society if it means surrendering core institutions. I believe that the gay agenda seeks to change the role of the family in America so fundamentally that it would cripple the country. The family is a core institution and must not be compromised. I believe this, having friends, colleagues and beloved relatives who are gay.

Another distraction was the White House Fellows Program. Secretary of the Navy Warner and Vice Admiral Hayward, soon to be CNO, recommended me for the program. It was an exciting, eye-opening ride to the final stages of the competition. A group of very successful 40-something executives from the Executive Branch, mostly political appointees, seemed to control the vetting process, which included interviews and a few group seminars. Only one, maybe two, military Fellows would emerge from the field of fifteen candidates. My PhD and my recent tour in Russia at a key time were all I brought to this game, but the other military men among the last few standing were combat veterans with chests full of medals who were clearly not of the John Kerry variety.

At one group seminar among competitors and young political appointees, we were discussing the politics and economics of oil. I suggested that we would be better off if we froze the level of imports to 1973 levels, sucked up the incremental costs of increasing demand, and forced the development of our domestic oil, gas and alternate energy sources, especially nuclear. At first, some of the contestants nodded agreement, but the political appointees actually sneered at my political naiveté. I was quickly dismissed as simply not understanding reality. Maybe it is true that I "just didn't get it." I have reflected on this exchange many times. I still don't get it.

One of the finalists for the White House Fellowship, a handsome, charming, and very bright Army Major, was a minority officer sporting, in addition to combat ribbons, a Legion of Merit. Colin Powell was selected and got assigned to Caspar Weinberger's office, then at the Office of Management and Budget.

The rest is history. He would be Chairman of the Joint Chiefs of Staff and Secretary of State. This was no early version of Affirmative Action. I would have selected Major Colin Powell myself. He was a high-flyer; I was a pedestrian, or maybe just a hitchhiker.

Powell supported the education of enlisted men and women at civilian institutions when I was President of Servicemembers Opportunity Colleges. As Chairman of the Joint Chiefs of Staff in 1992, General Powell said SOC was as important to active duty service members as the GI Bill was to veterans.

On the home front, an important family event was the arrival of "Pepper," an Appaloosa mare about 9 years old. She was skittish, having been used in frenetic barrels and stakes races and perhaps not treated very well. She soon settled down and became a beloved family pet who would die at old age after many happy years in our care. This, at last, was fulfillment of my promise to Wilma when we were teenagers. Her horses have been members of our family to this day. Pepper lies at peace in our front field.

Pepper and Wilma Kime
photo by the author

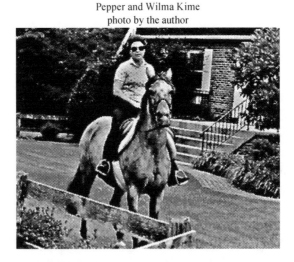

Chapter XII
Joint and National Intelligence

From the rarified air of the White House Fellowship competition, I returned to Joint Duty, assigned to the Defense Intelligence Agency and what seemed like certain career oblivion.

It was not long before I got baptized in the politics of making intelligence judgments in Washington. On October 6th, 1973, war broke out in the Middle East. Depending on your point of view, this was the Yom Kippur War or the Ramadan War, since the Jewish and Muslim holidays coincided that year.

The Syrians and Egyptians had been smarting since 1967 when the Israelis occupied the Golan Heights and the Sinai Peninsula. They, supported by a large coalition of Arab states, launched a surprise attack to recover these occupied lands on October the 6th. There were some initial Arab successes as U.S. analysts, including the Estimates Directorate where I was, watched. All hands were on deck. I was a backbencher among intelligence heavyweights who gathered to summarize their views of the situation. I was there to provide a perspective of potential Soviet involvement.

It was the most serious conflict with potential nuclear superpower involvement since the Cuban Missile Crisis. Both the U.S. and the USSR quickly and massively resupplied their client states during the conflict. But, as I saw the situation after the first days, it was not the USSR that we were in danger of misunderstanding.

The room was filled with pro-Arab sentiment, especially among the entrenched civilian analysts. These people seem to have been persuaded more by their sentiment than by the lessons of the 1967 War! Not shy, I piped up with my view that the Israelis had not gathered themselves and certainly had not yet expressed the Israeli Way of War. It was not clear to me why they held off as long as they had, *but they would surely gather their forces and strike decisively.* Disdainful glances were hurled from my civilian and military seniors. I was correct, but ignored. Within hours, the Israelis boldly crossed the Suez Canal and menaced the Egyptian Third Army. A UN-imposed cease-fire slowed the Israelis, but that cease-fire came apart, and they encircled the hapless Egyptians.

I was not privy to the feedback that senior intelligence advisors got after failing to foresee the obvious, but it must have been ugly, because military intelligence looked ridiculous in policy circles. A somewhat less cocky General, who was in the room earlier, caught me in a corridor a day later. He acknowledged that I had warned of a dramatic Israeli offensive, but he was more annoyed than gracious. I was told in no uncertain terms that it didn't help much to be right if you fail to convince anybody. He huffed off. He would get two more stars.

This was an important lesson, and one that had to be heeded if one were to have any impact as a mere "expert" among decision makers. Until you got to a position of serious influence, you had to make your case, sometimes to people who are clearly not the sharpest knives in the drawer.

Superiority or Превосходство

In analysis of Soviet intercontinental nuclear weapons and strategy, the word "Superiority" had special significance. The question was, "Do the Soviets seek superiority over the US in intercontinental nuclear capacity?" Superiority connoted the ability to attack with impunity. Any fool, of course, could say that the Soviets *wished* they had such capacity. The Holy Grail for intelligence was to find evidence that the Soviets thought that their wet dreams had come true, or that they could see a way to make them come true.

One Chairman of the JCS, beset by the evidence that Soviet weaknesses were mounting, faced with ABM and SALT treaties, and trying to defend ambitious defense budgets, was anxious for the Holy Grail. One piece of evidence was reported to be the long-sought evidence. Without revealing anything about sources, I can say that a there was consternation when I doubted the evidence. First, I was told I could not see it for lack of some extremely exotic clearance. It was so exotic that I had to be signed into it and out of it simultaneously! (I never understood this, and still do not.) Anyway, I reviewed the "evidence," and it was less than circumstantial.

I was in the doghouse with the morning briefers who thought they had a blockbuster for the Chairman. The "Team A" versus "Team B" debate that will be described below was a direct outgrowth of the frustration of Joint Intelligence to look into the murky realm of "intentions" and come up with convincing evidence of a successful Soviet drive for "Superiority."

When an old man sees a swimsuit contest and gets that special gleam in his eye, he might want to, but he just cannot really do it! The Soviets had the biggest, most phallic nuclear devices on the planet, but they just could not do it. "Superiority" for the USSR in the nuclear equation was not in the cards.

National Intelligence Estimates (NIEs)

There would be opportunities to make inputs that had high impact in the complex National Intelligence Estimates process that cranked out the final estimates that reached the White House, leaders on Capitol Hill and Cabinet Secretaries. I soon learned two very important things about this Process.

First, military intelligence experts might not prevail in the heated arguments and arm-wrestling over the meaning of evidence, but military players in the National Intelligence process had a chance to make their case. It was not an anti-military setting. This turned out to be very important. A Lieutenant Commander who did his homework and had credibility was respected in the interagency process more than he could ever be heard in the Pentagon where "senior" was mistakenly thought to mean "superior." (Fact of Military Life: superior officers are not all senior, and senior officers are not all superior.)

Second, CIA, under William Colby as Director, was an equal-opportunity intellectual environment. If you had a clue, he wanted to know. If you could put evidence together within a broad sociopolitical understanding, especially if you

could write it down with a little clarity, he wanted your help. I saw many times CIA appreciation of these things and CIA indifference to rank and position. It was not just Mr. Colby: until Bill Casey arrived at CIA, the entire Agency maintained an open, intellectual, and honest environment.

DIA occupied some of my time with Navy hardware-oriented and systems-related matters, and I did my best at those things. Some highly secret shenanigans were going on that involved both US and Soviet submarines. Most of this is in the public domain now. Americans should read <u>Blind Man's Bluff</u>, printed by Harper in 1999, to learn about heroes and events they may not know about. Anyway, some of these things involved those of us in intelligence. I was assigned some other interesting studies. For example, I wrote an assessment of Soviet oil and gas capacities and policies.

An Air Force Lieutenant Colonel working next to me wrote a study on what today we call terrorist training camps. In 1974 these were mostly anti-imperialist hate camps funded in the third world by the Soviet Union or, in some cases, by China or Cuba. In the Muslim world, they presaged camps we targeted after the 9/11/2001 attack. That it was a surprise to anyone that there were terrorist training camps in Pakistan and Afghanistan turning out people that would kill Americans is a shame. The 1974 study did not get much attention or any high level support.

My opportunity to shine came when I was assigned to participate in the political-military and military-strategic judgments in the critical annual CIA estimate of Soviet strategic intercontinental nuclear capabilities and intentions.

The Navy, and other players in the non-strategic or "conventional" parts of the U.S. establishment, undervalued this annual CIA estimate of strategic-level forces. This was shortsighted, because the conclusions from this effort permeated everything at both Defense and State and was vital to military strategy at both conventional and strategic levels of conflict. It was a big deal, and I was tossed into the middle of it.

I thrived. I was willing to work the long hours involved in repeated drafting and re-drafting that interagency pulling and hauling required. The best, most dedicated civilian analysts I would ever meet were engaged in this process. It was a very demanding environment that had no time for ideologues or sloppy thinkers. I brought familiarity with Soviet writings, a handle on past and recent academic analysis, and even some first-hand contact with Soviet military leaders to the table. I was not doomed as the folks who sent me to Joint Duty at DIA thought. It was not a bad place for a Navy misfit with my background to be.

I was invited to participate in Soviet-related activities outside the "office." When Georgiy Arbatov, the most influential academic in Russia, brought a delegation of military-strategic thinkers to the U.S., I was among the people who travelled and interacted with them. I helped with the Incidents at Sea talks when they were in the United States and maintained contacts with Soviet officers that would come in handy a decade later. And I got to see the bulging eyeballs of Soviet officers when we stopped with them at an ordinary Safeway store. One suggested that it was set up for them to see, like the *Potemkin Villages* of Tsarina Catherine's time. I was driving them to a dinner and had a little time, so I offered to go in whatever direction they ordered until we encountered another grocery store and we would visit it. They exchanged looks and declined.

Soon I was spending almost all my time as the DIA representative on national intelligence estimates. Of course, much of this business cannot be discussed here but, as I maintained during the intelligence process and throughout my time in uniform, the really important things are not "classified." I remain convinced to this day that, if we sent one copy of every classified piece of paper to the Russians or the Chinese, they would be just as confused as we are.

I was a participant in several National Intelligence Estimates. Two of them are worth special mention here.

The Soviet Navy was making a big splash on the world's oceans and getting a lot of attention, so a National Estimate on the Soviet Navy was commissioned. I was assigned to assist the CIA drafter who became ill, leaving me to run much of the process. Having written a dissertation on this subject only three years earlier, I had thought about the issues and was excited about testing what I had learned against all the evidence that intelligence could bring to bear.

There was a hitch. The U.S. Navy, though they provided unstinting support of my schooling and research, had never endorsed my dissertation. Many, and likely a sizeable majority, of Naval Officers and most naval analysts did not accept my view that the Soviet Navy was an inherently limited element of Soviet Military Power, in spite of its snazzy ships and highly publicized thrusts into the high seas. The U.S. Naval Institute sent every draft with my ideas on the Soviet Navy to "objective reviewers" who did not accept them. They were definitely not views that those wanting to justify US Naval budgets wanted to hear.

To support an effort to justify U.S. Naval forces, especially surface forces in the nuclear submarine era, the capabilities and intentions of the Soviet Navy were grossly exaggerated in American and Western Intelligence. Admiral Gorshkov played the advocates of American Naval power like a piano. Western analysis of the Soviet Navy, and for that matter, of other Soviet conventional military forces, was simplistic. Analysts refused to connect Soviet conventional military instruments to the context of escalation and the capabilities of the two superpowers to execute the various stages of warfare, especially nuclear stages.

On a less lofty strategic plane, the image of Russians who were ten feet tall was extended to the Soviet Navy, a highly technology-dependent force in a decidedly backward country. Russians are no taller than anyone else, and their boys did not grow up fixing their cars on their driveways. They had no cars and no driveways. Most had never seen a toaster, much less taken one apart. How on earth would they maintain a missile guidance system or a nuclear reactor?

The Estimate on the Soviet Navy turned out well. History has borne out the judgments in it. Look at the Russian Navy today! Thanks to some fine officers who valued integrity and objectivity in intelligence, the Navy did not hold my counter-institutional views on the Soviet Navy against me.

The second Estimate I mention nearly got me fired. CIA asked me to participate in the writing of a crucial National Estimate entitled Soviet Détente Policy. Soviet wheat purchases abroad, Soviet overtures on arms control matters, and growing economic malaise in the face of enormous Soviet military budgets, accompanied by Soviet dabbling in the Third World and occasional saber-rattling, all combined to present a mixed picture to U.S. policymakers. It was time to for a national assessment of Détente, or "Разрядка" as Russians called it.

Détente, a policy of relaxation of tensions, was like making love to a porcupine: it had to be done very carefully. The USSR had to be careful not to expose very real weakness. The US had to be careful not to project weakness where none existed. The danger on both sides was serious in a time of Mutually Assured Destruction, when miscalculation could be a disaster.

Huge equities were involved. Both Doves and Hawks in Washington were seriously interested in putting their own spin on the Estimate. This had become patently obvious when right-wing ideologues, claiming that our strategic assessments of the Soviets were in the hands of a left-oriented intelligence establishment, forced the creation of a "B" team to counter its judgments. They dubbed what they viewed as the effete leftist types, some of the toughest, most competent people I knew, "Team A." The "B" team, comprised of conservative scholars and politicians who, though not steeped in the intelligence, were convinced that the Soviet Union was using Détente policies as a strategy to gain intercontinental nuclear offensive superiority over the US. Team "B" was led by Professor Richard Pipes of Harvard's History Department.

Dr. Pipes was an articulate patrician-academic who had wide influence among conservatives and many military officers. He was a gifted, credible historian. I liked him and had admired his historical writings and brilliant lectures on Russian history. However, his political views and his understanding of international relations betrayed the knee-jerk simplicity of many political extremists and ideologues, and a hatred for Russia that many Eastern European émigrés - like Pipes - brought with them upon escaping to the West. It was sad to watch this fine gentleman and historian be drawn into what was essentially an ideological argument.

I can testify that those looking hard at Soviet military power and making judgments about it were not left-wingers. In fact, they knew better than most the damage that Bolshevism had wrought on the Russian people. They were a tough, coldly objective group as skeptical of Soviet motives and as patriotic as could be found. Most of these hard-nosed folks saw the potential enemy as seven or eight feet tall. Pipes and his cohorts insisted on painting them as ten feet tall.

The National Estimate on Soviet Détente Policy was argued and written in an environment soured and politicized by the Team B politicians who enjoyed a lot of press coverage. The press played up the "debate." My bosses in DIA, of course, being in the U.S. Military, could not be as openly "political" as the civilian Team B spokesmen, but they were, in fact, shamelessly rooting for Team B.

The DIA Director hired a right-wing ideologue as a "Defense Intelligence Officer," a job concocted to serve as a counterweight to the highly qualified National Intelligence Officer for the Soviet Union at CIA. She was an embarrassment in the company of the bright analysts at Langley, and quickly quit showing up where real evidence was discussed. She was obviously far out of her league. Analysts and officers under her purview, trying to be objective and reflect what the evidence indicated, were pressured to make the most negative possible judgments about Soviet capabilities and intentions. We call it "spin" nowadays in so-called "news." Politics, not facts, motivated such people. I ignored her. She reported directly to the DIA Director.

The Estimate on Détente, a powerful document that summarized Soviet strengths as well as its weaknesses and made important judgments about the predilections and prospects of our nation's nuclear superpower competitor, was sent to the White House toward the end of my tour in Defense Intelligence.

The Defense Intelligence Agency took exception to it. At the end of my tour I was called to the Director's office and chastised directly and personally. At least they recognized how much I was responsible for it.

Oddly, my immediate bosses, having heard the appreciation of those at the top of the National Intelligence Community, wrote a fine fitness report and recommended a prestigious award normally reserved to much senior officers. The Director downgraded the award by three levels.

Of course, it is easy now to point out that my colleagues and I were correct about Soviet Détente Policy. History is a powerful cleanser and deodorizer. It is sad, however, that military officers sometimes have to choose between integrity and objectivity and loyalty to politico-military institutions with axes to grind. I just could not make that choice. I calculated that I would survive having my loyalty questioned. And I did.

Parting Thoughts on Military Intelligence

The individual Service intelligence organizations, like Naval Intelligence, kept their noses to their respective grindstones and tried to provide intelligence to the forces that might have to fight. This meant that each Service intelligence organization's most important mission was "operational intelligence (OP-INTELL)," which was not my primary interest but was their primary job. Combatant commands in all Services need intelligence tailored to operational needs. Politics are not in their job descriptions.

Joint Military Intelligence, in contrast, proved to be utterly corrupted by politics and motivated not by facts but by defense budgets. At this level the "threat" must justify the budget. It is adjusted, or distorted, as necessary. I left the Defense Intelligence Agency thinking that the nation had erred by creating an intelligence arm of the Department of Defense and the Joint Staff, and that such an institution would invariably be more political than analytical.

The implications of this are important:

- The Services and the Department of Defense should focus on Operational Intelligence, information and analysis relevant to war fighting and the strategies for war fighting. HUMINT and socio-political analysis are key elements of Service and DoD Intelligence.

- Assessment of military power at the level of national strategy and policy is the province of National Intelligence. Assessment of foreign military power should be primarily a civilian enterprise that analyzes and assesses the entire socio-economic-political spectrum of the adversary. The military should, of course, make inputs into these assessments but should have a decisive role. Some experts on assessment of foreign military power should have experience in the Services and Department of Defense but they should not answer to the Department of Defense.

Chapter XIII
The National Defense University
&
The National War College
1976-1981

I did not have the slightest idea what the Navy would do with me in 1976. They probably didn't either. My career had no pattern to it. In the Navy an officer's career needs to fit the pattern of some career "community." I technically belonged to the Naval Intelligence Community, but I had never filled one of their billets. My billet in Moscow would become such a billet, but I was really sent there as a submariner before that happened. I was a career orphan!

Incredibly, a door opened. Admiral Thomas Moorer, the Chairman of the Joint Chiefs of Staff, a highly decorated aviator, WWII veteran, and former CNO, had been asked to speak at The National War College. During Q&A, he became impatient with the questions of the senior officer students there and asked, "Don't you people study the Soviet Union here?" A student replied, "We don't travel to Russia!" This reflected The National War College's curriculum, which consisted of a very general core course with guest lecturers from the government and academe, seminars, and an end of year trip to various areas of the world. It was a viewed as a year away from the grind of 16-hour days that all of them had experienced. It was a gentleman's course, a year off while awaiting orders, for officers who "carried Marshals' batons in their back pockets."

Moorer expressed annoyance that day to another highly decorated Naval Aviator named William R. O'Connell, a Navy Captain at the National Defense University. Moorer wondered aloud whether it made sense to keep such a useless place open, a view communicated to Vice Admiral Marmaduke G. Bayne, the President of the newly established National Defense University. Bayne was a submariner.

Captain O'Connell, an unconventional thinker, was asked what could be done about it. He called around and learned that I was in Washington. He called and asked me to come over to Fort McNair, home of the National Defense University and its constituent Colleges, the Industrial College of the Armed Forces (ICAF) and The National War College. I did.

O'Connell was a straightforward, profane, funny, and very intelligent man. He was not hung up on rank, career paths, or precedent. All he cared about was answering the question that had been posed to him about Soviet Studies at The National War College. He had thoroughly checked me out, knew that I was not on a normal career path, and seemed also to know that I, a Lieutenant Commander at the time, was more interested in doing something useful than satisfying the whims of some career planner. He said he had a slot for a full commander that was being vacated and, frankly, he was not sure what the guy currently in the job was contributing to the effort to educate senior officers.

The billet O'Connell had to fill was supposed to develop studies that would present the emerging technical revolution in analysis and management of systems to future flag officers in the military. He asked me what I knew about computers and the networks being operated, secretly then, by the Defense Advanced Research Projects Agency, or DARPA. (These people, not Al Gore, invented the Internet!) I told him that I had seen and used the network at highly classified levels, but I did not understand the technical side of it.

I had used the new DARPA system to gather and summarize classified information and evidence, but technical experts did all the hands-on stuff. I thought the quantitative analysis that I had seen in academe was silly and missed the boat on the most important subjective things. I was skeptical about the mission of the billet and did not think I could help much in it. Unlike my quantitative-oriented professor at Harvard, Captain O'Connell did not balk at this and asked me about the situation at The National War College and if I could help there. I told him I could and shared ideas about what I thought was needed.

In a couple of days he called again with a plan. Admiral Bayne had reviewed my experience and my record and was interested. He said that he was willing to essentially give up control of the billet if I would go over to the National War College, offer to help, and at the same time work on a project to find out what future senior managers needed to know about computer modeling in management. I told him again that I was weak on the technical project angle, and I was concerned that I would be several years junior to both students and faculty at The National War College. He scoffed at both of these reservations. I got orders in about a week and reported for duty in June.

Systems Dynamics

Before I could tackle the Soviet Studies issue at the National War College, I needed to try to fulfill my obligation to investigate the field of technical systems and modeling in management studies. I had the advantage of knowing nothing about it. I had to be guided then by a remark I heard from Vice Admiral William P. Lawrence, a former Prisoner of War, recipient of three Silver Stars, and Superintendent of the Naval Academy. This hero said, "The mark of a true professional is that he does the things he does not like to do as well as the things he likes to do." (I wish I could say that I heeded this advice at all times, but I did not.)

My plan was to survey the literature in the field and identify the major players, actually try to meet with these people, and write a report with ideas on how to organize and what to put into a course at the Industrial College of the Armed forces where the officer-students would be the senior managers of the huge defense acquisition and budgeting process. Doug Murray, skipper of IREX, would have declared it a "ten-minute job." I had about two months of the summer of 1976.

I located the nearly two-dozen professors and business people who were most prominent in the literature and talked to each of them by phone. It was an uneven group. Some seemed flaky, some seemed a little too sure that they had the Holy Grail, and some sounded like they had common sense. Anyway, the Captain, an Air Force officer who was going to teach management, and I would set out to meet personally with each of them. They were located all over the United States and we spent two weeks doing this. We got to peer into what futuristic-minded scholars saw as the future of computers in social realms. Simulation and modeling looked very promising, especially if the limits of quantifying subjective things were understood. Some places, like the University of Michigan's Management School, were ahead of others.

One concept that captured my imagination was a modeling technique at CIA developed by a fellow with the wonderful name of Schreckengost. He called the technique "Systems Dynamics." Simply put, it was a rudimentary language of symbols and formulas. Symbols represented activities and data on both objective and subjective inputs. Symbols had properties like valves, funnels, etc. You could manipulate and adjust the properties of the symbols of the model as you built it until you got it to behave close to the way that the real world worked. Then, you could try out variations on the inputs to the model and see what happened. It was rough, even crude, but it was at the leading edge of something important and was worth a look. I attended the short school on Systems Dynamics at the Agency. During the next year or two, I would co-teach a course on this modeling technique at ICAF where senior officer students would apply it to defense acquisition and budgeting problems.

We wrote the report, and it was entered into the curriculum process at ICAF. It had some impact. Some of the experts we had visited were invited to lecture in courses at the College. I also offered to lecture on Soviet political and military matters when they were relevant to the curriculum there. The Industrial College of the Armed Forces even listed me on their faculty and gave me a diplomma!

I paid my dues at the National Defense University, and it was not forgotten. A report of fitness, signed by an influential senior submarine admiral, would help as I was now, believe it or not, in another joint tour of duty.

The National War College

My reputation, good or bad, may or may not have preceded me at The National War College. What certainly did precede me was that the Chairman of the JCS and Admiral Bayne, a stern countenance morbidly feared by the two-star Air Force General who was the College's

Commandant, were unhappy with the curriculum and were sending some upstart over to fix it. I did not get a detectably chilly reception because of this situation: the military does not work that way. The first few days were very correct and wary. I was given a magnificent office but felt like a spy in their midst.

I approached the Dean of Faculty, a senior Air Force Colonel and Stanford PhD a decade senior to me, to clear the air. He was both very smart and approachable. I told him I was there to help, that I was a straightforward officer and scholar, and that I understood the Chain of Command. I had no intention of ever saying or doing anything related to the bosses at the National Defense University that I did not first discuss at The National War College. He could tell that I meant it. Colonel Hoffman, a fine scholar who had only recently arrived and who turned out to believe himself that the curriculum was weak on our major potential adversary, was visibly delighted and said he would really appreciate some help beefing up the Soviet Studies part of the curriculum. He personally walked me around the halls and introduced me. He briefed the General who appeared in my doorway a little later and was downright chatty. I was in! The faculty at The National War College included many outstanding future colleagues and friends.

The National War College is charged with teaching potential military flag officers and equivalent civilian executives throughout the government how U.S. national security policy is formulated and executed. An understanding of the context for national security policy is crucial. There were only two or three sessions on the Soviet Union at The National War College. No elective classes, more or less like college courses, existed, so a more in-depth exploration of potential major adversaries, the Middle East and South Asia, Latin America, etc., was not offered. Admiral Moorer was correct that this needed to be changed. A very strong faculty at the War College, many who were recent arrivals, thought so, too.

I asked for, and got, a six-week block of time in which to create a program of learning on the Soviet Union appropriate to the War College class. This class of approximately 120 military officers averaged about 43 years old. Virtually all had at least one Masters Degree and several students held Doctorates. All of them had held commands as senior officers and, except for the Naval Officers among them, a very high proportion would be flag officers. The 40 students from civilian agencies had similar credentials and were at similar career stages. It was a daunting task to come up with an appropriate program, but I had almost seven weeks!

I looked back at Professor Fainsod's lecture series at Harvard. It provided a common-sense set of domestic policy subject areas, though obviously some needed more attention than others. (Sadly, Fainsod had died in 1972. He lectured outside Harvard rarely, but he would have come for me.) Soviet Foreign Policy study needed to be tailored to focus on U.S. – Soviet relations, but the Soviet approaches to the Third World and vice-versa would also be highly relevant.

Soviet Military Policy needed serious attention. No wonder Admiral Moorer was unhappy.

Ordinarily, the process of building the core curriculum is a complex and slow process requiring endless coordination and approvals. This time, given the motivation from on high, it was quick. I got help and encouragement rather than obstacles. We started with a brush-up on history and a systematic walk through the elements of Soviet Domestic Policy. All students read Rick Smith's landmark book, The Russians. The sections on Soviet Foreign Policy were defined geographically and presented with the Soviet perspective in mind. Soviet Military policy began with the use of military instruments for showing the flag and moved up the ladder of escalation to intercontinental nuclear war. There were some "classified" sessions.

Readings were extensive. Virtually all of them were reprints of recent, highly relevant journal articles and excerpts from books, many written by the speakers they would hear. This approach is superior to reading a few books, and I used it in my teaching at Georgetown, American University, and the Naval Academy. It is now easy to employ this approach using the Internet, but then it required the efforts of several librarians.

Guest lecturers represented a Who's Who in Russian studies and U.S. policy making on the Soviet Union. Dick Pipes, an annoyance as "Team B" spokesman, was great on history as always. Kissinger came. Marshall Goldman of Harvard contributed world-renowned expertise on the Soviet economy. It was a parade of notables. I was absolutely amazed at the people who would come to the National War College and give their very best effort. I had the honor of delivering the base lectures on Soviet Military and Soviet Foreign Policy. After each lecture, there were student seminars to discuss it.

At the end of the study of the Soviet Union, we had a politico-military simulation that was a highlight of the year. Even senior, often cynical, commanders could have fun. Sense of humor comes with brains in most people, and it is vital to the smart people who must deal with the most sinister things. Imagination and sense of humor abounded among the talented National War College students. Each was assigned the role of a Politburo member and armed with a bio of "their" member, a description of what their responsibilities were, and information on what was known about their personality and behavior. Most students tried hard to play their roles, and some were very good at it. There were about a dozen student "Politburos." At the beginning of the day, each politburo was given a situation that had just evolved. About noon, and at about two-o'clock, they got intelligence updates that changed the problem. It was fun to see them, many dressed for their parts, play their roles. Most important, it was serious business with the threat of deadly conflict, and they learned a great deal from it.

Notes from the lecture on Soviet Military Policy led in 1980 to an article on Soviet military policy and strategy that appeared in many places including intelligence estimates, lectures throughout the United States, and in unclassified journals and books. These had some impact in their time but are now relics of the past, and it serves no purpose to repeat the details of defunct Soviet Military Strategy here. (We need new efforts to determine what may be relevant to the thinking of new nuclear superpowers.) My essay, entitled "The Soviet View of War," appeared in <u>Comparative Strategy</u>, Volume 2, Issue 3 1980, pages 205 – 221. An abstract follows:

"For the peoples of the Soviet Union, war is a very real possibility. They live on past battlefields and realize that, in the event of another major war, their country will be a battlefield once again. Consequently, theoretical constructs designed primarily for maintaining the peace rather than dominating the battlefield do not satisfy their desire for a strong defense. Unlike many Western military analysts, who focus on how a war might begin, Soviet strategists are more concerned with examining how it would end. This does not mean they neglect the political side of military power; rather, it merely reflects their conviction that the political utility of military power is a function of its combat effectiveness."

The National War College encouraged faculty to be active in the civilian scholarly community. I published quite a bit in <u>Strategic Review,</u> <u>U.S. Naval Institute Proceedings,</u> <u>Slavic Review,</u> <u>Air Force Magazine,</u> <u>Parameters,</u> and elsewhere including some classified places. I was an active participant in the American Association for the Advancement of Slavic Studies. I had more opportunity to present papers, give lectures, and serve on academic panels than most professors at civilian universities. The War College established the rank of Full Professor for an officer from each Military Service and I held that Professorship. On my own time in the evenings, I taught graduate courses in Soviet foreign and military policy at both Georgetown and American Universities, and each made me an Adjunct Full Professor.

My analysis of Soviet Naval Power appeared in several classified and unclassified forms during the 1970s when the Soviet Navy was at its zenith. I had concluded in my 1971 Harvard dissertation "The Rise of the Soviet Navy in the Nuclear Age," that the Soviet Navy was a spin-off of Soviet intercontinental nuclear superpower status. Since it has receded into history as that status has waned, it is not useful to dwell on the Soviet Navy too much. An article appeared in <u>Parameters,</u> the Journal of the Army War College in 1980, Volume X, Number 1, pp. 58-70. Here is the concluding paragraph:

T here was little the US could do about the new naval options open to the Soviet Union as a nuclear superpower. A great deal of latitude for political use of Soviet naval power, extending into denial and interposition roles vis-a-vis the US Navy, was a new fact of life in the nuclear age. So was a large range of strategic offensive and defensive missions. But there is no more reason for the US to accept parity, or something less, on the world's oceans than there would be for the Soviet Union to accept US conventional military domination on the European Continent. Only if the US can muster the will to do so can it remain the world's leading seapower in the nuclear age.

We made important changes to the academic rigor of The National War College. In addition to a more focused core course program, a strong elective program was added. Substantive college-like courses met weekly. Each officer-student took two courses. Papers were often required. Each officer wrote a paper. Courses were on the Middle East, Russia, Military Policy, China, Western Europe, etc.

There were no grades given yet as there were at the Naval War College, but it was not just a gentleman's course. I was given the new position of Director of Elective Studies in addition to my job as Director of Soviet Studies. They made me Associate Dean of Faculty.

US- Russia Military Education Exchange Visits

Lieutenant General Robert Gard, United States Army, who had become President of the National Defense University, was a strong supporter of what I was doing. He was also a Harvard PhD and a serious military intellectual. General Gard asked why there had been no National War College delegation to Russia. I said I did not know, but I would see if it could happen. It was not as difficult as it sounded. Insignificant things often take forever in the government, and important things can happen fast.

The Department of Defense and the State Department liked the idea, and a message to our embassy to explore the Soviet view of this was sent. The Soviets were interested in an exchange of military education delegations. We made arrangements. I would be the faculty leader and General Gard would be the Head of Delegation. The Soviet hosts would set the itinerary.

A faculty committee selected an outstanding student delegation, and I had the responsibility of preparing this group. All had performed well during the Soviet part of the curriculum, so it was a matter of supplementing those studies. They finished the equivalent of a semester-length graduate course in very short order.

The Soviet hosts rolled out a red carpet. We met senior officers at top level Soviet military schools, were treated to cultural events, visited the Soviet Space Center and met with cosmonauts. We were given VIP treatment at battlefields. We laid a wreath at their Tomb of Unknown Soldiers.

The National War College Delegation Moscow, 1977

CDR Kime and
Soviet Cosmonaut G. Titov, 1977
author's photos

The trip was a successful small step in improving U.S.-Soviet military contact. So was the return visit by a Soviet military delegation the following year. They sent older officers while we sent younger officers who were slated for bigger things. Otherwise the exchange was a mirror-image affair. I would see Soviet delegation members again later when on duty in the Soviet Union.

Before I departed The National War College, I had the opportunity to lead War College delegations to Romania, Yugoslavia, Japan, Korea and the Philippines. These were viewed as important opportunities by the U.S. embassies in these nations. We, escorted by our representatives there, met with the senior military and many civilian political figures in all these countries.

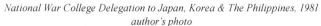

National War College Delegation to Japan, Korea & The Philippines, 1981
author's photo

The Military Mind

The only thing harder than getting a new
idea into the military mind is to get an old one out.
- Sir B. H. Liddell-Hart

Like most clever sayings, this one has some truth in it. Military officers, invariably charged with protecting and preserving a *status quo*, tend to be conservative in their thinking about sociopolitical institutions.

It is a mistake, however, to believe that military officers always want to fight past wars. My experience with hundreds of future senior officers revealed supple and inquiring minds willing to entertain different perspectives and different situations. This included willingness and ability to deal with situations that were more political than military. Left to their own devices, most officers I met would be innovators but in our system they are decidedly not left to their own devices.

In America, officers answer to civilian leaders, and they therefore are dealing with the reality that the civilian leadership perceives. Their civilian leaders are always a generation behind in appreciating the seriousness and the nature of the hostilities that they, and their military, might confront. Military innovation is not something civilian leaders in Congress or in the White House spend much time on. Politicians are reluctant to think about, must less prepare for, a war unlike the one most recently experienced. Except for defensive strategies, it would send signals that we would be reluctant to send. Civilian control of the military is a key part of our democracy, but it has this flaw: it is the civilian mind, and not the military one, that leads us to fight wars for which we are not prepared.

The American Way of War has traditionally amounted to mass mobilization in defense of the Homeland. In my view, we are not suited to "dabbling" or "intervening." America should be reluctant to change our approach and "dabble" with the lives of our children in uniform. The problem is that this would not prepare us for the conflicts that politicians, alas, cause us to fight.

Politics do not "stop at the water's edge" as Senator Vandenberg asserted in 1948. In fact, American politicians rarely resist the temptation to use foreign instability as fodder for their own political ambitions. This, from a plain and simple Midwesterner's point of view, is because it is easy to do. We are a very rich, somewhat isolated, and secure nation that can afford to use the misfortunes and misadventures of the rest of the world as a foil for our internal politics. At least some think we can afford it. American politicians, lucky just to be born in The Shining City on a Hill, are arrogant enough to think we can make the rest of the world over in our image. At least some think we can. These illusions are encouraged by an American population ever more aware of their great fortune, a little guilty about it, and sensing some obligation to share their fortune with a world that is not as well endowed and often dubious about whether they want to be like us at all.

So, American politicians take sides in guerrilla warfare, religious sectarianism, ethnic divisiveness, etc., often without much relevance to our national security. "If it bleeds, it leads" in news reporting and it becomes topical in our politics and even our morality. Clear-eyed assessment of the threat to the nation is rarely the primary consideration. Often "regional instability," or the need for access to "vital resources" are substituted for clear-eyed, unemotional assessment.

Sometimes Americans cannot resist outrage on humanitarian grounds when the cause is undeniably outrageous. Politicians are quick to talk glibly, almost antiseptically, about using "military instruments" in what seem to Americans as just causes but are in fact social, political, and military sinkholes.

We were not, and are not, disposed to fight the types of conflicts that politicians insist on waging and "sell" to the American people as righteous and just. This is precisely because we know in our hearts that we should not be fighting them, even when the cause seems right to the American Judeo-Christian mind.

If we insist on sending our men and women to fight in strange places for reasons that do not involve our vital interests, we must at least allow capable military minds to help us prepare.

I know that flexible, capable Soldiers, Airmen, and Naval Officers can do this. I met them at The National War College.

Navy Blues
The Navy Way or the Highway?

I had expected to be passed over for promotion to Commander because, though my fitness reports were fine, I had not filled the right career squares. It would not have been an unexpected or unfair outcome. My plan was to stay at the National War College as a Professor until I had served my twenty years and qualified for a modest pension. Then I would seek a civilian academic career, perhaps right there at The National War College where I was making a useful contribution.

As it turned out, I was lucky. I would go to the Soviet Union in 1977 and lead delegations to other countries as a Full Commander. Most of my students were still quite senior to me. Predictably, there was some gnashing of teeth about my promotion among officers who had filled the career squares and did not get promoted.

For Navy career planners, The National War College in the Seventies was viewed in the same bad light as Joint Duty. Among Naval Officers that got a year "off" to go to a senior War College, the most promising officers went to the Naval War College at Newport, Rhode Island. Far fewer Naval officer graduates of The National War College were promoted in the Navy than were officers from Newport.

All of the other Services promoted War College graduates, regardless of the College attended, at a much higher rate than did the Navy. In the Navy, attendance was encouraged for very promising officers only if they had a year to "waste." In the other Services, attendance at a senior War College was close to an absolute necessity.

There was growing unhappiness in the Department of Defense and the Joint Staff about the Navy's attitude toward Joint Duty and War College attendance. The last straw was when a Navy Commander who had held an SSBN Command with enough atomic firepower to destroy the planet got passed over for Captain while a student at The National War College. This caused quite a stink. I may have benefited from pressure on the Navy to do better with Joint Duty.

Still, Navy shoes dropped. I got a call from a senior officer and friend who delivered the message: The Navy liked me, I was not dead yet, but I needed to leave the National War College, and academic and joint jobs, ASAP. Specifically, I *must* get a seagoing Operational Intelligence job soon. I needed to be "re-Blued."

Later, the Director of Naval Intelligence, an officer I knew and respected for his intelligence and integrity, called me. He suggested orders to a Cruiser-Destroyer Group stationed in Norfolk. This was delicate for him, because he felt the pressure from the Department of Defense and the Joint Chiefs of Staff about the Navy's attitude on sending and keeping officers in Joint positions. It was unusual to be treated with such consideration: the Navy usually just sent orders as they did when I dared to question The System in 1973.

I drove down to Norfolk to check it out. It was worse than I thought. To summarize: I found an opportunity to work for an officer who might have been a student of mine but was three ranks senior to me. I would not get to be a seagoing part of the Wardroom or Staff where my experience and capabilities as a sailor would be relevant, but would instead be a briefer on information and analysis that I got from Naval Intelligence sources and a complex set of computers and information equipment. The Commander currently in the job damn near hugged that equipment when he showed it to me! It looked like something I could have done in my spare time when I was a junior Lieutenant. It certainly did not require a college degree.

Operational Intelligence, I understood after my tour in DIA, was the proper focus of the fine officers in Naval Intelligence, but I just could not do it. It was absolutely clear to me that I could contribute much more meaningfully as a Professor at The National War College. If it meant a shorter career in the Navy, so be it. If that was best for the Navy, I was prepared to pay that price.

I know that good Naval Officers would label me as a *prima donna* and remind me of Admiral Lawrence's opinion about what makes a true professional. I felt this criticism, which I know was voiced in circles that I respected. This hurt both professionally and personally.

The *dénouement* came in the form of a letter from the Chief of Naval Personnel in response to a request by the President of The National Defense University. NDU had written to the Navy to note that I was in the Navy's position of Professor and to seek assurance that I would be left in that position. The other Services had already enthusiastically endorsed the concept of Permanent Service Professors at the Senior Service Colleges.

This was the last straw to those in the Navy who brooked no such fiddling with The Navy Way. The letter from the Chief of Naval Personnel made it quite clear that my career was at an end if I did not start acting like a good Naval Officer and go to a Navy job befitting my proper station in life and years of service. The Old Navy had spoken!

I called the office of Vice Admiral Bobby R. Inman, who had been the Director of Naval Intelligence when I was working on National Intelligence Estimates and, though Navy and the other Services were sometimes at odds with positions that I supported, he was always cordial and supportive. Inman was a broad-gage thinker admired for his political assiduity on Capitol Hill and destined for four stars. I suspected that he valued differences of opinion in the intelligence process and could deal with deviations from The Navy Way.

It was an open secret that Admiral Inman was the guiding hand behind the careers of hundreds of officers. He had a remarkable memory for people, where they were, when they were due to move, and how they were performing. He was amazing. It was an unofficial fact that no senior intelligence officer moved without his initials on the paperwork, and this might have been true of many other officers as well. This, of course, was not something that folks like those who had written my latest career death threat liked very much.

Admiral Inman asked me over to breakfast at the National Security Agency where he was Director. It was a short meeting since he already knew everything about my situation and had already decided what to do. I was relieved that I did not have to make my case for staying put. His directions were simple: do not answer the letter from Naval Personnel. Just stay there and wait for orders. Of course, he knew that no orders could be issued without his approval. I waited.

One thing I did while I waited, at the suggestion of the Director of Naval Intelligence, was to spend a day every two weeks in his organization helping out and getting reacquainted at the highest classification levels. This enabled him to write an annual, concurrent, fitness report on me. This meant that there would be an assessment from a Naval flag officer in my jacket, along with all those reports by those Army and Air Force people who wore odd colored uniforms.

Fitness Report

The National War College is very attentive to the health and fitness of its faculty and students. These are middle-aged people highly susceptible to the maladies that beset Type A personalities. A Health Fair is held at the beginning of the academic year, and rigorous exercise is encouraged. This might sound a bit frivolous to bureaucratic bean counters, but it is not. We lost a couple of students to heart attacks during my time there. One of them was clearly a national asset and a great loss to the Army. This feature of the College was important to my future and may have extended my life. I played tennis at the lunch hour and still play, badly, today. I led a group called the "Over The Hill Gang" that met every day at lunchtime, beginning each year with a short walk and building up to a 6-mile run around Washington's monuments in a few months. I learned to take exercise seriously, and I know that many other officers did, too.

A life lesson that I learned later in life than I should have is also a health matter: smoking. It may seem silly to some readers to include the subject of smoking in someone's life story, but I do not think so. The average age of death of my parents and siblings, all but one dead today, is sixty years. All of them were smokers, except my mother. All but she had smoking as a primary cause of death. I have come to be a little fanatical on the subject, forbidding smoking before that became commonplace and refusing to hire anyone stupid enough to smoke.

While at Harvard and at the War College, I took up the habit of smoking a pipe. I smoked professorially, of course, not with the huffing and puffing of Popeye or Ed Wood. It was a typical professorial act of immature arrogance appropriate to academe. Before the War College exchange trip to the Soviet Union in 1977, my 10-year old son begged me to stop. I gave away my collection of pipes and have not smoked since. There is no Baptist like a Reborn Baptist.

Amusement at The National War College

My 40th birthday happened to be the day that we were trying out a new wireless microphone system for the main auditorium. I was delivering a major lecture that day on Soviet Military Policy. They fitted me with the mike an hour early and it worked fine. I turned it off and went to my office to go over my notes before the lecture. The secretaries in the Dean's office came in a little later with cake and there were a few hugs, which apparently turned on the microphone.

As the students and several senior guests entered the auditorium, I was complaining that it was no fun to wake up and find that you were just another Old Fart. There was more such repartee from the usually demure ladies as they ate their cake. All of it was loud and clear in the auditorium. The audio system worked! For the first time in my life, I got a standing ovation when I entered the auditorium. Future 3-star and 4-star officers sang "happy birthday."

Once after Vice Chief of Naval Operations Robert Long, a submariner, spoke at The National War College, I was walking with him between buildings. He asked me what boats I had served on and I told him, acknowledging that I was a relic and not one of the hot running submariners he dealt with all the time. As he was explaining that all submariners were submariners, a pigeon flew over and dropped its load on my dress blues.

My Harvard Professor, Secretary of State Kissinger, came to speak and I met and introduced him. As was customary, I offered a pit stop at the rest room before his lecture. Standing there, he asked if I had any suggestions before he went into the auditorium.

I said: "Professor, these students are in their forties. They will listen very carefully to everything you say for 45 minutes. After that, they have to pee." Surprised to hear such practical advice, he smiled: "That's good advice, young man." He followed it.

Chapter XIV
National Security Policy

Well the eagle's been flyin' slow
And the flag's been flyin' low
Lyrics from:Charlie Daniels Band song In America, 1980
used with permission of Charlie Daniels

Four things about U.S. National Security Policy bothered me in the Seventies. Since they were present everywhere in policymaking circles, they were reflected by the speakers and in the curriculum at The National War College.

Associate Dean of Faculty
The National War College, 1979

Author's photo.

Wrong Directions in National Security Policy

First, part of the focus on the Middle East was misdirected. The Arab-Israeli situation is not what I am talking about. I am referring to what became a buzz phrase: "Southwest Asia." It was almost as if the National Security Establishment was itching for military involvement in Southwest Asia.

Overconcentration on the politics of Southwest Asian oil was not matched by any thought of what to do about U.S. oil consumption or by recognition of the need for more effective political and economic policies in the region to combat Muslim radicalism and anti-Americanism. The deteriorating situation in Iran and the 1979 Hostage Crisis there understandably put a military spin on the treatment of the region, but it seemed as if senior officers were being conditioned for wars that we should never be drawn into.

The U. S. National Security Establishment did not look ahead with imagination in this vital geostrategic direction: it was part of a general drift in US policymaking circles toward involvement in Southwest Asia that was not in the nation's interest. In the following decades, this drift would carry America into dangerous and troubled waters.

The second focus in the curriculum that troubled me also had its buzzword: "interdependence." This buzzword morphed into the related buzzwords "globalization" "the global economy." It almost became a religious principle that intertwining the U.S. economy with the rest of the world was not just unavoidable but was an unmitigated good.

Some interdependence, of course, had long been a reality and a necessity and needed to be recognized at senior levels in the government. Increased interdependence was surely in the cards, but there was no attention paid to the downside for America and the need to guard against the negative influences on our economy. The attitude was that near total submersion of U.S. interests in an interdependent world was not only inevitable but was in our national interest.

Karl Marx in his 1848 Manifesto first discussed the economics of interdependence. It is a concept at odds with nationalism and capitalism in their pure forms. America long ago abandoned the pure forms of both nationalism and capitalism and understood that global integration would modify both of these, but far too little thought was applied to the philosophical and conceptual ramifications of uncritical and total acceptance of international economic interdependence.

It was a perfect storm of stupidity, greed and shortsightedness. Academics are always quick to applaud any One-World notion, and the State Department loves it, too. Interdependence played well to the politically correct and the touchy-feely folks who want an America "that plays well with the other children." Greedy, unpatriotic big businessmen and Wall Street were delighted with this attitude, and promoted it in government. They were happy to profit and avoid taxes as the U.S. industrial base and our workers were sold out in foreign markets.

National security policy, supposedly the primary focus of The National War College, was ill served by the uncritical acceptance of "interdependence" without due diligence in assessing the impact on America. The entire Washington policy establishment, by exaggerating the advantages of interdependence, dealt a body blow to American Exceptionalism and placed us on a path that would submerge America in the least common denominator of failed or failing Western states. Submerging America in this way fit the goals of some in policymaking circles.

The third thing I think was underemphasized at The National War College is related to the first one. The economics and the politics of oil were certainly discussed, but the imperative of energy independence for America was not. Big Business and government functionaries who were in the pockets of Big Business somehow managed to keep energy independence out of the discussion.

Environmentalists get attention from the left, but they only promote marginal ideas that appeal to intellectuals and cannot make us independent. Other countries are way ahead of us on this; the French clearly saw nuclear power, which does work, as a solution, even as left-wing Luddites in America shut down any talk of it. This is amazing in a country that has operated ocean-going nuclear plants *underwater* for over fifty years without an accident. A policy that would cap imports and force a more logical price for energy that would, in turn, make alternative sources of energy from wind, sunshine, and even oil more viable cannot even be seriously discussed.

The fourth erroneous direction of national policy was about the Great American Melting Pot. United States national security policy, the very instinct to protect and defend the nation, is rooted in *E PLURIBUS UNUM*. ("Out of many, one.") National strength and purpose flowed from America's incredible ability to absorb the talents and energies of immigrants from everywhere and meld them into a great culture and a great nation. In a well-meant but thoughtless and counterproductive attempt to spur equal treatment of black Americans, "diversity" was nearly made into a religious principle. "Celebrating diversity" became a battle cry for the Left.

This was no less than the dismantling of American cultural coherence and of its ability to adapt to its constantly changing makeup. It was a very important diminution of allegiance to the nation and to the willingness to defend it. We failed to understand the domestic and national security implications of separating cultures within America rather than embracing them, learning from them, and absorbing them as our own.

Peanuts and Patriots

One of the most important facets of national security is presidential leadership. Amazingly, a submarine Lieutenant got elected President! Jimmy Carter was the fifth straight President with Navy experience. Sadly, I never once observed any positive evidence of his Navy or submarine credentials. Only the anal-retentive attitude of a nuclear teapot operator survived from his Navy days. Not a smidgen of understanding of the military, of strategy, or a glimmer of "that which is not specifically forbidden is permitted" attitude was revealed by Jimmy Carter.

Lieutenant Carter should not have been promoted to President. He was a peanut farmer who apparently thought our country could be run like a peanut farm. The man's answer to the oil "crisis" of the Seventies was to shut off the hot water in government buildings and to charge public employees for parking in spaces that otherwise would have been empty. He was as clueless about real-world solutions to America's oil supply problems as the interviewers were in the White House Fellowship competition.

The significance of Carter's environmental dictums was summarized by the saying at the time: "If it's yellow, let it mellow: if it's brown, flush it down!" He shut off hot water in the Pentagon, caused officers to pay for carpool parking and had folks in Montana driving endless roads at

55 miles an hour under threat of losing federal highway funds. It was myopic madness.

This was a presidential administration for the feckless, post-Watergate,-politically correct, and touchy-feely Seventies. Jimmy Carter, a decent human being, was an enormous disappointment. Being a good guy was just not good enough. America drifted. Worse, at a time when our major adversary was flagging, we looked impotent. Ayatollahs thumbed their noses at us. Vietnam veterans slept in the streets. Officers in Washington were instructed not to wear uniforms daily so there would not be such a visible military presence there. In my view, this was a worse time to be serving in uniform than at the height of the anti-Vietnam protests. For those of us who had watched The Greatest Generation come home, sometimes in boxes, it was a painful time.

I was at The National War College when Ronald Reagan brought a hint of the 1950s back to the White House. He probably *knew* Beaver Cleaver! The current chatting class in Washington policy circles will undoubtedly sneer at this observation. They are correct that it is a bit naïve, but the observation is not off the mark. The "Shining City on a Hill" was the place where I grew up, and Ronald Reagan was saying that it was something to restore, NOT something that Americans should feel guilty about. It was *not* inevitable that America would be submerged in a stew of failed Western states. Americans desperately needed to hear that America was still a great country in 1980, and they need to hear it again now, 30 years later.

By capturing the hearts and minds of ordinary Americans who were fed up with the bad-mouthing of their country, Ronald Reagan rescued conservative thought from the Right-Wing radicals and John Birchers and opened up a non-reactionary conservatism to all Americans. He gave Southern Democrats, genuine conservatives who resonated with much of America, an intellectual and philosophical place to go when the Democratic Party no longer believed in conserving the aspects of American culture that they wanted to conserve. Some in the South have been slower than others to realize this.

A caveat is in order here. Reagan Republicans captured Independents and Democrats who had been alienated by a Democratic Party that no longer represented them, but the Republican Party did not gain a permanent grip on these voters. Many of these "Reagan Democrats" have been since alienated by rightward shifts in the Republican Party, and the George W. Bush presidency made these voters once again feel that they were not represented. By 2008, the Party of Reagan could no longer claim to represent the thoughts of the crucial bloc of voters who wanted to preserve the essence of American culture but accept sensible change. Many of these voters ended up voting for Barack Obama, and those voters represent an important intellectual and conceptual battlefield of the future.

American conservatism is deeply rooted in liberty and freedom and harks back to the same Western philosophical tradition that many so-called American "liberals" claim as their heritage. In fact, American conservatism is very much part of "The Liberal Tradition in America" that Professor Hartz at Harvard described in his book of that name. Americans have bastardized the words "liberal" and "conservative." We have confused these concepts with the machinations of political parties.

It is important to understand that mainstream American conservatism is not reactionary. "Conservative" does NOT mean to return to the past. It means to preserve what is worth saving from the past while adjusting to change for the future. Samuel Huntington, the famous Professor of Government at Harvard and scholar on American politics, observed that "liberal" and "conservative" Americans argue less over *what* they believe than over *how seriously* they believe it. The important thing to most who call themselves "conservative" is to *preserve what is essential in society while adjusting to the change* that the march of time presents. Many who would call themselves "liberal" agree. They would, of course, argue over specifics.

The British political thinker Edmund Burke believed in changing with the times while retaining whatever works and still applies from the past. Ronald Reagan, who had been a Democrat, was a conservative who understood, instinctively, what this meant to an America facing serious, and needed, change.

A nation did not have to be weakened to correct errors in its past: it could grow and thrive.

It could even be A Shining City on a Hill.

Chapter XV
Return to Russia

One day the Director of Naval Intelligence called and asked if I would be interested in going back to the Soviet Union as the U.S. Naval Attaché in 1985, about five years away. This clearly implied the Navy was going to promote me to Captain! I had only recently made my number as a Commander. I said that it might be better for the Navy if I went in 1983. He noted that they had not yet identified a candidate for 1983, that the Joint Staff was getting very hard to please on such assignments, and that I would be easy to get approved. It would obviously put pressure on the Navy promotion system. He would check. In a day or two he called back and said it was possible to send me in 1983 and I immediately accepted. The orders that Admiral Inman said to wait for were going to come! My plans to transition to a civilian academic career would be put on hold. My exile in the Joint environment was going to end. The Navy wanted me back!

It would be remiss not to acknowledge the fact that the flexibility and imagination of senior officers in Naval Intelligence had a lot to do with my survival and promotion in the Navy. Many of the Directors of Naval Intelligence, including Admirals Rectanus, Shapiro and Butts, were submariners but some were not. Rear Admiral Tom Brooks is one of them. All of them saw the wisdom of having Naval Intelligence officers who knew the culture and language of potential adversaries, even when the Navy at large was dragging its feet on establishment of a serious Foreign Area Officers Program.

The Office of Naval Intelligence has been around since 1882. It has a distinguished history, most of which cannot be discussed here. Besides the tens of thousands of Naval Officers who toiled in secrecy and made untold contributions to national security, some became well-known. These include:

Eric Garcetti, Mayor of Los Angeles, California
Bobby Ray Inman, ADM USN

Mark Kirk, United States Senator from Illinois
Mark Lippert, a U.S. Ambassador to South Korea.
John P. Stevens, Assoc. Justice of the Supreme Court
William O. Studeman, ADM USN
Byron White, Assoc. Justice of the Supreme Court
Bob Woodward of *The Washington Post*

Leaving The National War College was bittersweet. Naval Officers are not supposed to "homestead," but the National War College was a place to serve where I felt that I was doing my best and doing some good. Many people go through life, in and out of military service, and never feel like that. I will always be grateful for that opportunity and am indebted to the splendid military scholars who tolerated and encouraged me there. In my second career as an educator working to get the best possible education for military members and veterans, it was vital that I knew many, maybe most, of the senior commanders in all the Services by their first names.

Departing The National War College in 1981

author's photo

I was overjoyed about the opportunity to serve again in Russia, but I had to tell Wilma. She did not blink an eye. We had a couple of years to get ready. She would just have to quit her job and give up tenure again, ship everything we owned in several directions, brush up on Russian, figure out schooling for the kids, sell the cars and buy a new one, board out the horse, find temporary homes for two dogs and a cat, rent the house, buy two years worth of household items, and find some arctic gear to wear. Ten-minute job! No sweat!

It took a year and one-half to get to Moscow. I spent several months heading the desk of the Soviet and East European Affairs Division of the Attaché Affairs Directorate, where I was responsible for managing the administrative details involved in selecting, sending, and supporting attachés behind what we used to call The Iron Curtain. This was a way of "paying my dues," and I survived it. Since desk jobs required only 8 or 10 hours a day, it provided time to start getting family affairs together. After that duty, I attended a "refresher" at Attaché School, which, mercifully, was short. Wilma meanwhile had begun attending the Foreign Service's Russian Language School. I joined her in January of 1983 and was paired with the future Army Attaché who had also served earlier in Moscow and was a graduate of the Army's Russian Language Institute in Garmisch, Germany. The two of us were treated to a specially tailored program that was run by native speakers for about four months.

We had to be sure that the family was situated to handle another Russia tour. Our daughter, Lauren, had graduated from VPI and would teach in West Virginia. Our eldest son, Barry, had completed Law School at Arizona and would practice in Tucson. Our son, Carl, claims to this day that we abandoned him and moved halfway around the world when he was sixteen. He was scarred forever, to hear him tell the story, which is only partially true. He had completed all the requirements for high school in three years, had clobbered the Scholastic Aptitude Test, and had won an NROTC Scholarship to the University of Virginia. Carl would have to shuttle back and forth to Moscow during holidays and travel in the Soviet Union and Europe extensively. This plan solved the major family concerns we had with the timing of the tour.

We arrived in Moscow in June of 1983 before I "made my number" as a Captain. I had been wearing a Captain's uniform for almost two years. I had been serving in a Captain's billet since I was a Lieutenant Commander. But "making your number" meant that your rank relative to other officers in other Services actually began and, very important, you got paid at the new pay grade. This meant that bureaucrats in

Washington would only pay to ship household goods at the weight allowance of a Commander. The difference was huge, especially given the need to send a lot of stuff to Russia. An enormous bill for overweight shipments eventually caught up with me. I thought about fighting it but decided to ignore it and see if it would go away. I'm still ignoring it.

Overt Observation and Spies

The reader has probably heard that military attachés are spies. This requires some explanation. Technically, representatives of the US Military Services are overt observers of their host countries. They carry diplomatic passports with the privileges that diplomatic status confers. The host understands that a Naval Attaché will want to travel wherever he can and see whatever he can see. They know that what is seen will be reported. The host has the problem of managing what the attaché sees. The attaché pushes the envelope to see what he can see. The host puts up with this in return for a similar arrangement with the attachés it sends abroad.

This, of course, requires some gamesmanship but it is not a game. Important things can be seen and heard and an astute observer can make significant assessments. Society cannot be hidden and neither can the largest army on earth. If one believes, as I do, that the most important things in a country are not classified, and quite often are not military, the role of the overt observer is crucial.

An understanding of the capabilities and intentions of a potential enemy, the Holy Grail of military intelligence, is more likely to be had by an overt observer of social, political, and economic reality on the ground than by a hardware-oriented "bean counter" holed up somewhere in a windowless room.

This said, some military representatives sometimes slip out of their roles as overt observers and become spies. Russians do it often. UN "diplomats," who do not even have counterparts in their host countries, are usually spies. American military and Naval Attachés would not hesitate to latch onto any information that they could gain access to, but they are not really spies.

Kime Family in Red Square.
New Year's Eve, 1983

Captain Kime and the Assistant Naval Attachés
Inspecting Seabee work atop the US Embassy

author's photos

Korean Air 007 Shootdown

On September 1, 1983 a Soviet SU-15 fighter shot down Korean Air Flight 007 (KAL-007) flying from New York to Seoul via Anchorage. Sixty-two Americans, including U.S. Congressman Larry McDonald of Georgia, were among the 269 who perished. Three other U.S. Congressmen were 15 minutes behind in KAL-015. I was the senior U.S. military attaché in Moscow at the time.

That fall had been a tense time in general, and in particular in the Kamchatka Peninsula region. The Soviets feared that the U.S. would dramatically surpass the Soviet Union with an effective strategic defense breakthrough, and U.S. talk about its Strategic Defense Initiative rattled them to the core. Our plan to deploy Pershing Missiles in Europe, and a huge Naval exercise in the North Pacific annoyed them. There had been past flights over Soviet territory without Soviet response for which Soviet officers had been criticized by the political leadership.

There was a heightened Soviet alert in the area as the Soviets were getting ready for a missile test on the peninsula. There are plenty of reasons in retrospect to think that Soviet Air Defense personnel were in a trigger-happy mood, in addition to the fact that Soviet Air Defense had shot down planes in the past.

KAL-007 strayed off course innocently enough. A Soviet jet fighter pilot was ordered to shoot it down. It was not an accident. For days and weeks afterward tensions were very high, with Soviet denials, charges of provocation, some lies about supposed warnings given to the airliner, and close operations between U.S. and Soviet maritime units that threatened to get out of control. One communication was directly from our Navy to theirs. I was ordered by secure means to deliver the message to the Soviets.

The Soviet Ministry of Defense controlled all contacts between foreign officers and their Soviet counterparts. I insisted on talking directly with the Chief of the Soviet Main Naval Staff, Fleet Admiral Nikolai Chernyavin and was told that I would have to deliver the U.S. message to the Defense Liaison Headquarters. I said I would be there in two hours. A translation into Russian was prepared, and I arrived at Headquarters in a chauffeured car.

The Colonel who escorted me from my car to the meeting was flummoxed: I had arrived with no assistants, State Department officers, or translator accompanying me. He ushered me into a very impressive room that looked like it belonged in the Winter Palace. Standing around the immense table was an array of very senior Soviet military officers. It was impossible to identify all of them. There were empty chairs on my end of the table and there was a remark about my coming alone. I said: "I have a message from my Navy. I am a Naval Officer. I do not need help to deliver a message." There were smiles and respectful nods.

A Soviet Army general delivered a soliloquy about U.S. provocative activity, the need to reduce tensions and better reflect the spirit of the Incidents at Sea Agreement, etc. He read the written statement as if his heart was not in it. I delivered my message, we all stood, and I departed.

My tiny role in the KAL shootdown incident was insignificant in the big scheme of things, but it made a difference in the way the Soviets treated me. Of course they did not cut me any slack on matters like travel and access to anything, but they treated me with respect. I think the Soviet Navy contingent at the meeting was pleased that a Naval officer came alone to the meeting, and the word got out. When I saw Fleet Admiral Chernyavin, a submariner, at a formal reception, he looked me in the eye and was willing to have a conversation. I also ran into him in civilian clothes at a second hand store in Moscow, he exchanged greetings, and we noted our shared interest in old Russian things and Russian history. Sailors the world over are bound by something that soldiers and aviators do not share. The Sea is a common master and great leveler. Sailors may be adversaries, and they will fight each other, but they also understand each other.

The officers who ordered and executed the KAL shootdown were not rogues: the Soviet High Command and their political masters were totally responsible for the environment in which an air defense general ordered a civilian airliner to be shot down. The bosses in Moscow created the situation and they knew it, but the event was a shock to them, too.

An analogy worth considering is this: When U.S. Air Force General John Lavelle ordered bombing of North Vietnam in 1972, causing international and domestic outrage, he was doing exactly what he had been conditioned to do and was led to believe was what the President wanted him to do. His firing and demotion was pathetic pandering to a U.S. domestic audience. By the way, the career of the Russian Commander of the Far East Military District when KAL 007 was shot down did not end. He eventually became, in 1991, the Deputy Minister of Defense and the Commander in Chief of Soviet Air Defense Forces.

Diplomatic Duty

Social responsibilities during this tour were greater than a decade ago when I was a relatively junior officer. It was also true that the climate for contacts with foreigners had changed some for the better, and this impacted relationships between foreign representatives. The Chinese attaché would come to my apartment in the U.S. Embassy for a chat. (Admiral Rickover would have had a fit!)

Both Indian and Pakistani representatives were accessible. The Algerian Military and Naval Attachés were downright friendly, though the latter would get drunk and spoil social events. Once, because he had started a fight while drunk, I had to evict him from a wonderful weekend outing at a Russian resort called "Zavidovo." This was a taste of how the

Communist big shots lived. There were steam baths, and snowmobile rides and even "private" individual cottages for all my Naval Attaché colleagues from other countries. I hired a local farmer with a horse and old cart to give the kids a ride. We were lucky that the Russians let us hire the whole place. I still do not know why they did.

Wilma and I "entertained" quite a bit. We are more "horse people" than social butterflies, but this was an important part of our duty. Ambassador Arthur Hartman let us use his elegant residence, Spaso House, for a white tie "dining out" for Naval Attaches from around the world. God knows where his butler got the elegant roast beef for that event. The rumor was that he was plugged in somehow to the same folks that provided meat to Kremlin bigwigs. My going away reception was at a restaurant he helped me to hire where whole goats were roasted on a spit. Entertaining was not our "thing," but like Naval Officers everywhere, we found a way to get the job done.

author's photo

Sea Entry and Exit

One of my duties was to enforce the agreement between the U.S. and the Soviet Union that Naval Attachés could enter and exit the countries at several points by sea. My assistants and I frequently entered and exited from Leningrad to and from Baltic ports. We exited from the Far Eastern Port of Nakhodka, in a Russian ship, at least once a year. It is common to do that today, but during my time in Russia a trip to the Far East was an adventure, and a chance to see people and countryside not seen frequently by Americans.

The Ports of Murmansk and Arkhangel'sk in the Far North were more sensitive, and we did manage to get clearance to those cities, but an exit by ship was not in the cards. Entrance and exit from Odessa was done fairly frequently, but only to ports on the Black Sea Coast. The Soviets refused to permit my exit to a foreign port in Turkey or Greece.

Wilma Kime at the helm of
Royal Viking Sky
Baltic Sea 1985

Captain Kime aboard Russian ship "Khabarovsk"
Sea of Japan 1984

author's photos

Seabees in Moscow

As the senior US Naval Officer in the USSR, I had the pleasant duty of watching over the large Seabee contingent involved with the construction of a new US Embassy. They did not work for me, but I got to present awards and promotions, as well as taking care of any problems they encountered. It was good to have thirty or forty sailors around!

Reenlisting a Seabee
author's photo

Graveyard Watch

The most important events during my 1983-85 tour of duty in Moscow involved the Grim Reaper. Soviet Politburo bosses dropped like flies. This happened just as all the contradictions in Communist Party rule were coming to a head. Brezhnev died. Yuri Andropov, the KGB Chief, succeeded him, but lived only 15 months longer than Brezhnev.

Andropov, though an intellectual, was a sinister figure who brutally removed people for corruption and economic failure. He was an intellectual in many ways, and he understood that the Communist system did not work. Had he been healthy, we might have seen a serious reform of the Soviet system that would have been something like Aleksei Kosygin had in mind in 1965, and such a reform might have prevented, or delayed, the collapse that Gorbachev's more dramatic *Perestroika* precipitated.

Ordinary Russians understood that the changes at the top portended a fundamental shakeup of the Soviet system. They paid rapt attention when Andropov started gathering up the crooks and cracking down on the corruption that had been part of everyday life for decades. As noted earlier, he executed the "Butcher of Moscow." Most of the economy had been "under the table" for years and only the "connected" people could get anything out of the Soviet economy.

Other Russian thinkers had recognized that full-blown Socialism would not work if rammed down the people's throats too quickly, if it would work at all. They understood the importance of incentives and opportunity in an economic system, even if they accepted Marx's criticism of unbridled Capitalism. Andropov and eventually Gorbachev were throwbacks to the early colleagues of Lenin who disagreed with the pace and nature of the Russian Revolution.

The disappointment and cynicism of ordinary Russians, many of whom understood the ideological tensions in the Communist Party noted above, was palpable when Konstantin Chernenko of The Old Guard took the reins after Andropov died. It was a last-ditch attempt of the Old Guard to hang on to power. Chernenko was a step backward for any hope of reform that might rescue the faltering Soviet system. Chernenko did fire the Chief of the Soviet General Staff, Marshal Ogarkov, who was pressing for more spending on defense at a time when even the most jingoistic of Soviet Nationalists knew that more spending was not possible. This gesture by a dying old man was too little and far too late.

Unhappiness with Chernenko's leadership was quite openly reflected. This startled the Old Guard and made Gorbachev's ascendance inevitable. Chernenko was dead in thirteen months. This time Politburo colleagues accepted Andropov's choice, 54-year-old Sergei Gorbachev, the first Communist Party leader born after the Great October Revolution of 1917. When he ascended to the Politboro at age 48, Kremlin watchers marked him as the leader of a new generation of leaders. He was clearly a protégé of Andropov and astute Russians understood that he represented a "new broom."

When Gorbachev took over, I sat next to a lady from Tomsk on a bench outside the Bolshoi Theater. "What do you think of Gorbachev?" I asked. Her response was swift: "The crooks had better watch out." Change was in the air.

Vice President Bush
& Embassy children, 1984
author's photo

Vice President George H. W. Bush shuttled to and from Washington to attend funerals. He has big feet: arctic weather shoes big enough were provided by one of my assistants. Such funerals were impressive affairs with magnificent music played in such sorrowful, somber, and low dulcet tones that buildings shivered. It seemed to reflect something in the Russian soul.

Dissidents

When they think of dissidence in the Soviet Union, Americans usually think about Alexander Solzhenitsyn and other famous Russian writers who were often in exile in remote locations. These brave people were indeed leaders and heroes who exposed the flaws and inhumanity of the Dictatorship of the Proletariat. But these are not the dissidents that I think about. I do not think that they are the ones that most frightened the Communist Party Politburo. It was a much more broadly based dissidence that spooked them. They could manage a few Solzhenitsyns, but the wave of general dissent that began to emerge during the Thaw was a threat to the survival of the regime.

What amazed me was the wide and deep layer of dissidence that lay close to the surface in Russian society. Dissidents were not hard to find. Even during Khrushchev's Thaw in the wake of Stalinist Terror, when the leadership thought that loosening the reins a bit would be manageable, the depth and breadth of opposition to Soviet dictatorship was surprising even to Communist Party leaders who had long been wary of the Russian thinkers, including colleagues of Vladimir Lenin, who disagreed with their policies. Ordinary Russians, as well as Kremlin leaders, were not oblivious to the ideological differences that lay just beneath the surface of a system that looked solid to many Western observers.

Russians under the Communists knew how to lie low and keep their powder dry. In addition to a canny ability to entertain more than one idea at a time, Russians have an artistic streak that is seasoned with a healthy dose of cynicism. Willingness to climb the ladder in a hierarchical system of power does not, in a population like this, mean love of the self-serving and self-perpetuating Communist government. Even many in the Party were not true believers. Also, the Party itself always included those who would not have done things the way that Lenin and Stalin did them. There were lots of silent sympathizers with Stalin's enemies, Trotsky and Bukharin, who would have introduced Socialism more slowly and carefully than Stalin did. He was unable to send them all to labor camps, though he tried his best. Several schools of thought were still alive. (Stalin came by his paranoia honestly!)

A vast countercurrent flowed beneath the surface of Soviet power. We could see the painters, poets and writers who would stick their necks out and even talk to some of them, but the most important thing about them was that they were not alone. The bottom line for the Communist Party leadership was that their margin for error was much thinner than their superpower adversary, the United States of America, thought it was. Steel is strong, but some steel is flexible and some is brittle.

The Soviet Union was strong but brittle. Assessments of Russia before the fall of the Soviet Empire often missed this point. The reader might recall the Team B vs. Team A debate in the 1970s discussed earlier. Powerful voices in the West, some with vested ideological, economic and military-strategic interests, refused to see what was before their eyes. Russians knew in their bones that a new Time of Troubles was coming.

Opiate of the People

Religion, the "Opiate of the People" in Communist thinking, was suppressed, but it could not be stamped out. Khrushchev was buried in the Orthodox churchyard at Novodevichiy Monastery. (This was not only because he was denied a place in the Kremlin wall for his Communist heresy and hare-brained schemes.) Brezhnev's mother had a religious funeral which he dutifully attended. Visits to numerous closed churches invariably found older folks caring for the sacred place for the time when it would again come to life. Easter remained an important time in Russian life. My family, and other Christian visitors, were received with open fanfare at St. Sergius, Russia (called Zagorsk by the Communist Party.)

Dissident painting that restores Moscow churches demolished by Communists
Painted for the author in 1985. photo by the author

Western analysts for some reason had trouble understanding this reality in Russia. Many pointed to the fact that only old people risked Communist wrath by openly supporting the Orthodox Church. This was silly. Where did they think the old people came from over the decades? Of course, Orthodox believers protected those still young, but as old age set in they took up their positions at the church. The truth is that their obstinacy was tolerated by local bureaucrats who were loath to take on their families and neighbors.

The proof of the vitality of the supposedly submerged Russian Orthodox Church is clear. When the Communist system collapsed, it took no time at all to reopen the churches to enthusiastic worshippers of all ages. A good example is the Cathedral of Christ the Savior in Moscow. Located within sight of the Kremlin, it was demolished in the 1930s and became the site of a huge swimming pool in the 1950s. In 1992, a fund was started to rebuild the church and over a million Russians donated. The pool was demolished in1995 and the church was rebuilt by 2000.

Before the Fall: Out and About in Russia

I enjoyed conversations with ordinary people in ordinary settings. I found that one cliché is mostly true: ordinary Russians think like working class Americans -- at least like the Midwestern Americans I grew up with. I had found this with the young people I had spent time with in 1961. Youth, even in the "Dictatorship of the Proletariat," were bound to be more uninhibited than older people. Their elders, of course, carried the baggage of The Great Patriotic War (WWII) and the Stalinist Terror that submerged the Russian peasant outlook so familiar and congenial to Americans.

Older folks, remembering the Stalinist days, were more wary of foreigners. It had to be difficult to ignore the story, often repeated in the press, of a mythical child-hero named Pavlik Morozov who had turned his parents over to the tender mercy of the Stalinist Purges. The War hung over the Russian people like a perpetual black cloud. Husbands, sons and brothers were missing everywhere they looked, leaving tired, aging women to do most of the work. They were always trying to catch up with the rest of the world, and they simply did not have the human horsepower to do it. The built-in excuse of the war, and the refuge of alcoholism did not help.

Intellectual and political dissidents had a tough job shaking these people out of their doldrums. But, of course, young people keep coming. They have opinions, expectations. A major expectation was that the Soviet Superpower would not fail.

The Old U.S. Embassy in Moscow
Home of the Kime family in 1983 - 1985

author's photo

The KGB remembered that Khrushev's "Thaw" had seen brazen dissidents come out of the woodwork. During my 1971-73 tour, even with Strategic Arms Treaties and an emerging Détente, the KGB ran a taut ship, and people were reticent around foreigners. During the leadership instability and the rise of Gorbachev in the 1980s, Russians began to open up again. Remember that Politburo boss Andropov was head of the KGB! Their humor, common sense and pluck began to show. I sent reports entitled "Vignettes from Moscow" that reflected this. It is amazing how many people read them. The CNO, fellow submariner and future Secretary of Energy Jim Watkins, told me that he read them and some were read in the White House.

Author, his dog & grandson, in Hills Lenin

The Embassy instructions discouraged bringing dogs to Moscow, but I did it on both tours there. I made a practice of walking my dog at odd hours and would often exit the Embassy after midnight and let her do her business in a little park off the alley that ran alongside the building. I know that the Soviets thought all sorts of nefarious things went on during these perfectly innocent walks, and I was pleased that they devoted some resources to them. I liked walking my dog and she was a conversation-starter in Moscow. Russians love dogs, too.

During this period of change, I had an interesting incident with one of the burly policemen, "militia" in Russian, who stood guard outside the Embassy, mostly to keep desperate Russians from rushing inside to claim asylum.

One day I exited the embassy and one of the militiamen hustled after me, grabbed me by the shoulder, and turned me around. I thought: "here it comes," another incident that will end up in the papers. I looked him in the eye and was prepared to object and resist. He smiled and said helpfully, "You are unzipped!" I could not help laughing at the situation. Afterward, the guards at the Embassy door always grinned when I went in or out. Of course, they still had a job to do, and so did I, but the atmosphere had changed a little.

On the 40th anniversary of the defeat of Germany, and to commemorate the role of the United States' resupply of Russia through the ports of Murmansk and Arkhangelsk, Ambassador Hartman and I travelled there to throw a wreath on the water to honor the sailors of the 78 convoys that braved German U-boats to supply wartime Russia. One of my assistant attachés and I were invited aboard a Soviet fishing trawler.

Our reception in Murmansk and on the trawler was cordial, as would be expected of a diplomatic event, but there was more to it than that. People in The Far North remembered the incredible significance of the American effort to help the Russians at a terrible time. They saw the military aid passing through their area on the way to battle fronts where Russian soldiers were in very serious trouble. Stalin could shift official policy on a dime, but ordinary Russian people did not forget.

Aboard a Russian Fishing Trawler in Murmansk in1985
author's photo

"Progressive" Americans decry expressions of "American exceptionalism" and seem uncomfortable with their country behaving like a leader on the world stage. These people are in tune with the elites of other countries who resent the fact that America is exceptional. Ordinary people abroad seem to understand it. Russians certainly did. Even Third World diplomats serving in Russia did. Foreigners seem to understand that being exceptional and being a bully are two different things. I cannot understand why American Progressives are unable to make this distinction and act as if we are pushing the world around if we recognize that we have good things going for us. And they seem to be saying we should feel guilty about it and even apologize for it! This does not make sense.

One attaché's daughter had been in a bad auto accident and suffered terrible cuts on her face. The Russians were going to just let the scars remain. The attaché asked me to get the required medications "from America." I did. Another attaché had ruined the tires on his car on Russian roads and could not find replacements. Good old Firestone Tires were in his hands in a week. He was grateful, but not surprised.

Our maid, whose daughter was getting married, saw a wedding dress in our Sears catalog. Nothing remotely like it was available in Russia. We ordered it and, when it came, there was amazement that, not only did it have all of the buttons on it, there were spare ones! Several Russian girls got married in that dress.

I do not know how many Russians, who tended tiny plots in the countryside for their food, used Burpee seeds that my family provided "from America." These were treasured gifts that were shared widely. Some of those vegetables and fruits at the *rinok* had American DNA. It is a sure bet that generations of those seeds have been collected and passed to others.

Shortages

An old Russian saying, "The shortage is divided among the peasants," captures some of the Russian cynicism, humor, and reality. Reality is standing in a long line for a scrawny Bulgarian chicken, or one or two foreign oranges in a country that used to have plenty of food. It is carrying an "*avos'* or string bag in your purse in hopes you might spot something, anything, worth buying. *Avoc'* means "just in chance."

There are two reasons for the Soviet Union's shortages. First, there is the obvious fact that the Soviet Socialist system could not produce food where it obviously could be and had been grown. Even when a bumper crop appeared, they could not effectively gather, store and transport it, something the Kulaks that Stalin murdered did with no problem. Second, the ruling class appropriated any desirable products. A decent cut of meat or a palatable wine was almost impossible to find for the rubles used to pay ordinary Russian workers, no matter how many rubles one accumulated.

The importance of this, like the importance of broad and deep dissidence below the surface, is that the Soviet system had a "superstructure" – political system -- that looked strong and healthy but a "base," or civil-economic foundation, that was brittle and potentially unstable.

The ruling class benefitted from thorough corruption in the distribution of goods but was not unaware of the danger that it posed for the system. In fact, the "Butcher of Moscow," who supplied Party big wheels in Moscow, including Brezhnev himself, with the finest foodstuffs, was executed when Andropov took command. It was an intentionally symbolic act made public: The Soviet News Agency said Yuri Sokolov, a well-known figure in Moscow, was guilty of taking bribes and "illegal machinations with food products" and had been sentenced to death. Appeals were short in the KGB's Lyubyanka Prison. The paper Evening Moscow announced that the sentence had been carried out. For better or worse, death penalties in Russia do not require twenty years of hand wringing to be carried out. The lesson to the public is more important than the possibility that the individual might have not been given "due process" in the proceeding.

It may seem that my observations of the Soviet Union focus too much on the failures of the Communists to keep pace with the developed world in material ways. I am convinced that the tangible, material failure of the system to advance the economy and technology is critical to understanding the country. Material progress was essential. The policies of the Communist leadership for the final two decades of Soviet rule were direct results of material failure. It had promised a rosy future for current pain for decades. The war was a half-century old and it was an ever weaker justification for Russia's lagging development into a modern state. The Party's grip on power was directly related to its ability to produce real, visible progress. The leadership's credibility was fading.

Lenin himself, after dissolving an elected Constituent Assembly by force and declaring the Communist Party the rightful ruler of Russia, made it clear in 1917 that economic and technological development was the key to the justification for Communist rule. He said, "Communism is Socialism plus Electricity." Actually, he delivered on electricity, but it was downhill after that.

The Russians clearly saw that the Communists were always behind and, except for the excuse that the Germans had retarded Soviet development, it was difficult to understand why Western Democracies had *both* development and freedom. The Communist Party had no way to explain why the gap with Western Democracies grew wider every year. Russian ability to continue funding a gargantuan defense establishment was waning as American innovation accelerated. Everyone in Russia sensed this.

Russian Racism

One unpleasant similarity between Americans and Russians is a history of racism. Quite a few Americans were attracted to Socialism during our Depression and moved to Russia. Most had grim experiences, but the American blacks who made this move encountered vicious racism. I met a couple of American students in Russia who were minorities, and their stories were revealing. Black students from Africa told us sad stories about life in Soviet universities and in Russian communities. It was not safe to be out at night, and it was very dangerous for a black man in the company of a Russian woman.

Racist jokes common in the US in the Fifties were often heard in Russian, though most often aimed at Central Asian peoples or the peoples of the Caucasus, such as the Chechens, who are Muslims. The Chechens brought contempt upon themselves; they have a strong criminal element that plagued the cities and controlled the concentration camps of the Gulag. They are the Sicilians of Russia: The Mob.

Non-Russian peoples had difficulty getting permission to live in the big cities but would fly in for short periods with their fruits, vegetables, and homemade wares. Some slept wherever they could. They made what was good money back in their homelands. Russians paid handsomely for the food that they carried in, but they were an underclass in the big cities and the butt of racism. Many, of course, were Muslim and unwelcome in a Russia that, despite Communist propaganda, was Russian Orthodox, if not openly churchgoing.

Russian fear and loathing of the Muslim world was not new with the Bolshevik Revolution. There has been a tension between the Russians and peoples to the South and East since the recovery from the Mongol Yoke, well before the rise of the Romanov Dynasty.

Soviet Central Asia

This is a fascinating part of the world. On reflection now, I wonder how the ham-handed Soviet Machine ever managed to dominate these people. Then, I realize that they never really did dominate them. It was as if the Soviet Communists had dipped their hand into a deep well of water and, when they pulled it out, it was as if they had not been there. To be sure, the Communist Party brought electricity, modern communications and mechanization to the Silk Road, and they positioned thousands of Russians there to operate it, but they did not suppress the culture, language, and religion of a region far older and wiser than the upstart Soviet Russia.

Peoples from here had stormed across Eurasia, murdering, raping, and ruling for thousands of years. Some tribes formed populations north of the Black Sea. Caravans roamed back and forth over the Silk Road and socio-political entities rose and fell over the years. When I was at the University of Louisville, Professor Israel T. Naamani, taught his 19 year old student not to believe Soviet claims that these nations were all part of a homogeneous Soviet Union. He said that someday we would understand the Russian concern for this part of the world and why the Tsars and Commissars were wary of it and wanted to control it. There were too few experts on this region in the U.S. and we needed more of them.

Like in the Baltic States, Russians populated the Central Asian Republics with enough people to sustain political control until the 1980s. The Soviet Union tried mightily to cobble together a Russia-dominated empire from these disparate peoples. The language of commerce and in schools was Russian, and the technical personnel were Russians using Russian instruction manuals. Locals who succeeded were Party members. But a visitor could feel a suppressed culture that remained strong in their hearts. They had roamed the Silk Road for countless centuries, crossing borders with impunity, including those of China and Russia. They knew mathematics and astronomy when Russians still did not have a name. Their dance and their music evoked centuries of history that Russia did not know.

Walking the markets and bazaars, one sensed that these people had been places and seen things that had no place in "Socialist Reality," the rubric that State-sponsored "artists" and "writers" were supposed to depict. That Realism, crass depiction of workers and peasants with hammers and sickles, was not the real world that the Central Asian peoples understood.

I saw a baby camel, and an old fellow said he would trade it for my 11-year old daughter. He was probably not kidding. He was sincere when he said the camel was worth more than a mere female. I held my daughter a little tighter. I found an old foundry where several men were repairing old copper and brass pots and jugs. They seemed high, probably on hashish, and were very friendly to an American who strolled in. We negotiated long and hard over several pots and jugs, or "Kuvchens," and I got them down to ten rubles. They respected my toughness as a negotiator, but I gave them their original asking price anyway. My son and I left with a heavy burlap bag of old copper and brass. I had to haggle with Aeroflot to get it back to Moscow.

These old fellows had a "wait and see" attitude about politics. They did not take it at all seriously, as nearly everyone did up north in Russia. In the Provinces to the South and East, it was as if current political facts were a temporary wave among the waves of history. "This, too, shall pass." They were right.

Old Central Asian Copper and Brass

"Three Turks and a Gypsy"
Russian Lithograph

photos by the author

During a journey to see the old cities and the architectural, ethnic
and intellectual heritage of the Central Asian nations that had been
temporarily absorbed by the Soviet Union, we saw people standing in
the aisle as an obviously overloaded plane took off. Some were carrying
live chickens! A little goat was aboard, apparently to meet a bad end at
a wedding somewhere. Marx, Lenin, and Stalin would have been totally
out of place.

There was one positive result of the Soviet era for the five former "stans"
in Central Asia. All are still secular governments today, and stable
compared to Afghanistan, Pakistan. They do have burbling extremist
insurgencies, but they keep them fairly well under control. These five
governments call themselves democracies now but they are no more
democratic than the Soviet Union was. America should let these sleeping
dogs lie and resist the temptation to try to force "real" democratization
on them.

Getting Around: Aeroflop

We flew Aeroflot (Nicknamed "Aeroflop" by our children) to everywhere
in the Soviet Union that they would let us visit. Aeroflot itself was
sometimes an issue in trying to travel to remote areas. There were
places that, though technically "open" to travel, were effectively closed
because of the poor safety records of Aeroflot, especially where one

and two engine aircraft were involved. I tried several times to visit Yakutsk in Siberia because I had written a paper on Soviet Oil and I was interested in how they coped in such an inhospitable place. The New York Times managed to get its correspondent Hedrick Smith there to do a feature story, but I never made it. I was told that it was not a safe place for diplomats to travel. I pressed them and finally they said that travel in the old one-engine Colt Aircraft was not permitted. There were always rumors in the air about airplane crashes that were not publically acknowledged.

Travel into Central Asia on Aeroflot in the winter was about as bad, but my family made it on twin-engine aircraft. They had to jump-start an airplane in Khiva, an ancient town in Uzbekistan.

Once, Wilma and I were returning to Moscow from Batumi down on the Black Sea near the Turkish border. There was almost no seating inside the airport and the passengers had been left waiting outside in 100-degree heat for a four-hour flight delay. There was only a foul, open, Central Asian toilet that stunk to high heaven and no water. I could see that the pilot had arrived and the plane had been fueled. Finally, I demanded an explanation from the "authorities," two peasant ladies at a loss to handle the situation. One of them blurted out, "There are thunderstorms in Moscow." I asked patiently why that was a problem here in Adjaria in Southern Georgia, four hours away. She hung her head and mumbled: "The pilot is not instrument qualified."

It is difficult to forget the trips out to Siberia in Aeroflot craft. The first time I flew to Khabarovsk, a major strategic city at the confluence of the Amur and Ussuri Rivers on the Tran-Siberian Railroad, the backbone of the Aeroflot long-range fleet was the same as the old TU-95 "BEAR" strategic bomber. The flight took nine hours. There was virtually no heat and you could hear every piece of equipment on the airplane.

Forewarned that no food or drink would be offered, I carried a bag with two Fresca soft drinks in it at my feet. In two hours, the drinks froze. A flight in 1983 was much better: there was a newer Ilyushin aircraft, and we were offered a piece of boiled chicken that only had a little bit of green mold on it.

The Trans-Siberian Express from Khabarovsk to the Port City of Nakhodka, as train trips often were in Russia, was a trip back into the past. The coaches are old and comfortable. There was a *dezhurnia*, invariably an old peasant lady who really seemed to care if you were warm and who kept a huge hot water tank boiling to make tea. At little towns along the Chinese border, peasants met the train and hawked warm meat pies and other peasant fare. The only negative part of this journey was a surly KGB contingent that hated both the Americans and the Chinese.

Among the "technology" we dealt with in the USSR was the elevator in the Embassy. This ancient device was a legend in the diplomatic community. It broke down frequently, including when VIPs, such as then-Vice President. It was always filthy because of the ever-present snow and mud that was tracked in. LBJ got stuck in it and was not amused.

Once, when Rear Admiral Hayward was there for the signing of the Incidents at Sea Agreement in 1972, he turned to the Acting U.S. Naval Attaché, Lieutenant Commander Kime and said, "You need to get this thing cleaned up." Fourteen years later, after he retired as Chief of Naval Operations, he was stopping at the Moscow airport on the way to Japan. I invited him to stop by for dessert at a dinner party in my quarters. I met him below and, as we got into the elevator to stop by the office, he smiled and said, "I told you to get this thing cleaned up!"

Капиталисты (*KAPITALISTI*)

Eight decades of unrelenting propaganda about the virtues of Communism and the evils of Capitalism had a devastating effect on the future of Russia. This propaganda was, along with a ready supply of alcohol for the masses, the opiate of the Russian people. It was numbing to the brain, but part of the ordinary Russian's survival to go with the flow. A strong but relatively small intelligentsia knew better, and even ordinary people understood that the images they were being fed were propaganda, but they lived in an Alice-in-Wonderland world where "we pretend to work and you pretend to pay us" was the prevailing ethic. It was a black and white international environment: Communism is utopia and Capitalism is the incarnation of evil and voraciousness.

Russians invented a wonderful machine that gobbles up snow. It has long arms that reach out, gather in snow, and stuff it into a voracious maw. Like a huge insect it eats everything it can grab. They call this monster a Капиталист (pronounced kap-i-tal-EEST.) The name reflects both Russian humor and the Russian Alice-in-Wonderland perception of reality.

Ordinary Russians had been conditioned to think of Capitalism not in the tamped-down and socially tempered form that it became in the West, but in the raw, vicious form depicted by Karl Marx in 1848. Understanding this view is crucial to understanding what happened in Russia after Communism fell.

Self-styled Russian "Capitalists" behaved exactly like the machine that gobbled up snow. Brighter, more aggressive, young Party members were in the right places to grab state property and control vast areas of the economy as the grip of the Communist Party of the Soviet Union slackened, then let go precipitously. They turned the simplistic Communist image of modern day Capitalism into a horrible reality, a self-fulfilling nightmare for Russians.

Assets that had been built at enormous cost to simple people by a hideously inefficient and corrupt Communist system were turned over to the greediest and most vicious among the survivors of the Soviet collapse. Marx's image of Capitalist barons separated from disenfranchised masses, perversely, became more nearly true in Russia than it was in America.

A Soviet Vietnam

The Soviet war in Afghanistan hung constantly in the air during our 1983-85 tour of duty. The Soviets, supporting a friendly regime in Kabul against Mujahedeen opponents, had intervened in 1979. My friend and fellow poker player, Adolph "Spike" Dubs, who was Ambassador in

Kabul, had been murdered earlier in the year there. The country was unstable.

The invasion of Afghanistan did not fit the way Russians think about the use of force. Russians do not dabble with force: they smash things. A convicted criminal gets two bullets in the head, and the bill for the lead is sent to the family. A plane that violates Russian airspace is shot down. Tanks visit Hungarians or Czechs who take too many liberties. Russians will try other solutions, but their patience has limits. There is a saying: "Russians are slow to saddle up, but we do some fast riding." Whacking the Afghans was not repugnant to Russians. Not succeeding at whacking them quickly and totally was unacceptable.

The Soviets got themselves, Vietnam-like, entrenched in an intractable conflict for a decade. Soviet conscripts began coming home in boxes in a steady stream. It was impossible to hush it up, and Russians were fed up with it. How could the Communists be the awesome superpower that they claimed to be every day in Pravda and be helpless in a fourth-rate country? It felt like the American helplessness in Vietnam.

Over 14,000 Russian soldiers were killed in Afghanistan. Hundreds were captured, and some said that many of these were forced to accept Islam. Over 50,000 Russian soldiers were wounded, and 10,000 of these were permanently disabled. It took the Soviets over nine years to get out of Afghanistan.

It was a black hole for blood and treasure, and after all that had been wasted, there was absolutely nothing to show for it. The impotence of the Communist Ruling Class was revealed in Afghanistan, and the deep opposition to the war was a major factor in the fall of the Communist regime.

In 1984, I asked an old fellow about Afghanistan and he just did not know what to say. He did not want to be unpatriotic, something Russians would never be no matter what government was in charge. Referring to our elderly President Reagan, he blurted out that "your old 'Baba' could make the same mistake!" I told him he was wrong, not knowing that, like in Vietnam where we got mired down a decade after the French debacle there proved it was a stupid idea, the US would indeed make the same mistake in Afghanistan!

Diversion: from Paris to Russia's Past

During this tour of duty in Russia, we were able to escape the rigors of Soviet life several times and travel abroad. Our family had escaped to Greece and the Greek Isles in 1974 after a year in Russia. That trip, in addition to being a great family adventure, helped me better understand Russia. During my 1983-85 tour of duty in Russia, I resolved to travel abroad when I could. After visiting Scandinavia, Germany, Italy, Japan, Yugoslavia, or even China, return to the Soviet Union had a somber reality to it in the mid-1980s. It was always like going back into the past, into a place where history weighed heavily on the present and promised little for the future.

A trip to Paris had an unusual end. Our family visited Paris after New Year's Day 1985. On a flight back to Moscow, Omar Sharif, who was making the film "Peter The Great" in the old Russian town of Vladimir, where the Romanov Dynasty began, was on board. The plane was diverted in a ferocious snowstorm to Leningrad. The Soviets had no idea what to do with this bunch of foreigners. The KGB in Leningrad could have not been pleased with such unwanted guests.

My family, using a suitcase for a table, broke out cards and played Euchre. Sharif, a world-class bridge player, was taken with this sight, especially our children who had played cards since they could talk and played well.

We were shuttled to the best hotel Leningrad could offer, and Sharif gave his seat on the bus to Wilma. The next morning, he complained that his major regret was that he could not get French wines in Russia. I told him I could solve that problem, since I had wine shipped to me through diplomatic channels via Helsinki. He invited us to visit Suzdal' and Vladimir, home of the Romanovs until Moscow became Russia's Capital in 1326, and watch some of the filming of Peter The Great.

We enjoyed a journey back into pre-communist Russia, complete with troika rides in the snow, as his guest. On the way, we visited The Pearl on the Nerl, a beautiful little church on the Nerl River that required a long trek in the snow. It was plain on this trip that, just behind the sinister Communist façade, awaited a glorious history that would reappear as soon as the Marxist pretenders yielded the Tsars' throne. This Russia out of the past reflected the culture and charm of a people who had been smothered in an ideology unworthy of it.

Captain and Mrs. Kime enjoying a Troika ride
in Suzdal, Russia 1985
autor's photo

Parting Thoughts on the Soviet Union and Russia

I left the Soviet Union in 1985 with a strong sense that the fraud perpetrated on the Russian and other peoples of the Soviet Union could not be sustained for very long. The Russians, a hopeful but cynical people, had been aware of this fraud for a long time, and there were ever more open mutterings about it. The incessant drumming of Communist propaganda was becoming more and more absurd.

I could not help recalling the Honors thesis that I wrote in 1962 at the University of Louisville. That thesis dealt with Communist propaganda immediately before they exploded a 100 megaton nuclear weapon in the atmosphere and immediately thereafter. I was in Russia beforehand and was exposed to shameless statements that the USSR would never do such a thing at the time they were preparing to do it. After the explosion, propaganda turned 180 degrees in a single day. This had to insult the intelligence of anyone who could read.

The Russian language has a future tense, but the Soviet Union as it was then operating did not. In the mid-1960s, fairly radical reform had been discussed, and it was clearly again time for some serious thinking about reform of the system. After Chernenko died, Gorbachev brought serious reform. The question was whether the Soviet Union, an ungainly conglomeration of nationalities dominated by a Russia that was failing to keep up with the rest of the developed world, could survive it.

Lenin said, "Scratch a Russian Communist and you will find a Great Russian Chauvinist." Maybe because Russians are more homogeneous, they are more nationalistic than Americans. Though the Soviet Union was a tightly controlled system of nationalities, it was Russian nationalism that I, and many other students of the USSR, saw as the glue that had held the system together in spite of forces that would eventually pull it apart. Russians are patriotic nationalists, and the Communist Party counted on that. They miscalculated when they thought this Russian patriotism meant that Russians would absorb blatant incompetence and failure to make Russia keep pace with the civilized Western world.

It was, after all, the Russian language that was taught everywhere, Russian designs for electrical systems, housing, dams, communications and the infrastructure upon which Soviet progress, such as it was, was based. It was a Russian military establishment, a Russian police force, and KGB that ruled. It did not seem likely that Russians would give up control without a fight.

We saw the enormous flaws in the system, but Sovietologists overestimated the influence of Soviet military power and underestimated the willingness of a tired old regime to let power go. Reflecting back on the six or so decades of Soviet rule, it strikes me that we were too quick to accept as permanent what turned out to be a Soviet aberration in Russian history. *The Bolsheviks were always a temporary blight on the history of Eastern Europe!*

Underappreciated and under-analyzed by so-called "experts" or "Kremlinologists" are the short time spans between major events in the tumultuous Soviet political and economic history. The system was always being adjusted for fundamental flaws. The entire history of the Great Bolshevik Experiment, the length of Stalin's life span, was a blink in time. It was a powerful, sometimes outright threatening, phenomenon, but *the USSR was never permanently established*. Consider this brief historical sketch:

Russia had been around for a thousand years and the Romanov Dynasty was in place for three centuries before the Bolsheviks, in the midst of a terrible war, Russian helplessness, and impending famine, seized power. It took Lenin and the Red Army five years to end up in charge. It was only a couple of years before Lenin died. Some Ukrainians fought until 1924. It took three more years for Stalin to take total command of the Communist Party. He then spent over a decade imposing terroristic policies on his people: purges, murders, and elimination of the peasant middle class. In 1939 he agreed to a pact with fellow terrorist Adolph Hitler.

Stalin was dead just 14 years after this. During this decade and a half, Stalin exhibited fanaticism and insanity and was "ruling" an occupied country part of the time. When Stalin died, a new Purge seemed to be coming. Reformers were quick to dispose of Stalin's certifiably insane running mates, including "the demon dwarf" Beria, and saw the need to return Russia to her artistic and creative nature. This experiment ebbed and flowed for a decade.

Khrushchev was ousted in 1964, more for "harebrained schemes" than for failure to pursue "Communist" orthodoxy. His successors knew that the economic system did not work. The early Brezhnev-Kosygin regime in 1965 seriously considered significant economic reform, but this attitude lingered only a few years. Then, as Russians watched Americans on the moon, the leadership clearly understood that they were getting ever farther behind.

In the 1970s, Brezhnev and an aging leadership tried overtures to America and the West and entertained an interdependence where Russia, because she was an intercontinental nuclear superpower, might be accepted and left alone with its one-party anachronism of a government. This lasted through the Seventies, during which time

Soviet wheat crops failed and, though Americans were flying around the moon, they kept shooting themselves in the foot with Vietnam and Watergate.

At the turn of the Eighties, Afghanistan was the most dramatic of Soviet overreaches in a feckless attempt to demonstrate that the Soviet Union was a viable international player. It fell flat. The Politburo was tired and aware that the Great Bolshevik Experiment, really only a half-century old, had failed. They could kill everyone on the planet, but they could not make a decent automobile, grow grain in Europe's Breadbasket, or even subdue pesky Muslims on their border.

America had shaken off the silliness of the Seventies and was awakening in the early 80s. Talk of Strategic Defense Systems that might actually work and the Shining City on a Hill profoundly worried the Old Guard in the Soviet Union. The world looked dangerous to a bunch of old, sick, men in Moscow who plainly did not know what to do.

National suicide, an option that Stalin might have entertained, or loss of power for the Party, was a real risk if, once again, radical approaches to "rebuilding" the country were not considered. The Old Guard was faced with an imperative: brighter, more flexible, and younger voices, like Andropov and his protégé Gorbachev, had to be heard. It was a tense three years in the 1980s before the dying began. Gorbachev brought the ultimate "Thaw," called "Perestroika," and this was the beginning of the end.

Taking Leave of Russia

Navy Contingent says Good-Bye. Moscow, 1985

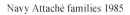

Navy Attaché families 1985

I have suggested in this Story and will continue to suggest things that would improve Navy policies. Based on my experience over the decades and the perspectives I have gained as an unconventional Naval Officer looking at the institution from a different angle, it may seem that I am critical and ungrateful. That is not true. I am deeply grateful to the U.S. Navy for the opportunities it provided me to serve at a time when U.S. – Soviet relations were of critical strategic significance. My debt to the Navy far outweighs the contributions I was able to make. My gratitude to the Navy for opportunities both as a scholar and as a Naval Officer cannot be overstated.

As a student of the Great Bolshevik Experiment, I was fabulously lucky. The US Navy allowed me to:

- visit during the Thaw in 1961 as a Midshipman;
- study the Soviet Union and Russian at Harvard;
- serve for two years as a Lieutenant Commander during the first Soviet strategic overtures to the West;
- help to write the estimates on the USSR during "Détente;"

- teach Soviet Studies at the senior military school in America, The National War College, Georgetown and American Universities, and later at the US Naval Academy;
- publish extensively on Soviet affairs;
- serve on delegations in US-Soviet relations in the 1970s;
- and, as a Navy Captain, serve as U.S. Naval Attaché in Moscow when the Politburo began to disintegrate and the end was near.

Chapter XVI
Navy's Political-Military Directorate: Politics in the Pentagon

In the middle of my tour as U.S. Naval Attaché in Moscow, I was in Washington and had an appointment with Admiral James Watkins, the CNO. This talented submariner was a broad-gage thinker who would later be Secretary of Energy and Chairman of Ronald Reagan's AIDS Commission. I am certain that Admiral "Ace" Lyons, Head of the Incidents at Sea Delegation that was in Moscow while I was there, had told him of the off-the-beaten-path tours about Moscow that I had taken with him. He knew I had handled communications with the Soviet Ministry of Defense during the Korean Airline shootdown, had seen some of the reports I had written, and wanted to discuss perspectives from Moscow. He produced a chunk of a propeller from a Soviet submarine that had been embedded in a U.S. warship. It was all shined up and had an engraving on it. He asked if it was OK. Engraved on it, in Russian, was a famous understatement that all sailors understood: "a collision at sea can ruin your entire day."

His staff had suggested he give it to the head of the Soviet Delegation soon to arrive to discuss the Incidents at Sea Treaty. It would be given when the Soviet Admiral made a call on the CNO in his office. What did I think? He knew that I would not mince words and that I was not afraid of repartee with Russians. But I said I would not do that in that particular, formal situation. (Maybe over cocktails after ice was broken and a few sailor stories had been exchanged?) He nodded. I do not know what became of the chunk of propeller because I was back in Moscow, but I think that meeting had something to do with the orders I got out of Moscow.

It was unprecedented for an intelligence officer to be assigned as Deputy Director of the Navy's Politico-Military Directorate. It was a plum job on the Navy Staff that had several post-command Navy Captains, each with his own staff, reporting to it. Politico-military issues that came before the Navy were vetted by this position. The Navy was sending me to the best political-military job it had at the rank of Captain for any officer, let alone one with my unusual background. I would often act in an admiral's stead. This was a job in the coveted E-ring of the Pentagon and in the heart of the Navy Staff. It was like being welcomed home! I got orders.

The Pentagon Treadmill Disease

OP-61 was a chance to be back with the Navy, but it was part of the Pentagon rat race. Officers arrived before sunrise and went home after sundown. It was absolutely imperative that one arrive before the boss and leave after he does. If every subordinate and every boss does this, everyone is always there! Jobs were expanded to fit the optics of one's service in the Pentagon. The image of working to exhaustion was crucial to a Pentagon fitness report. Some officers spent the middle of the day at the POAC, the Pentagon Officers' Athletic Center, in order to make the day fit this bizarre requirement. Families did not fit in the Pentagon routine.

A process that demands at least three signatures on any piece of paper fills time in the Pentagon. If one "signature authority" made a change, even to fix a typo, the previous signatures had to be redone. Majors, Lieutenant Colonels, and Commanders carried the papers around and waited for the signatures. Though some senior officers had awesome responsibility and worked very hard in their office and at POAC treadmills, I never saw a job that could not have been done in eight or nine hours of focused, efficient effort. Crises, of course, are excepted.

Good officers know a real task when they see one, and they will, and do, stay as long as it takes to get it done. They love doing real jobs. The tragedy of the Pentagon is not that fine officers toil long hours on serious issues: it is that fine officers spend long hours on short, frivolous tasks.

The Navy was not immune to the Pentagon Treadmill Disease. I was amazed, after seeing junior officers in their early twenties with massive responsibility and authority, to find Commanders in the prime of their life and capacities treated like college interns. These officers, remember, are marking time after years of awesome responsibility as seagoing officers while waiting for the brass ring: Command at Sea. Some would return after command for another turn at the Treadmill! I reflected back on the time when I realized that I had balked at the requirement to mark time for a decade before I could get a command. Again, I admit that maturity is needed for command at sea, but I knew that I had done the right thing.

Still, it was Navy, and better than the rest of the Pentagon. We were lean and mean compared to the other Services that had far more officers on their staffs, usually a grade or two senior to Naval Officers in the Pentagon. This could be confirmed by taking attendance at the POAC. Wags had dubbed the Pentagon "the World's Largest Kindergarten" and "too small to be a country and too big to be an insane asylum."

Pol-Mil

I was the filter, or as junior officers might say, "bottleneck," through which all politico-military issues that would be briefed to the CNO had to pass. We also fielded the "hot" items that arose every day, analyzed them and did a quick summary and recommendation on how the Navy should deal with them in the Pentagon policy mill. The CNO, a member of the Joint Chiefs of Staff, had to be up to speed when, in the famous "tank" where the Service Chiefs met, the issues were addressed. A senior post-command Captain headed each of five small staffs that kept track of geographic areas and one that handled submarine and associated issues. These reported to me.

The Director of OP-61 was a Commodore. The Admirals in the chain of Command largely ignored this gentleman, a very bright man who would be sent to a dead-end job and retired, so I ran the place. His successor was a dynamic and successful officer who retired as Commandant of the Industrial College of the Armed Services with two stars. He had a doctorate in Nuclear physics from Stanford and was in the job awaiting promotion and assignment to run an aircraft carrier task force. He was a fine, competent officer and quick study, but happy to let me handle the issues.

I did my best in this environment, working the usual 80-hour weeks without POAC time. The problem was not that it was demanding. Good Naval Officers thrive on all-consuming assignments. Otherwise, warships would come to a stop all over the world. The problem was that much of the work in the Pentagon was a waste of time and energy. Most issues were obvious. Some required a brief look, and some were extremely serious, but all required a piece of paper. Never has so much talent been applied to such a wide array of things in such a wasteful way as in politico-military issues in the Pentagon.

Some truly sophisticated and intelligent senior officers of all of the Military Services were involved in the pol-mil process all the way up to the Chiefs of the Services and the Chairman of the Joint Chiefs of Staff, but the bottom line in the Washington policymaking world is that politics is not the purview of the military and it rarely makes much difference what was ground out by politico-military staffs in the Military Services.

The reader might recall that, on matters of intelligence, I came to the conclusion that the Services should focus on operational intelligence in their respective spheres and that the Department of Defense should focus on the bigger picture. Otherwise, judgments on the military arms of potential enemies would suffer from a "ten foot tall" syndrome aimed at justifying Service budgets.

A similar conclusion might make sense on political-military affairs and military strategy. Bigger picture assessments might be best done at the Joint and DoD levels. This is not to say that the individual Services should not cultivate and maintain military and political strategists, but the senior jobs for officers so trained and educated should be at the higher policymaking levels in the Joint and DoD environments. This is not, of course, compatible with Navy's historic view of Joint Duty, but it makes sense today, especially given reduction in forces and a distinct shift in US policy toward joint plans and operations.

Stardust

As mentioned earlier, my reporting senior had the rank of Commodore. The rank of Commodore is a venerable one, but one that one-star Naval

Officers hated. The Navy had annoyed the other Services for years with their practice of pinning two stars on Captains the minute they were promoted to one-star rank and giving them the title "Rear Admiral." They were paid as one-stars until they actually made the next rank, but the practice of wearing two stars rankled the other military services.

Actually, the practice made some sense. There are Navy Captains in lots of jobs occupied in other Services by one-star officers. These jobs, like mine in OP-61, had senior Captains reporting to them. The Navy had done this for decades. Many of the Navy Captains with at least as much responsibility and authority as one-star officers of the Air Force or Army are called "Commodore" by tradition. They still wore the uniforms and drew the pay of Navy Captains.

The Navy practice made some sense, at least to Naval Officers, but it fell flat in the "Joint Environment" which was growing in power. Sometimes there was, for example, a one-star Air Force or Army Officer who was senior to the Navy officer in the same organization wearing two-stars. These were people with big egos, playing in "the world's largest Kindergarten", and there was hate and discontent. It was another case of the Navy thumbing its nose at the Joint Environment.

For a brief period in the early 1980s, the other military services prevailed, and one-star Naval Officers wore one star and were called Commodore. They hated it. The Navy scuttled the title of "Commodore" for one-star officers in 1986, but they still had to wear just one star. Such was the stuff of Pentagon politics!

Potted Palms

In the Pentagon's E-Ring one gets a glimpse of the rarified social life that would await a new flag officer. There were often calls for officers to attend social or diplomatic functions. The State or Defense Department would specify that they wanted "a flag officer." Our civilian betters wanted to see firsthand the prestige, and the cool uniforms, which the system conferred upon a chosen few. And, of course, this gave the civilians a chance to assert their seniority.

In almost every case some one- or two-star fellow who did not have the slightest clue would be sent to decorate some cocktail party. I felt sorry for them. I suggested that we dress up a potted palm with all the medals we could find and put some stars on it. A junior enlisted man could transport it cheaply. If this was too obvious, we could just let the enlisted man wear the uniform. He would not have to talk, and we had some candidates that had fewer years on them and would wow the ladies. This suggestion fell flat, of course, but I heard it repeated in the E-Ring hallways.

The Promotion Paradox

There were signs that some powers-that-were in the Navy still thought I might be useful to them for a few years. I did not pursue the potential of this because it was increasingly clear to me that my out-of-pattern career had run its course. Finally, I understood something that is not often understood about the military: an officer can be clearly cut out for making decisions and running things, but fail because he is not a good subordinate.

Naval Officers, who are trained and given significant responsibility early, are more often suited to run things than they are to be good subordinates. Perversely, the route to successful flag officer jobs has more to do with being a good, absolutely reliable, blue-and-gold subordinate than it has to do with the ability to command.

In senior jobs, the trick is not to make a detectable error and be absolutely reliable to your senior command. It is called "pattern maintenance." To succeed in a well defined, disciplined culture, you must reflect the culture's pattern and totally subordinate yourself to it. As one obtains senior rank, closer adherence to the culture's pattern is required.

The Navy rank of Lieutenant Commander is the pivotal one. We need for these leaders in their thirties to actually run the Navy. Someone has to make things operate and train the youngsters in their twenties who shoulder huge responsibility and thrive on the attitude: "That which is not specifically forbidden is permitted." Once one becomes a senior officer, full Commander in the Navy, the emphasis shifts decidedly toward Pattern Maintenance. The Navy has a wonderful saying that encapsulates this: "The Navy is operated by Young Studs, Old Fuds, and Lieutenant Commanders."

There is a paradox in this. The things that make excellent seagoing officers are precisely *not* the things needed of the most senior officers. The Navy, to its credit, makes good leaders out of the majority of junior officers. *Not all good leaders are the outstanding followers that senior officers must become.* "That which is not specifically forbidden is permitted" is an attitude that cultivates good leaders, but it will bring a Captain or a junior Admiral to a screeching career halt. You can command a ship, but you had better not get a reputation for rocking the boat!

I have often reflected on this paradox. It is the main reason that we train the best people we can find for two decades and then push the majority of them out of the Navy and onto the streets in their early forties. The civilian world scoops them up because they are good leaders who have actually *done* something and shouldered big responsibilities. The Navy does not know what to do with them. Only the Government could sustain such a wasteful process!

These observations are not meant as criticism of the Navy. The Navy system makes huge contributions to civil society by serving as the training ground for future political, business, and manufacturing leaders. The military serves as a kind of "School of Capitalism and Democracy" in this role, so in the end the expenditure of military resources might be worth it to the nation.

In America, the military at the levels where it touches national policy is, and must be, subordinate. An officer who is slow or unable to adjust to this fact in the competition at higher levels of rank will fail. Most of the officers in the highest ranks in the military are bright enough and competent enough, but they are professional, practiced subordinates.

I did not understand through all those years in the Navy that, though I love the institution and always wanted to find the best way to serve it, I was a terrible subordinate. I still am. A civilian position of responsibility, if it was reasonably independent, was what I was cut out for. I was one of those that the system needed to put on the streets after two or three decades. I belonged in academe.

Time to Go, Again!

It seemed clear that Naval Intelligence, though the Admirals there were friends, and even students of mine, did not have a clue what to do with me. One told me flatly that, for a senior Naval officer, I was "eccentric!" It did not seem wrong when he said it. I did not fit any of their most senior positions and would not have taken one of them if it had been offered. I needed to move on, and I could not see a way that I could stay in a Navy uniform and be useful.

Sensing that the time had come, I made it known in June of 1986 that I was going to retire from the Navy that year and seek an academic job in the Washington area. Wilma and I looked for, and found, a wonderful horse-country property in Clifton, Virginia. As we were closing on the property, our world changed.

On July 1, 1986, Admiral C.A. H. Trost became Chief of Naval Operations. A submariner, he relieved James Watkins, the submariner discussed earlier. Vice Admiral Charles Larson was the head of OP-O6, which had cognizance over Navy politics and strategy, and over OP-61 where I was assigned. I had known him since I was a candidate for the White House Fellowship. (He was the first Naval officer to ever win one in 1968.) Chuck Larson had two submarine commands and was soon to don four stars and become Commander of the Pacific Command, the largest military command on Earth. He had been Superintendent of the Naval Academy and would return there later as a retired 4-star Admiral.

Admiral Larson called me at my desk in the Pentagon at about 0630 as I was poring over the usual three-inch pile of morning message traffic from all over the world. He asked me why I was leaving the Navy, since I was in a promising job and there were senior people in the Navy who wished me well. I told him that I knew I was a square peg in a round hole and that I belonged in an academic job. He already knew this and had an answer ready.

Admiral Larson asked if I would be interested in going to the Naval Academy and looking for a civilian academic job from there. He threw in a sweetener before I could answer him: they would assign me one of the big houses on famous, historic Porter Road. Flabbergasted and flattered, I blurted out; "Where is Porter Road?" He laughed out loud, because every Academy graduate knew and revered Porter Road and its stately row of Captains' houses. He noted that maybe I was just what was needed there. I would be the first Director of an academic division at the Academy who did not wear The Ring. I should drive over and check out Porter Road.

Like Ado Annie in *OKLAHOMA*, I could not say no. Here was a chance to pay the Navy back for its incredible tolerance of me and do it in Navy's inner sanctum, which also sounded like a challenging academic environment from which to look for a civilian academic job.

Author's home at #10 Porter Rd
US Naval Academy
author's photo

Chapter XVII
The U.S. Naval Academy
Issues in Officer Education

I told Wilma, who had just found her Dream House in Clifton. She, a Navy wife, did not flinch. We would have to move into the Clifton home and sleep in makeshift beds for a month to establish it as a "residence" for tax purposes and find a renter. Having finally collected all our goods in one place we would move all of it again. Pepper, her Appaloosa mare, would have to be boarded out near Annapolis. Stephanie, age 13, would have to change schools, again. Ten-minute job. No sweat. We were moving to the Naval Academy.

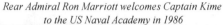

Rear Admiral Ron Marriott welcomes Captain Kime
to the US Naval Academy in 1986

author's photo

Duty at the Academy is as good as duty gets. The people are first-class and friendly. It is a beautiful place and a tight-knit community. I never heard a word about my being an odd career type. I did get some good-natured ribbing about not having The Ring.

The first Superintendent during my tenure there had been a student at the National War College where I was his faculty advisor. The second was the senior student in my Sub School Class a quarter of a century ago. Though the latter sometimes wondered aloud why we had all those "Bull" courses, and wondered why my office was better than his, I was among friends.

The Naval Academy, though oriented too much toward engineering, is a solid academic institution. Its faculty is mostly made up of civilian scholars who would be accepted elsewhere in academe. Some military officers hold academic rank. I was accepted as a Full Professor and taught courses on Russia.

The Division Directors, who are responsible for a few academic departments, are senior Navy Captains. I had the Political Science, Economics, and Modern Language Departments. Faculties at the Academy are mostly civilians who could compete with faculties elsewhere. Division Directors serve the functions of Deans at civilian colleges. There is an Academic Dean who serves as what would be a Provost at most institutions. All this adds up to a very fine college, but one limited, in my view, in some ways.

Engineering Officers

Some might guess that, in saying that the Academy is limited, I would be talking about the crushing non-academic demands on the time and energy that are placed on midshipmen. Indeed, the demands are great, and sometimes they are excessive, but this is not what I'm talking about. The young men and women win an intensive competition to get admitted to the Brigade, know that they are in for a tough program, and have the stamina to handle it. I'm not positive that I would have been able to handle the nonacademic demands of the Academy, and I admire those who do. More power to them!

One thing that limits the Academy is that it is decidedly an engineering school. It is a very good undergraduate engineering school but this, in my view, limits the Academy's ability to provide the American People what they need in a Navy.

The Academy has made significant improvements in the correct direction that are discussed below, but I think more still needs to be done to expand the worldviews of midshipmen. There should be a larger segment of required liberal arts courses. No student should leave the Academy with the contempt for "Bull" courses that too often is expressed by senior Naval officers.

Bull

I studied Chemistry and Physics in college and I served as a Chief Engineer. If it were really true that there is only time to teach one thing, I would teach the STEM courses. But it is not true that there is only time to teach engineering skills in an undergraduate engineering curriculum. There is time to provide a solid core of broadening coursework. I do not object to a single course at the Academy: I do object to the fact that Midshipmen are conditioned to consider the Liberal Arts bulls--t.

While is true that many of the challenges to junior officers in the fleet will be engineering challenges, taxpayers fund the Academy to produce Naval Officers whose *most important* challenges will not be technical ones. Naval Officers must be well grounded in Engineering and the Sciences, but equal weight should be given to English, History, Government, Economics and Foreign Languages. Otherwise, officers are not as well prepared to do the leadership, management and policy jobs that taxpayers expect them to do. Sadly, the non-engineering part of the Academy has long been called "the Bull Department." There have been Superintendents who promoted this view.

The Naval Academy was, in my day, not a great environment for a scholar who believed that an understanding of human social and political intercourse is just as important as the understanding of technology and the physical universe. Vietnam War hero and Academy Superintendent William Lawrence tried to adjust the balance between these perspectives at the Academy in the 1970s, and some adjustments were made, but it was still decidedly an engineering school.

I did not understand until I was a senior officer that Naval Officers succeed primarily on narrow Naval expertise: as they get ever more senior, their success is determined much more by Pattern Maintenance of the Navy culture than by extending themselves into serious policymaking realms that demand sophisticated social and political savvy. Perversely, the best way to get to 4 stars and a job with sociopolitical policymaking clout is to avoid any such thing for as long as possible!! It was a career-ender in my day to waste much time in the realm of "Bull." A PhD indicated "Bullshit Piled Higher and Deeper."

Throughout my career in the Navy, I heard Naval Academy graduates assert the mantra: midshipmen needed to spend their time on science, math, and engineering. A good Navy seagoing officer can do anything, including policy at any level in any place. Besides, any idiot can handle the squishy, sociopolitical stuff: the "Bull." Academy graduates carry this attitude about social and political matters into the Navy at large. For many years this has prevented the Navy from keeping pace with the other Services in the effort to understand our adversaries.

This was incorrect and silly, as many Admirals who donned 4-stars would discover, but the hubris about "Bull" extended far and wide in the Navy, and caused a great many talented officers, who saw an environment that valued plumbers more than philosophers, to leave the Navy. This hubris did not seem to be lessened by repeated failures to grasp the fact that the things that draw America toward war are neither scientific nor technical.

Foreign Area Officers (FAOs): A Major Step Forward

There was a brief period in the Seventies when the Navy toyed with the idea of career patterns for Foreign Area Specialists somewhat like what the Army had in place. The Army had struggled to find the right fit for FAOs in its personnel system, but it recognized the value of Foreign Area Officer education and assignment long before the Navy. There were attractive career possibilities for Army FAOs. I thought, briefly, that there might be a formal career pattern like this in the Navy. It turned out better for me than I hoped, but it would be an ad hoc thing, not in a recognized specialty. Other politico-military oriented officers got stopped in their tracks.

As noted earlier, I wrote an impassioned letter to the Navy to encourage better education of officers to understand foreign societies and languages. This Masterpiece of Incisive Thought and Analysis was, I am sure, put into what was a large pile of impassioned letters from impertinent officers. The entire Foreign Area Studies concept for the Navy was beaten down in the Seventies. This was a serious mistake in Naval Intelligence, where serious focus on what was called Human Intelligence (HUMINT) could have greatly improved the institution.

Naval Intelligence, perhaps in large measure because of the operational needs of the nuclear submarine community, became almost totally absorbed by the bean-counting and submarine-tracking specialists called OP-INTELL officers. This made operational sense, and it was and should have been the primary focus of Navy Intelligence at the time, but it was a pity. The Army and Air Force grabbed the influential jobs in the military that dealt with important judgments about our international friends and enemies because they educated and promoted HUMINT officers to make those judgments. A Naval officer had to risk his and his family's future to do what other Services encouraged officers to do and rewarded them for doing it well. Navy missed the boat.

The Navy took a major step to correct this in 2006 by establishing the Navy Foreign Area Officer (FAO) Program. This, thirty years after I wrote my impassioned letter and after the initial effort to create a FAO system failed, is all I could have hoped for in the early 1970s. The Navy now ties education and practical foreign affairs experience into a career pattern to which a talented officer can aspire. It even has the possibility of attaining senior rank in FAO billets! This is a lot of Bull!

Particularly positive for the future of this effort, the disciplines of concentration are tied, in the Implementing Instruction, to the major Navy command areas:

FAOs will be appropriately apportioned among four disciplines and eleven sub regions: EUCOM/NAVEUR - North Africa, West Africa, Europe, Russia and Eurasia; CENTCOM/NAVCENT - Middle East and South Asia, East Africa; PACOM/PACFLT - Northeast Asia,

Southeast Asia, India and South Asia, China; and SOUTHCOM/ NAVSOUTH - Latin America and the Caribbean.

Criticizing a great institution like the Naval Academy must be done with care. After all, it does what it sets out to do as well as it possibly can, and no one, including me, can do better than that. I believe that the Academy sets out to do too much engineering and not enough to give midshipmen broader sociopolitical perspectives. This remains true today, but the Naval Academy has taken some important positive steps. The terrorist attack on 9/11/01 had a powerful effect on the attitudes throughout the US National Security Community about the importance of politico-military education. The Navy, which needed this jolt more than most institutions, responded well. Today, some programs that already worked are supplemented by newer efforts.

The Naval Academy Foreign Affairs Conference (NAFAC)

One thing the Naval Academy did very well in spite of the institutional attitude about "Bull" was NAFAC. I was responsible for this. Every April, the Academy sponsors the largest undergraduate Foreign Affairs Conference in the United States. The Chief of Naval Operations came personally every year I was there. There was a faculty advisor and a large midshipman contingent that made it work. Midshipmen ran this operation: they handled the many details of housing, feeding and organizing the activities of hundreds of students from all over the United States. Major issues were addressed. Each midshipman wrote a paper and these were presented and judged. Guest speakers included the likes of Secretaries of State and Defense.

These Conferences were the Naval Academy at its best two decades ago, and NAFAC continues today. Issues of the scope that should concern future officers are addressed. Midshipmen are intermingled with their civilian peers while immersed in delicate political and social issues. The leadership and hard work of these future officers, which is amazing, teaches them a great deal about dealing with the real civilian academic world. For a short period, they are operating in an environment that any Ivy League University would envy. Of course, the Academy cannot do this all the time, but it should make more attempts to mix its student body with the rest of America and to address the kinds of issues that midshipmen will have to confront as Naval Officers in a broader world. Today, the Academy's International Programs Office, which did not exist in my day, is responsible for trying to do this.

The author at the Naval Academy Foreign Affairs Conference in 1987
author's photo

Naval Academy International Programs Office

This office, created in 2005, represents a major improvement since my days at the Academy. Undoubtedly, much more is done today to expose midshipmen to the international political environment, since previously the only event of note was an annual International Ball, a black-tie event to honor the foreign officers at the Academy and to broaden international exposure for the midshipmen. I sponsored this event to which young people from all the embassies in Washington were invited.

Currently, several dozen international midshipmen and a few international officers from several countries are at the Academy, and many U.S. midshipmen spend some time at foreign academies. Some midshipmen spend a semester abroad either at a foreign naval academy (Spanish, French, Japanese, or German) or a civilian university for language study (Arabic, Chinese or Russian). There are 4- to 6-week immersion programs during the summers in the seven languages taught at the Naval Academy. Faculty lead training programs to areas of their expertise. Some take part in summer training aboard foreign ships.

Honor

From the US Naval Academy web page:
http://www.usna.edu/About/honorconcept.php

The Honor Concept of the Brigade of Midshipmen was established by midshipmen to urge everyone to carry out their duties with the highest sense of personal integrity and honor. It represents the minimum standard that midshipmen are expected to follow. Honor, integrity, and loyalty to the service, its customs, and its traditions, are fundamental characteristics essential to a successful naval officer. Lying, cheating, and stealing are intolerable in the brigade as in the Fleet, and may be cause for separation from the Naval Academy. The emphasis is on "doing what is right" rather than simply not breaking the rules.	*Naval Academy Honor Concept:* "Midshipmen are persons of integrity: They stand for that which is right. They tell the truth and ensure that the full truth is known. They do not lie. They embrace fairness in all actions. They ensure that work submitted as their own is their own, and that assistance received from any source is authorized and properly documented. They do not cheat. They respect the property of others and ensure that others are able to benefit from the use of their own property. They do not steal."

When I arrived at the Naval Academy as a Division Director after over two decades in the Navy observing the behavior of and attitude both Academy and ROTC midshipmen and officers, the pretense to superiority over their civilian peers in "honor" seemed a bit hypocritical and hollow to me. After all, there is no formal honor system in the fleet. Navy men and women in the fleet are held to the same standard as the rest of America. They are not expected to lie, cheat or steal.

Lying, cheating and stealing were bad things back in Indiana where I grew up and even at the humble University of Louisville where I was in the NROTC Program! More Americans would agree with the Honor Concept than with the Ten Commandments. It is Motherhood and Apple Pie. Some would say it is picayune to suggest that there can be too much motherhood and apple pie.

My concern with the Academy's honor environment is not how it is articulated. It is that the absolute aura of the Honor Concept paradoxically coexists with a "beat the system" attitude that permeates the Brigade of Midshipmen. Future officers become "Sea Lawyers," and the system, if not the Honor Code itself, becomes a force to be circumnavigated. Rules, and the Honor Concept, become quite literally interpreted. "Breaking the rules" becomes a game.

Academy midshipmen who misbehave are not bad or even unusual kids, but they are kids in spite of the Academy's pretense that they are junior officers already "better" than their peers on the "outside" in pedestrian civilian schools. Not so. Like their counterparts at civilian colleges, they are young people still in the process of becoming mature officers.

Academy midshipmen are generally brighter, more committed, more physically in shape, and probably, as a group, better officer prospects than their civilian peers because of the rigorous selection process and the money invested in their training. They have yet to prove that they are better human beings. Printing an Honor Concept does not make them better. Such a code does no harm, of course, if it is understood as a high standard applied to normal human beings, not to some super race. So understood, it would be a better guide for midshipmen who will sometimes fail. It would also be better for those in charge who have to manage situations when midshipmen behavior is not perfect.

Midshipmen at the Naval Academy indulge in misbehaviors that I have seen from normal, bright youngsters at civilian schools, but they have to rationalize their behavior in terms of an absolute code. It is nearly inevitable that there will be situations when the code must be "finessed" or just ignored. It is reasonable to question whether this is a healthy thing for future officers. The fact that the punishment is severe "if you get caught" does not make the question less important.

The Naval Academy is a place of honor. But I am not convinced that the Naval Academy balances its absolutism about honor with the pulling and hauling between normal young people and the system of rules and controls that they must cope with in the real world. The Navy is in the real world. Balanced thinking about such things is important in the education of all young people. It is even more important for future officers.

The Debate: Academy or NROTC?

The second major limitation of the Academy is even more difficult to address. This is the fact that the institution selects a cadre of students not typical of American youth and educates them separately from their peers. Powerful alumni and many decision-makers in a grateful nation would insist that this makes the Academy the great institution that it is! It is a fine institution in many ways, but I disagree that separation from society is a strong point.

There has long been a debate about the relative merits of NROTC and Naval Academy educations. A strong argument can be made that we need the officers from both sources, but it is not a frivolous debate.

I have first-hand experience with both NROTC and the Naval Academy and have observed the performance and the careers of the graduates for years. It is clear that there should be some serious thought applied to the way we prepare officers and some changes should be made.

Separate and More than Equal?

This is first and foremost about education, not training. The value of being *educated* in civil society is immeasurable for citizen-officers, which is what all American officers should be. A future military officer, like everyone else, benefits from classrooms with students, and even professors, who look, smell, act and think differently than they do. The snotty kid with the earring might not make sense, and the professor might introduce radical ideas, but it is important to hear what they have to say. That snotty student and the professor need to hear from future officers, too.

The Academies, with their much more homogeneous student bodies, tend to perpetuate an Officer Class. Militaries worldwide have some degree of a dynastic Officer Class, and America will never be immune from this tendency because the military is naturally somewhat insulated from civil society. However, the Founding Fathers envisioned militia-oriented military power to defend the nation, and a military that emanates from American society and its institutions. West Point provided leadership with elite training that long dominated the Army, but America did not cultivate and institutionalize a "warrior class" like other nations did. Officers from various walks of life fought with and led Americans in war. Foreign militaries have strong elite officer traditions—kings and tyrants don uniforms and lead a Class of Officers. Not in America. To the extent that our military academies train and perpetuate an elite officer corps, it should not be celebrated as a good thing.

This presents a dilemma. If we want an Academy, it will be separate to some extent and it will perpetuate an elite corps of graduates in which the country has made a large investment. This means, if we accept the notion that an officer corps should look and act like America, that attention must be paid to mitigating the things that make Academy graduates separate and elite. It does not mean mirroring the least common denominators in American culture; rather, it means rising from that culture and being able to lead and improve it.

My experience suggests that the active duty Navy and the realities of duty in the fleet do a fairly good job of mitigating the flaws in Academy education over a period of five or six years. Reality does not somehow confer the broader education and exposure to the radical professor that Academy officers will need later, but the good officers will succeed at managing, and learning from the snotty kid they did not deal with in college. And, after that time, the non-Academy officers catch up with the vocabulary and the shoe-shining.

After that time, some work needs to be done to adjust the promotion system to mitigate the inherent unfairness of the Academy Old Boys' Club. This must be done carefully at pre-flag levels where what is needed most is better recognition of exceptionally talented officers from all sources instead of preordination of youngsters who excelled at the Academy.

Training in the values, behaviors, and the appearance of an officer corps that is charged with doing things that civilians do not do is obviously best done in a military setting. Training at the Naval Academy is superlative. Training in the NROTC Program is much less rigorous, but covers the essential bases. My experience suggests that in two or three years the difference between sources of commissioning, as it pertains to military performance, bearing and aptitude, balances out for good officers. It takes two or three more years for average ones. In the end, individual motivation and performance in Navy uniform outweigh prior knowledge of military culture gained in an undergraduate program.

It is about balance. The argument between the two concepts could go on forever. It probably will never go away, given the fact that education at an Academy is very expensive and subject to challenge. No one is absolutely right or wrong. I have seen that the best NROTC graduates outshine the average Academy graduates and vice-versa. Similarly, the best NROTC institutions are at least equal to the Academy in producing excellent officers and the Academy is among the very top institutions in the country. The Naval Academy tries once in a while to alter the balance in the direction of a broader education, but reaction soon sets in. NROTC programs would benefit from more rigorous training, especially in summers, but civilian educators, some hostile to ROTC, will not support this.

And, again, there is cost. It costs far more to send a young man or woman to the Naval Academy than to other commissioning sources. I would argue that maintenance of Navy culture at a core institution by maintaining the Academy is worth some of the difference in the cost and worth the problems associated with creation of an elite culture.

Both options will be retained. This is a political reality independent of merit and the facts. Still, I think Congress should pay attention to the issues of balance, and of maintaining an officer corps that reasonably closely represents American society. They should make some changes.

Some of the other points in this chapter suggest the need for discussion of change.

Education at the Academy needs to be as important as training, and the education itself needs to be weighted more in favor of sociopolitical subject matter than is currently the case. ROTC would benefit from more of the Academy attitude about service, and academic rigor in the various NROTC institutions needs to be closely monitored.

Perhaps the "semester abroad" for Academy Midshipmen should be at a State College or University. An "Exchange Program" for a semester between midshipmen at the Academy and in ROTC Colleges might be a good place to start.

Navy "Role Models"

I never complained about the Navy ideal of what an officer should look like. It was nice to have the world think that we all could be in the cast of Top Gun. I introduced Charlton Heston and Glenn Ford, who were playing Naval Officers in a movie, to a Soviet Delegation once and did not bat an eye. It did not hurt any of us to have to work hard to help keep the Navy Top Gun image alive. (And it wowed the fat old Russian officers!)

But the Navy ideal type did some real harm. Physical appearance dominated the Navy's concept of a "Role Model." Once, at the Naval Academy, when we were setting up a leadership event for midshipmen to attend, one of the brightest officers I ever saw was excluded. He was an Academy graduate and was so amazingly talented that he was selected for four stars, but he was excluded because he "was not a good role model." This gentleman weighed about 350 pounds and could not win the weight battle. Another officer in the same weight range was recognized to be extraordinary in every way, including in command. His career ended at a fairly senior place, but he was not accepted as a good role model. There are many such cases that readers probably know. The Navy, in training its officers, should be an institution that has high standards but the flexibility to embrace exceptions that yield nothing in terms of competence, diligence, and honor.

Professor

Teaching is the occupation of scholars. Scholars need to keep up with their fields and need time to stay abreast of their fields through continued study and research, but they are not scholars if they do not teach. Administrators at the Academy teach courses, not as many courses as I would have them teach, but they were teachers. Most were good teachers.

I think administrators should teach at all colleges, and especially at the Military Academies. I wish that far more officers on active duty would be qualified to teach on a first-class faculty and would do so both at the Naval Academy and at NROTC institutions all over the country. Anyway, I taught, and I found it to be the most rewarding thing I did at the Academy. The Midshipmen were wonderful. They were bright and inquisitive. My only criticism is that they gave the "Bull" courses short shrift, a reflection of the general attitude about "Bull" at the Academy.

One of my favorite stories about teaching at the Academy is revealing: I insisted that my students learn some specific facts about the Soviet Union and the reemerging Russia. Most Midshipmen are quite literate and can write good essays about almost anything. Their attitude was that, with a modicum of study, they could do fine on essay tests in the "Bull" courses. They were not entirely wrong. I required a couple of essay answers and several specific identifications of items from readings and lectures on the midterm and final exams.

One of the identification items on the final exam in 1987 was a fairly obscure but rising politician named "Boris Yeltsin." One student obviously did not know who Yeltsin was but otherwise did fairly well on the rest of the exam. He got a B+ on the final and in the course. It was his only "B," and he asked to discuss it. We met, and he complained, "Who cares about Boris Yeltsin?"

Ten years later, when Yeltsin was President of Russia and I was President of a Consortium of Colleges and Universities, I got a phone call from a Lieutenant Commander. He introduced himself: "Captain Kime, this is Lieutenant Commander ---- and I am calling to tell you that I know who Boris Yeltsin is!"

Military faculty

Supplementing the civilian faculty at the Academy are Naval Officers on active duty assignments. The Naval Academy does not, like West Point, provide career pathways for such college faculty in uniform. This works well for the Army and might be a good idea for the Navy in a few cases, the practice of sending seagoing Naval Officers and marines to the Academy strengthens both the fleet and the Academy as long as the officers are qualified to teach. The Naval Academy requires officers assigned to the faculty to spend three years there in order to have time to learn their jobs and also have time to teach enough to make the tour effective.

I was asked if I would accept a marine Captain in one of my Departments, Political Science, for just a two-year tour so he could get on with his career. He had been selected for the Leftwich Leadership Trophy as the outstanding Captain in the Marine Corps and had the first of what would be three Masters degrees. I replied that I would take him for two minutes if that was all I could get. Captain John R. Allen was one of those youngsters that everyone can see would be a flag officer and I had the great pleasure of noting that fact officially. He eventually became a 4-star general and U.S. Commander in Afghanistan. The Naval Academy faculty benefits enormously from the services of such active duty officers. General Allen returned to the Academy as Commandant of Midshipmen.

Political Football

One duty of Division Directors at the Academy is to sit on the Academic Board. This is a difficult, generally negative, function. Midshipmen in serious academic trouble come before the Board. Their entire record is laid out, they are interviewed, and a vote is taken. They either are retained or they pack their bags. The experience, sad as it sometimes was, proved to be enlightening for an educator. I also sat on the Admissions Board and was fully aware of all the considerations involved in bringing these young people into the demanding Academy environment. In a year or so, it was obvious when, in the admissions process, it was time to warn of future failure.

Football players frequented the Academic Board. This was no surprise, but it was a disappointment to me. We set some of these young men up for failure to serve the whims and memories of the alumni. Several times I was reminded that, at Army-Navy games, we faced football players across the line playing for Army whom we had not admitted! We lost every Army-Navy game while I was there. This was serious stuff to the alumni.

I suspect that some athletes were admitted as special cases outside the Admission Board's purview. This, if so, violates the Honor Concept about "doing the right thing." In any case, the formal admissions process was guilty of accepting several candidates a year who simply could not get through the academic program. I knew to a near certainty that some of them, especially young men sent for a year to the Naval Academy Preparatory School, could not pass Plebe Chemistry or Thermodynamics. This meant that, for each questionable admission, a bright young man or woman who did not play a major sport did not get the opportunity to attend the Academy. I still regret this.

I know it is an unpopular view, but I think the Military Service Academies should compete in Division II or III sports. It is not the athlete who might be a candidate to play in professional sports, especially football, who the nation needs to be a Naval Officer. It is true that the Navy benefits from seeking athletic young people who excel at team sports. There are plenty of such candidates who can compete at the Division II or III levels, excel at academics, and be successful midshipmen and Naval Officers.

This is a taxpayer's and a Professor's view, but a view consistent with the Naval Academy's Honor Concept. It is a dedicated Naval officer's view. I question the integrity of a system that admits students who cannot complete its academic program at the expense of a candidate who is a better potential Naval officer.

Lucky Bag

I had some assignments while at the Naval Academy that were out of the ordinary. I seemed to be the officer in charge of the "Lucky Bag," the Navy version of "lost and found," where miscellaneous things often landed.

Chinese Navy

I took the two-semester course on China at Harvard and was intrigued by the history and politics of the place. Sino-Soviet relations were a huge consideration in the study of Russian foreign policy, and the period since the rise of Mao Tse Tung in 1949 was crucial in this relationship. It still is. The best China scholars maintained that Mao's flirtation with Marx was a matter of convenience and that China would find its own way between the prevailing ideologies of the Cold War. Indeed it is doing that, and both Russia and the United States are coping with the result.

In the spring of 1987 there was an exchange of Naval delegations between the U.S. and China. I was selected to be part of the U.S. delegation to China, which was given the Red Carpet treatment. A Chinese plane was provided to travel all over the country. We met with political and senior Chinese military figures and visited Chinese ships. I was reminded of Soviet obsolescence and sorry state of appearance, but the Chinese, both military and civilian, had a more forward-looking and prideful attitude than the Russians. This is manifested more and more as time passes.

In war, I would rather face the Russians than the Chinese. The Chinese are probably more dedicated and more capable warriors. Couple this impression with the new realities in conventional and nuclear warfare that are emerging, and it seems that the "Chinese Threat" in this century is at least as serious as the "Russian Threat" was in the last century.

US Navy Delegation to China, 1987   *Aboard a Chinese Submarine 1987*

author's photos

One thing really impressed me: a civilian escort told me that, years from then, we would see modern Chinese cities that would arise in the next two decades and that fear of Capitalism would not slow their development. He was right. China seems to understand Capitalism in the 21st Century better than Americans do. Their "State Capitalism" might not be strong on human rights and democratic principles, but it might actually work better economically than our stew of Democracy and Social-Capitalism and our "service economy" that has replaced American innovation and individual worker productivity.

Joint Study

In 1987, as part of the military transformation following the Goldwater-Nichols Act, I was selected to participate in a study of the Senior Service Colleges: The Army, Navy, Air Force, and National War Colleges. This was actually about whether these institutions were doing an adequate job of integrating Joint Studies into their curriculums, as well as looking at the their relative academic rigor. This task was dripping with inter-Service rivalry issues and reeked with the Department of Defense's current emphasis, and Congress' insistence, on improving "Joint" cooperation between the military Services.

The House Armed Services Committee Chairman was intent on enforcing better Service cooperation with the Joint Staff. A retired Air Force 4-star officer controlled this study. There was a "No Navy folks need apply" attitude: I was the token Navy representative. The retired Air Force General, a Louisville graduate, ostentatiously ignored me. The

National War College, an alma mater and past home of mine, was "Joint" to the core so it faced no challenge from this study on that score.

In the end, The Naval War College was judged the most rigorous of the War Colleges because the superiority of their rigorous academic program was clear, but the Navy was criticized for lagging behind the other Services in sending promising officers to attend the other War Colleges, a conclusion probably written before the "study." Joint education and more attention to sending promising officers to joint duty were emphasized. It is now required for officers to get their "ticket punched" with Joint Duty or their careers will be truncated.

The Naval Institute

During my tenure at the Academy, in my spare time, I was active at the United States Naval Institute. The Institute, established in 1873 to discuss military history and strategy, is situated at the U.S. Naval Academy. It is a private, non-profit forum that publishes its own journal and many books on maritime-related matters.

I was elected by the membership, then about 100,000 active and retired Naval Officers, to serve on the Institute's Board of Directors. The Chairman of the Board was Carl A.H. Trost, whom I had known since my early Moscow days and who was then Chief of Naval Operations. My final tour at the Academy and my opportunity to serve on the Institute Board was partly due to Trost's influence, I am sure.

While serving as an elected Director at the US Naval Institute, there were many opportunities to participate in our evolving Naval history. For instance, we initiated the Naval History Magazine. I was also on the Editorial Board of the U.S. Naval Institute's monthly journal, Proceedings. I read every draft article submitted to the journal. This was a lot of work, but one of the most informative and educational duties that I have ever performed. In Proceedings, we published many articles of note. Among these were pieces by an up-and-coming Naval Commander, James Stavridis, who later became the Commander of Supreme Headquarters, Allied Powers in Europe (SHAPE). Captain Bill Manthorpe, my fellow Assistant Attaché from my Moscow days, also had several perceptive articles in <u>Proceedings</u> that analyzed the capabilities of the Soviet Navy.

The many books published by the Institute include such popular bestsellers as Tom Clancy's first book, <u>The Hunt for Red October</u>. We had to grapple with the issues of managing the success of that blockbuster. While I was there, the Institute published the bestseller <u>Flight of the Intruder</u>, by Stephen Coonts.

Since my days at the Naval Institute, things have changed. The technical revolution in communications has altered the place of the print industry. Newspapers are on the way out altogether, and the jury is out on journals and magazines. The younger generations are not inclined to join and to communicate the way that past Naval Institute members were. Membership dropped off. The USNI <u>Proceedings</u> has been flexible and creative in this changing environment. They have opened up membership and participation to an increasingly aware and communicative enlisted force. Governance and Editorial Boards reflect new constituencies.

The future of the Institute will be a challenge. There was some temptation to resort to a corporate model and an advocacy role, which would have diminished the quality of the publications. This was vigorously resisted by the membership. At this writing, all is well. The Institute is changing into a 21st Century outfit that I am proud to say still publishes an occasional piece by this author.

Alumni

My position at the Naval Academy had responsibility for alumni affairs. One Superintendent, aware of the odd situation where the only Division Director without The Ring had this responsibility, and maybe a little concerned about it, tried to talk me out of it. I felt his pain but insisted on discharging my duty. It was part of my determination to learn as much as possible about the Naval Academy and its graduates.

One of the events at the academy every year was the 50th anniversary of an Academy Class. One of the first and most delightful phone calls was from a Class officer planning its 50th anniversary. Incredibly, it was my old NROTC skipper, Captain Vincent Schumacher, the officer who had sent me to Submarine School a quarter of a century earlier! He had been convinced that the Navy needed officers from the civilian academic world and was beside himself with joy that one of "his" officers was a senior Captain at his *alma mater*. I made certain that every Class got the respect and attention that it deserved, but his Class got my very best effort. He rubbed it in a little, telling the Superintendent that the performance of that NROTC guy was stupendous. The Alumni Association, a very influential player in Annapolis society, treated me as if I were a member.

The Naval Academy is the home of "The World's Largest Cocktail Party." This is an annual gathering of Academy graduates in September after Plebe Summer is over and the academic year has begun. Cocktails are followed by a dinner in the mess hall, where 4,000 men and women take three meals a day. It was my responsibility to make this happen.

It was an amazing event. We had over 3,200 graduates present representing every class since the Class of 1918. Ninety-year-old graduates and their wives had witnessed over 40% of the nation's Naval history. I had ambulances standing by, and used two of them.

In addition to the 50th anniversary Class that had a major reunion, several other Classes had events. Winners of Congressional Medals of Honor, Navy Crosses and Silver Stars ate and drank together in Maury Hall. Rarely do so much brainpower and intestinal fortitude gather in one place. They ate like plebes, swapped lies, and harassed one another for old times. I am the only officer to have had this responsibility who does not have a Ring, but I felt like a member of that very special family one September evening each year.

Letting Go the Anchor

In 1989, it was time for me to go. I had contributed everything I could to the Naval Academy. Though, as my comments above reveal, I take exception to some aspects of the education at the Academy and with the uneven playing field for Academy and non-Academy graduates, I have tremendous respect for the institution. I hope it lasts forever: I would mend it, not end it.

At the retirement of senior officers at the Naval Academy it was customary to have a parade of midshipmen. This did not seem appropriate in my case. I had not been the kind of career officer that the Navy would want those midshipmen to emulate so why should they waste their time parading for me? I would much rather that they had one more hour to study English or History! I declined a parade and all other retirement events. We loaded up a rental truck with all the stuff the Navy would not move and headed for Clifton. My uniforms, like Harry Truman's suitcases, were carried up to the attic.

The Navy sent me a Legion of Merit in the mail.

Chapter XVIII
Servicemembers Opportunity Colleges

As it turned out, Navy retirement was neither retirement nor entirely leaving military service. It was more like changing uniforms and duty stations. My uniform would be "purple:" I would work for service members who wear all the nation's military uniforms.

I had sought a senior job, president or dean, on a civilian academic campus. I was interviewed for quite a few. Some faculty members on search committees were impressed with my academic credentials but had a morbid fear that a retired military man might start calling cadence at faculty meetings. I should have marched for them. Other colleges clearly valued and highly respected military experience and offered positions. In the end an opportunity presented itself that could not be resisted.

In 1989, The American Association of State Colleges and Universities, acting on behalf of a Board representing DoD, the Military Services, and the major higher education associations, appointed me President of Servicemembers Opportunity Colleges, or SOC. This vindicated my gamble not to compete for promotion in uniform but to hold out for an opportunity in higher education. No admiral's position that I could hope for would have been better for me. Now it was my duty to see that it was better for the nation's military.

New Uniform, and new President, Servicemembers Opportunity Colleges in 1989
Author's photo

SOC is a consortium of colleges and universities dedicated to the education of the nation's servicemembers and veterans. This consortium operates in the higher education community and answers to a Board of presidents and representatives from national higher education associations and the Military Services. Over 1900 colleges and universities agreed to abide by a set of principles aimed at facilitating the civilian education of servicemembers while they serve on active duty.

Every year thousands of servicemembers complete Associate and Bachelor degrees at civilian institutions that are affiliated with SOC. The Department of Defense funds SOC, which functions administratively as part of The American Association of State Colleges and Universities, where I became a Vice President.

This unique partnership between the civilian and military world was created in 1972 when, because of the unpopularity of the Vietnam War, there were poor civil-military relations in America. Servicemembers and veterans were having a difficult time on campuses and some leaders in both higher education and the Department of Defense created SOC. This is a unique organization, situated between the Department of Defense and higher education, with responsibility to express and serve the needs of both of them. It was an honor to have had the opportunity to lead SOC and to pay back the military, as a civilian educator, for the educational opportunity that I enjoyed while serving in a Navy uniform.

A tremendous upside of this position was that the family could return to the retirement home in Clifton, Virginia that we had bought three years earlier. Wilma's horse, Pepper, would return to her barn, and soon we would have three horses there. It was a 27-mile commute to the center of Washington where SOC was housed, but it was a great compromise between city work and country living. We are here in Clifton as I write. Pepper is at peace in the front field.

I arrived at Servicemembers Opportunity Colleges at an interesting time. The Director who I replaced had done a terrific job of creating and assembling a system for integrating the curriculums of colleges that offered degree programs to military men and women at military locations around the world. This was a difficult task that required participating colleges to accept the credit of other colleges and to limit their residence requirements. As his tenure came to an end, it was time to further broaden the role of SOC in the partnership between the Department of Defense and higher education.

SOC was ahead of its time. The requirement that colleges and universities compromise on the amount of residency needed for a degree was too demanding for many institutions. Demanding acceptance of credit for learning in the military workplace was revolutionary. The requirement to interchange courses on an equal basis in advance was quite a leading edge concept when SOC introduced it.

My two predecessors, Dr. Arden Pratt and Dr. James F. Nickerson, deserve the credit for these ideas. I took on the challenge of building on their creativity. The degree networks started in the Army would grow and change to fit the needs of all the Services, eventually to include the Coast Guard. Eventually, the challenges of Distance Education, to include courses delivered by Internet, would be integrated. As the National Guard and Reserve Components became more thoroughly integrated in the deployments of the All-Volunteer Force, SOC added programs to help with the education of those servicemembers.

We set about reinvigorating the partnership between higher education and the Department of Defense. The Services and the Department of Defense were engaged at every opportunity at the policy level. My contacts from The National War College often came into play, since I knew many of the 3-star and 4-star officers.

SOC became more visible. We published articles on the higher education issues involved in the education of active duty service members and veterans. I made my arguments in Army Times, Air Force Times and Navy Times that military enlisted men and women had to be *educated as well as trained* in order to perform in modern combat situations. Numerous higher education publications published our arguments on behalf of military people and their families. Dr. Clinton Anderson and I published a book on the 30-year history of SOC. We published Issue Papers that were sent to decision makers.

There was a SOC representative at every meeting that we learned about. I lectured, pulling no punches in representing both the requirements of higher education and the needs of the Military Services, at state and regional Military Education Councils. I travelled and lectured in almost every state and at military bases everywhere. It was not long before SOC was recognized as a strong national voice for the education of service members and veterans.

A Luddite Reformed

The first thing I saw in my office when I reported aboard at SOC was a computer and printer on my desk. I told the lady showing me around to "get them out of here." Andrea Baridon, a plucky and bright lady who had been at SOC for a decade, knew better. She suggested that she get rid of the printer and leave the computer, an imposing big Macintosh "for a while until she could move it." She hinted that I might not be able to do without it, and handed me a thick instruction manual on Microsoft Word. She turned the computer on for me. She knew what she was doing, and what I needed to do. I did not want the SOC Staff to see me as a grouch, especially Andie, who was obviously the spark plug in the place.

I also did not want to look stupid. I took the book home, read it, and understood some of it. The next few weeks were a tutorial. I figured a lot of it out, but the staff answered a thousand questions. When I was able to use Word, Andie gave me the Excel book. This was before e-mail and the Internet, but SOC's Degree Networks were automated, and publications crucial to SOC publicity and communications were developed on the Mac. It was a tool that I did not have to master, but I had to be able to work with it. SOC would produce hundreds of brochures, posters, manuals, and books by computer.

To my amazement, it was almost fun. I discovered that the systems approach that every submariner has internalized is exactly what the Macintosh computerizes. It was painfully, mercilessly, logical. I liked it.

SOC is a computer savvy place. Everyone at introductory pay level is a Program Assistant. Program Managers and Project Directors do their own correspondence. Everyone has a Mac and a job to do with it. SOC keeps up to date with computers and software. This, I realize, sounds pretty obvious and routine today, but it was a whole new world to me and to a lot of managers of that time. By the way, Andrea Baridon was the Associate Director of SOC when I retired.

Key West

At SOC, we had a bright committed staff with a terrific sense of humor. Like with the crew in a submarine, you could count on such people to do their jobs and have some fun at it. It was a delight to manage a place where meetings were not necessary because, like good military people everywhere, the staff was on top of all the issues. There are a hundred stories from my time at Servicemembers Opportunity Colleges with these imaginative and fun-loving people, too many to relate here. A typical story is about a conference in Key West.

My deputy, Dr. Clinton "Andy" Anderson, was, like me, one of the elders in the military education community. The two of us often travelled together and we were close friends. On one occasion, our twosome of old guys arrived at one of the capitals of the gay community and needed to rent a car. We were told that the modest vehicle we had reserved was unavailable. Of course, a flashy, huge 4-door Oldsmobile with all the trimmings was available at the same price. We took it.

Key West is really a small town with one main drag where local couples parade their stuff. All the hundred or so attendees at the conference, including those who manage the funds allocated to SOC for such things, were walking up and down the main drag visiting the colorful shops and restaurants there. We had no idea how it looked, so Andy and I drove down the main drag two or three times looking for parking. It was a sensation. Only when we saw folks pointing and giggling did it occur to us that we looked like two old Queens.

This was too good not to exploit. Dr. Barry Cobb was Director of DANTES, the DoD entity that supervised our funding. He and I were good friends. Andy was super sensitive to criticism. I talked Dr Cobb into backing Andy into a corner and asking him what the hell he was doing parading up and down the main drag in that massive rental car. He reported that Andy was so embarrassed that he kept up the charade for quite some time.

Battles to Educate Military Men and Women

There is a fundamental struggle that is always present in the development of the men and women who enlist in the nation's Military Services. There are those responsible for training service members to accomplish their military missions, and there are those who are trying to help those service members, on their own time, get the same high-quality education that their civilian counterparts can obtain. Military training and civilian education, though they overlap, are really two different things.

Submariners are trainers first, and I was and am a trainer. All officers are. I was always quick to say that military training should and must come first. America does not maintain military forces as an extracurricular activity. The priority is clear.

The question is: can we carve out time and provide resources that enable servicemembers to better themselves, making them more effective soldiers, sailors, and marines? And can we do this without subordinating or limiting their education to the vocational orientation of their military career? These may seem like straightforward questions with easy answers, but they are fraught with controversy. Funding is always lacking. Ideologies are not.

Most military officers I know put training first, but they are also strong proponents of education for enlisted men and women. If enlisted men and women can earn Associate Degrees with solid general education included, they will be much better equipped to handle the politico-military situations on the modern battlefield where even junior military men and women must deal with complex situations. Better yet, if they can achieve a Baccalaureate Degree, they are much better able to handle the responsibilities of senior enlisted positions, and some can become officers.

Unfortunately, budget-oriented bean counters and some narrow-minded officers do not think this way. I saw cases where very senior officers attempted to restrict off-duty education to the vocational subjects of a servicemember's training. The little-picture perspective of some senior officers never ceases to amaze, but it is not surprising. Remember that a majority of them were raised to think that general education is "Bull." The number one reason enlisted volunteers join the military is for educational opportunity that can lift them up in their stations in life, but it is constantly necessary to fend off decisionmakers who would limit that opportunity.

Attempts to restrict enlisted men and women to vocational studies have been focused on the Associate Degree level. The surest way to keep blue-collar people in their "place" is to ensure that they have little opportunity to advance beyond the Associate Degree. If resources are concentrated to vector enlisted people into vocational, terminal Associate Degree programs, enlisted personnel are manipulated to extend their active duty commitment but are limited in their educational horizons. Some decisionmakers suffer the illusion that limited horizons will encourage more, and better, sailors to reinlist! The funding that is provided by Congress for voluntary education of a servicemember, on his own time and of his own choice, is not intended to be limited in this way.

The Air Force actually institutionalized the concept of limiting education to vocational areas with limited general education. Legislation that permitted creation of a "Community College of the Air Force (CCAF)" was hidden in a larger bill and did not get the scrutiny of those responsible for education. CCAF enabled the military, not civilian higher education, to issue degrees for so-called "academic credit" judged not by college teachers but by vocational military personnel.

Though supplemented by a limited number of civilian courses, CCAF ensured very little interaction with civilian students and professors. It was a terminal degree, not totally accepted into baccalaureate studies. Periodically, some ambitious trainers in the Army and Navy would explore imposing this concept on their enlisted personnel, and the CCAF itself has tried to expand its power to other Services, usually by hiding the concept in other legislation.

Military–issued associate degrees are divorced from the policies and practices that are the province of the civil sector in America. In my view, they are worthless as educational credentials and are the opposite of what the country needs. What the country needs are military people *trained* by military professionals and *educated* by policies and practices determined in civil society. Civil society reigns supreme in America.

The criticism above does not apply to graduate military degree programs which are aimed at specialized higher education and which are at least equal to what civilian institutions provide in quality.

The baccalaureate and graduate programs of the military, like those at the Academies, are very carefully kept in tune with the policies and practices of civilian higher education. They are accredited by solid regional accreditors. Standards in American higher education have been maintained for many years by a system of regional accreditation associations. For example, the Southern Association of Colleges and Schools accredits institutions in 11 states in the Southern part of the country. In terms of academic credibility and quality, accreditation by a regional accrediting agency has been the gold standard in America. A solid indicator of this is that every baccalaureate degree that is required as a minimum academic qualification for commissioning an officer in the U.S. military is a regionally accredited degree. Why should a degree conferred upon an enlisted person be anything less?

There has been an ongoing battle in America for years over accreditation. There are those who would substitute other accrediting regimes for the longstanding regional accrediting organizations. Many proprietary institutions, where the monetary bottom line trumps any academic one, would set up their separate "accreditation" systems and insist that the Federal Government recognize those systems as equal to the accreditation systems long used by academic institutions.

Distance education, based on courses delivered by technology and devices separate from classrooms and the presence of other students, complicates the accreditation picture. Some courses and programs are good and some are not. Some types of accreditation will not take a student to a higher academic level. Some are restricted to lower vocational levels. Some courses will transfer to other colleges and some will not. SOC works on these problems

Large amounts of money are involved in the voluntary education of service members. There are charlatans who would take the tuition assistance money provided to service member and provide no, or practically no, real education. There are fine institutions that are just the opposite. It requires a strong partnership between higher education, the Department of Defense, and the Military Services to sort this out. SOC is that partnership.

On the Record: Educating Active Duty Men & Women

Arguments for educating military enlisted members appeared in many places. Those arguments are even more salient today. The best summary appeared in the Naval Institute <u>Proceedings</u> in August 2004:

> War, some say, is too important to be left to the generals. This is debatable: great Secretaries of State have been generals and DoD has been well run by politicians. But the thinking behind this notion is worth contemplation. What is the relationship of broader, critical thought to the military mission at all levels of combat? How important is education when the

socio-political elements of the use of force are growing and sometimes overshadow the military elements?

At the executive level the U.S. military establishment has not ignored this question. A strong educational system of undergraduate education, Service War Colleges, postgraduate opportunity, and joint duty works fairly well, and DoD has at least as respectable a record as that of the Department of State of posting capable, politically astute people to sensitive posts.

Modern war is becoming too complex to be left to corporals or sailors as we have trained them in the past. We do not think much about the working levels of our military when it comes to the social and political elements of military presence and the use of force. This in spite of the fact that most of the socio-political interface with potentially hostile populations these days is at lower levels. Our history, our military traditions, and the necessity to train more intensely for the modern battlefield all militate against putting time and resources into broader education for our enlisted people.

But we must. No longer can the sailor be regarded as a working class person who is "sly and cunning and to be watched at all times." Neither is the soldier or marine an automaton to be trained not to question orders rather than educated to be a critically-thinking, armed, ambassador who must act correctly on a small piece of a complex socio-political battlefield. The thinking cannot be left to superiors who get the education and wear the brass. This is a technological and a social reality.

It is useful to remember that the military is one of many employers in our society. It is a huge and unique employer, but in many ways the military is subject to the trends and forces that buffet other employers. One of these trends is the growing importance of education in the workplace. To recruit, grow, and retain modern workers, especially those who would become leaders, corporate executives are learning that technical and social realities in the civilian world require education

well beyond the training that they have always
understood and accepted as a cost of doing business.
The military corporation is in the same boat.

Today, voluntary educational opportunities for
military enlisted personnel are greater and tuition
assistance is more accessible than ever before. Tens of
thousands of service members are going to school. What
then, is the problem?

The positive environment for voluntary
postsecondary education is more a result of recruiting
and retention calculations than of an understanding
that we need a professional enlisted force whose
leadership elements are both educated and trained. Such
an understanding - a vision for enlisted education - is
needed to avoid allowing voluntary education to become
merely another "people program" instead of a crucial
part of the personal and professional development of our
military workforce. A comprehensive vision of enlisted
education would also prevent education programs and
dollars from becoming just more resources for military
trainers, certain death for development of critical
thinking capacities.

For example, we must avoid the tendency to channel
service members into degree programs linked to their
military occupational specialties. True, for some. these
vocational programs are appropriate and probably often
contain as much broadening education as some service
members want or are capable of completing. Vocational
options should certainly be maintained. They must not
become, connected as they are to occupational training
at Service Schools, mere extensions of training. The
price of encouraging this is high. Minimal broadening
and mind-stretching coursework is taken. Pursuit of
higher levels of education and conceptual development
can be stifled.

Technology harbors some serious traps for both
civilian and military higher education. American
higher education, after a going through a "next

big thing" phase, is coming to realize the limits of distance education. It is not a panacea. Certainly some work can be done on the internet, for example, but there are serious concerns that important aspects of the educational process are getting short shrift. At a minimum, it is obvious that such study is not for everyone and that highly capable students can get more out of it than can average or less academically oriented students. Our service member students are terrific, dedicated adult students, but they must not be automatically assumed to be prime candidates for independent study on the web. The military is quick to seize on what they are told is newer, faster, better and cheaper, and we easily fall into the trap that the allure of web-based coursework represents.

It is an error to channel our students into educational options, technology-driven ones or vocational ones, that do not fulfill the promise of real educational opportunity that many joined up for. It is also bad business for the military corporation.

If we want to compete with civil society for capable youth and with industry for a competent modern workforce, we must maintain educational options for our enlisted service members that are as rich and varied as those of their civilian counterparts One of the difficulties in doing this is that the military likes things neat and higher education is a diverse, messy operation. Military voluntary educational programs must resist the temptation to over organize, direct and supervise. For real education to take place, a student must have choices, make sacrifices and do some hard work. For many, this will require the inconvenience of the classroom, and for others technical modes of delivery will work, but for most it will be a blend of various colleges and different modes of educational delivery that will serve them best. This requires patient management and does not lend itself to quick fixes. And spoon feeding, a trainer's habit, will not work with serious education.

It was encouraging to hear that CNO Vern Clark at the 4th Annual Navy Workforce Research and Analysis Conference on March 29, 2004 said "When I dream about the future, my dream is of a Navy where all the Chief Petty Officers have college degrees."

Educating Veterans

This country has a checkered history on the education of veterans. The good news is that, after a long fight for veterans, we finally got it right.

I was honored to serve on the Veterans Advisory Committee on Education (VACOE), a Congressionally-mandated Committee appointed by the White House. I was appointed a member, then Chair of VACOE, for several years. At that time VACOE, which had senior representation from all the powerful, well-known veterans' organizations, was very influential. Periodic reports on the status of veterans' education, which was in terrible shape, were shared with these constituencies, Congress, and the presidents of all the higher education associations.

Veterans were denied a decent GI Bill in the aftermath of the Vietnam debacle. They were punished by an ungrateful nation with a weak GI Bill that did not enable very many to go to college. It fell far short of the cost of a reasonably inexpensive education at a public college or university. Veterans, older and often with family responsibilities not shared by traditional students, could not actually use the GI Bill. They had joined the Services and had even sacrificed a large part of their first year's pay so they could have an effective GI Bill. The country reneged on the promise. It was a national scandal.

As soon as I was appointed to VACOE, I did a quick study of the number of veterans that actually used the Montgomery GI Bill and the number that had paid the $1200 fee to become eligible to receive it. I was astounded to discover that blue-collar youngsters who had enlisted primarily to get an education but could not use the GI Bill had paid more money **into** the fund than those who could actually use the Bill had taken **out**! In the early 1990s the country had not only reneged on its GI Bill promise to veterans, it was making money on it.

The VACOE took this mess on. It was delicate, because the Department of Defense, which funded SOC, had long resisted increasing the GI Bill. There was serious work to do to convince Defense proponents that the GI Bill could be improved without causing military men and women to leave the Services. The Department of Defense, without a shred of evidence other than a "study" it had bought and paid for, continued to assert that the nation could not provide a viable GI Bill without badly damaging military recruiting. Congress, especially the Senate Armed Forces Committee, uncritically accepted this nonsense.

From my point of view, this meant making two points. First, America had to keep its promise and fund an education at least at the level of a four-year education at a public college or university. Second, the Department of Defense had to come to grips with the reality that it was up to the Department of Defense and the Military Services to make staying in the military more attractive than leaving it!

At one point, Congressmen meeting with VACOE said flatly that, since there was no public outcry, nothing much was going to be done. VACOE, joined by superb veteran advocates from the VFW and other national veteran organizations with chapters in every Congressional District, formed an organization called the Partnership for Veterans Education. All the major national higher education associations joined this Partnership. Letters signed by influential educators and veteran advocates in the nation began to land on the desks of legislators.

As Chairman of The Veterans' Advisory Committee on Education, there were several opportunities for me to testify before Congress and have a direct impact on the arguments over the GI Bill. The Partnership for Veterans' Education added weight to this testimony.

It did not happen all at once, but we did manage to make it increasingly possible for veterans actually to go to college. Several incremental improvements were passed. Finally, after the wars in Iraq and Afghanistan produced a new generation of combat veterans and the deficiencies in the GI Bill became too visible to ignore, VACOE efforts got serious attention. The attitude on the Hill changed. Senator Jim

Webb tapped this new attitude and was not bashful in demanding a GI Bill that was more generous than most of us thought possible. It passed.

We had made enormous progress, but more needed to be done to repair the damage done to veteran education in the past. After the passage of a new GI Bill, scholars met to discuss ways to take advantage of the new opportunities to improve the education of veterans. I was asked to give the concluding address, and it was summarized in: **Improving College Education of Veterans**, Edited by C. Hopkins, D. Herrmann, R. B. Wilson, B. Allen and L. Malley. Published by Create Space, Charleston, S. C. July, 2010, Chapter 25, Endnote Address.

A veteran can today go to college on the GI Bill, something not possible a decade and one-half ago. Colleges and universities now maintain Memoranda of Understanding that lay out responsible policies for managing veteran education funded by the GI Bill.

My job as advocate for a viable GI Bill was done. I resigned the Chairmanship of VACOE as the new GI Bill got on track.

Russia Redux

In 1995, as president of a consortium of colleges and universities, I was invited to lecture at an education conference in Moscow, along with Servicemembers Opportunity Colleges Associate Director, Dr. Clinton Anderson. This was a chance to see the results of the decline that started when I was the U.S. Naval Attaché a decade earlier.

We stayed not far from the apartment house my family lived in on my first tour in Russia 23 years earlier. I took the venerable *Krasnaya Strela* (Red Arrow) train to Leningrad, now properly called St. Petersburg. Once again, I visited the peasant markets, rode the subways, and talked to common folk on the streets.

It was a time to reflect on the remarkable decline of the intercontinental nuclear superpower that the USSR had so recently been. Everyone knew that the Soviet Union was very ill, but the precipitous death of Soviet Communism surprised practically every foreign analyst. This is not a source of pride to so-called Kremlinologists, but it is the truth.

Those who say differently are as guilty of historical revisionism as the Communists were!

I thought that there would be a prolonged and dangerous Soviet decline followed by an attempt at radical reform that would extend farther and faster than the reforms suggested in the early Khrushchev era and by Premier Alexei Kosygin in 1965. Such reforms would probably fail, and there would be a conservative reaction to them and some turmoil. I did not think the entire Soviet System would fail so quickly and disintegrate into its constituent republics.

Death did not become the USSR. All the promises of the ruined system came apart. Pensions, inadequate at best, were not paid. Public school teachers, and other non-ideological servants of generations of Russians, went hungry. They had no Party position from which to divvy up the spoils of State Communism. A Marxist caricature of Capitalism had been allowed to run amok. The worst Soviet images of Capitalistic monsters appeared out of Soviet rubble. It was a self-fulfilling nightmare. Beggars lined the streets.

The Russian Orthodox religion was rejected by Communist ideology as the "opiate of the masses," but the Church survived the Communists. Communist Party leaders had been hypocrites all along: many were from religious families and some had Orthodox funerals. It was like much of the Soviet world where appearance trumped reality. In the end, the Communist Party succeeded only in adding a new opiate, alcohol, the only thing that the Soviets did not dare to try to control. Now, the Church was free and a national addiction to alcohol remained.

The Russian military after the fall of the Soviet Union was shown for what it really was: a massive, awkward, hulking Gulliver. It was more quantity than quality, much like the Eurasian landmass where it dwelt. Russians absorbed the French Army in the 19th Century and the German one in the 20th with sheer space and bulk. That was not enough when faced with 21st Century technology. The Soviet Navy, a limited extension of intercontinental nuclear capabilities, soon faded back into obscurity.

Nuclear weapons were also bigger than they were better, but they were real and really dangerous in the hands of a dying Party and now a struggling nation. The nuclear genie cannot be returned to its lamp, so it must be managed. It remains a threat to America, whether in Russian hands or spread elsewhere. The SALT Agreement was renewed in 2011. We need to follow up with rigorous inspection and monitoring.

Analysts used to say that Russians longed for the Tsars of their feudal past. This was often said to explain the Russian love of their tormentor, Stalin. I did not ever fully accept this, but it has some truth in it. Russians seek freedom like all human beings do, but they respond to strong national leadership. "National" is the key word. Russians have a high tolerance for corruption but a low tolerance for disarray and incompetence of leadership.

After the 1995 visit, I concluded that *there were Russian "Times of Troubles" ahead. Part of the trouble will be a conservative Russian nationalist reaction that suggests the rise of a strongman more than the rise of democratic institutions.*

This conclusion was easy for a longtime observer, and the prediction came true. It is just as clear that the situation at this writing in the second decade of the 21st Century in Russia, with its Caricature Capitalism and crony government, cannot be sustained in the Russia that I know.

Wake-up Call

In 2003, I got cancer for Christmas. I was scheduled for a physical examination in January of 2004, but Wilma was due for a mammogram in the fall of 2003. I went with her in November so we could make just one trip. It saved my life. The doctor administered the dreaded finger wave and was concerned about the prostate. Not an expert on such things, he insisted that I see a colleague upstairs at Bethesda National Naval Hospital (Now called Walter Reed). I was there in minutes and this doctor wanted to take biopsy samples. Bad news came back quickly. The urologist, a diminutive lady with fearful responsibility, was very concerned and was not enthusiastic about the longer-term approaches to my cancer. This was not the slower, old man's prostate cancer that is amenable to such treatments.

An operating room was made available at the first opportunity. This was a blessing. There was very little time to fret about it, and there really was no decision to make. They removed everything that was suspect or liable to be affected. I woke up and began the months of Hell that recovery involves. Tubes dangled from uncomfortable places, and the check-ups were as bad as the surgery, but I had been lucky. The entire organ was full of cancer. I would have been dead if I had waited three months for the physical. Instead I was, unsteadily, back at work in a few weeks.

The lesson from this ordeal is obvious. Men should not mess around with prostate cancer any more than women should ignore the prospect of breast cancer. Many men do this. I tell every adult male I know to heed my story.

Time Is Up

My brush with mortality reminded me, once again, that there is a time for all things. It was time for me to end my tenure at Servicemembers Opportunity Colleges. I had done all I could do to advance the educational opportunity for service members. The staff at SOC was very strong and had been well prepared to continue without me. The truth is, they might even do better without me!

I had done the things I saw that were needed when I arrived. I was a strong supporter of traditional approaches to education that were carefully supplemented by the radical new concepts of SOC. Those concepts had become less radical and more accepted during my tenure. The International Adult and Continuing Education Hall of Fame inducted me for efforts at Servicemembers Opportunity Colleges.

Another special honor was the President's Medal from the University of Maryland University College, a flagship institution among those that educate service members. It was awarded at graduation ceremonies in Heidelberg.

By 2005, when I departed, higher education was changing faster than I was! The integration of new communications technology into the modes of "delivery" of education, something that I encouraged only with reservations, was moving too fast to suit me. There were big savings to be had in reducing, or eliminating, the classroom. Budgeters wanted to save, and entrepreneurs always want to increase profits. I still do not believe that a complete education can be had sitting alone with a computer. Perhaps some of the requirements can effectively be fulfilled in that way, but very important parts of the personal growth that comes with education happen only in the company of others, in the flesh, with different backgrounds and competing ideas. Only in very rare cases is solitary exposure to information adequate for an education, in my humble view.

As with most things, I believe that change must come but at the least possible cost to the things that should be preserved. It was time for a new approach and new energy to be applied to obtaining the best possible education for service members in the changing context. SOC's mechanisms were effective, its reputation and influence was strong, and its prospects for making huge contributions in the future were bright. It needed new leadership.

When I left SOC, the American Association of State Colleges and Universities, on behalf of all the national higher education associations, gave me the Nickerson Medal of Merit for contributions to the education of military men and women and veterans. The Department of Defense gave me its highest civilian award, the Defense Civilian Distinguished Service Award.

We went home to Clifton.

Kimes' Cove in Clifton Virginia

author's photo

Chapter XIX
After the Journey
Russia, Geopolitics, and War

This Officer's Story has journeyed from a Hoosier boyhood to Submarine duty, then to Harvard, Russia, National Intelligence and the National War College and back to Russia. After that was The Naval Academy and a career in higher education, military and veteran affairs. It is inevitable after observing the world from these quite different vantage points that reflections on political and military matters remain.

Some judgments after a long journey are not very important, or they are likely to be quickly overcome by the march of time and change. These would serve little purpose here. What might be useful are assessments, based on decades of observation and analysis, on:

- Russia in the 21st Century
- Changing geopolitical reality: America in A New Geostrategic Age
- The changing military environment: A Second Nuclear Age
- An American Military Doctrine for the 21st Century

1.) **Russia in the 21st Century**

> *"Russians have more words for 'bribe'*
> *than Eskimos have for 'snow'."*
> Peter Pomerantsev

The prognosis for Russia is only fair. She will not die but she will be the Sick Man of Europe for a long time. Ironically, the phrase "Sick Man of Europe" is usually attributed to a Russian Tsar, Nicholas I (1796 -1855) who was talking of the Ottoman Empire. Nicholas' reactionary reign began with a revolt, was marked by corruption, grappled with dissent, and ended in defeat in the Crimean War. History would have confirmed a sad prognosis for Russia when he died.

In the 21ˢᵗ Century we see a Russia still struggling with a corrupt
and debilitating recent past. When the Bolsheviks took over in 1917,
Russia was not on its way to the modernization enjoyed by Western
civilizations. Seven decades of Bolshevism kept Mother Russia barefoot,
pregnant, and isolated. She stagnated in comparison with an outside
world that was roaring ahead.

At this writing Russia is a quarter of a century removed from the
Communist scourge. A serious revolution has occurred, but Russia is no
better off. A strange concoction of Tsarism and Cartoon Capitalism has
emerged. A new Russian Time of Troubles has set in.

The old Russian Time of Troubles (1598-1613) was between the end of
the Tsars of the Rurik Dynasty and the rise of the Romanov Dynasty.
Russia was in a mess with false rulers, war, and economic disasters.
Russia rallied around a strong ruling Dynasty. The Romanov Dynasty
lasted for three centuries and provided some colorful history, but it did
little to advance Slavic Culture or Russian development.

Enter Lenin, Stalin and the Bolsheviks. The truth is that these
opportunists did not care about Russia at all. Their idea was to spark
a world Socialist Revolution by starting in a prostrate, hopeless place
where everything was ripe to fall apart. Serious historians, who read all
their stuff and chronicled all their moves, would object to this shorthand
and point out that it was all a bit more complicated, but this is the
essence of the matter.

Lenin & Co. were disappointed that the REAL Revolution never got off
the ground and they argued interminably about why and how to proceed
to get the pesky Germans and others in the West to get on with it. The
bottom line: Bolshevik intellectuals thought Russia was a necessary,
painful backwater. However, Stalin, a thug and not an intellectual, was
plenty happy to make Russia a place for "Socialism in One Country," as
he put forth in 1924, the year Lenin died.

All this from a century ago is important because it explains that Russia,
to put it bluntly, was ruled by political gangsters who did not care about
Russian Culture nearly as much as they cared about the development of
Socialism and Communism for the world. To be sure, they *based* their

international revolutionary hopes on a strong Russian nationalism and the consolidation of Russian power more and more as time passed, but the fact is that the Communist enterprise only lasted seven decades. It left the place in a mess.

A love for Mother Russia and a long history of acquiescence to the power of the Tsar remained after the Soviet Union fell of its own weight. These persist in the 21st Century, and are about all that ordinary Russians have.

Russia in this century is not especially gifted. Though it should be able to feed itself, since it used to, that is not always easy. Analysts have remarked that to grow crops you need moderate temperature, water, and fertile soil. Russia has all these, but not in one place. We who study Russians love them, but they are not Germans (maybe that is why we love them.) The harsh truth is that Russians are not going to build a Mercedes Benz. They built missiles and nuclear submarines by scraping all the cream off the top of the economy and they could not sustain that.

They did best at extracting and selling natural resources, which is what Third World countries, not superpowers, do. Remember that the most ardent world revolutionaries did not dream for a second that global Communism would or could be led by Russians. Even Mao Tse Tung, a supplicant, but from an ancient culture, could not bring himself to defer to Stalin when they met in 1949. Stalin had the arrogance to leave Mao waiting outside his office! What Russian would treat the Chinese like that in the 21st Century? China is growing while Russia wallows in a pathetic nationalist revival sans economic progress.

Maybe this somber assessment of Russian prospects will change later in the century. Things do change and the pace of change can be fast. But there are no signs of this at all. New technology is absorbed in Russia a bit faster nowadays, but it is not created there. Political reform might be simmering here and there, but there does not seem to be any universal desire for "democracy" or whatever it is that we have in the West.

There are demands on Russian leadership that are not fully understood by Western politicians. Even Tsars are not totally free to act. The price of staying on top in a place like Russia, as the Communist Party found out in the 1970s and 1980s, is that you cannot fail to satisfy the love and pride in Mother Russia.

She is poor and bedraggled, but She is a demanding Mistress.

A current (2015) example is instructive. In 2014, Crimea -- a region which was part of Russia up until 1954, and is still heavily populated by ethnic Russians -- voted to return to the Russian Federation. As of this writing, in 2015, the eastern Ukrainian city of Donetsk appears to be quickly following suit. Vladimir Putin has had little choice but to support ethnic Russians who would break away from Ukraine. It is not an exaggeration to say that his legitimacy is at stake on the issue.

All Russians know the treasure that was invested in the Donetsk region. All know that Russians populated and ran it. Cousins of Russians have travelled back and forth, and lived across the borders. Ukrainians were not subdued as members of the USSR until after Lenin died in 1924. Up until that time, Ukrainians were still killing Russians. Westerners who think all this is just ancient history are mistaken.

Russia will, at bottom, have to look inward to cope with economic, technological and socio-political realities, and this fundamental insularity will keep her behind the rest of the developed world. Do not, however, expect Russia to be passive at her periphery or, when she can be a visible player, on the world stage. It is in these places where the Russian leadership can recover a little past glory and satisfy Russian nationalist fervor.

It is up to Western political leaders to recognize and manage the realities that govern Russian leadership. There are more limitations than opportunities among those realities, and this can be managed to the benefit of the West, but doing so requires a sophisticated and deft approach. Russia can be mishandled to the detriment of everyone.

2.) America in A New Geostrategic Age

During my career I have, like other students of geostrategic thought, been strongly influenced by the Three M's: Makinder, Mahan and

Morganthau. Their images of world power are good places from which to understand how the world has changed.

MacKinder (1861-1947)	*Morganthau (1904-1980)*	*Mahan (1840-1914)*
Sir Halford John Mackinder, a founder of geopolitics, used his Theory of the Heartland to instruct idealists like Woodrow Wilson after the First World War that control of the Eurasian Landmass was key to world power. He saw geography as a dominant force and the Eurasian Landmass as the "Pivot of history." Mackinder wrote: "Who rules East Europe commands the Heartland; Who rules the Heartland commands the World Island; Who rules the World Island commands the World.	*Hans Morganthau's Politics Among Nations is a mid-20th Century classic. He was an international political realist who saw the key role of the interests of nation-states, backed by all of the elements of power that those states could bring to bear. What those interests are and how those elements of power are applied were the stuff of international relations. He later added moral considerations to his thinking, but Morganthau's basic 1948 model remained intact.*	*Admiral Alfred Thayer Mahan, the great American geostrategist of the nineteenth century, held that it was command of the seas that was crucial to world power. Mahan talked of controlling strategic points and dominating enemy fleets. This was revolutionary thinking indeed to Great Nations whose Armies had long dominated military thought. Command of commerce and "communications" outside the landmasses, Mahan theorized, could be decisive.*

Mackinder's Western myopia seems a bit quaint these days when Asian shadows are cast, as they were a thousand years ago, over the great landmass. But the point about world power residing in the heart of Eurasia still requires some thought even if it must not dominate our thinking. Geography has shrunk, but it has not gone away.

Steve Kime

The thinking of Alfred Thayer Mahan was revolutionary thinking indeed to great nations whose armies had long dominated military thought. And it was intoxicating for those who were natural sea powers. Command of commerce and "communications" outside the landmasses, Mahan theorized, could be decisive.

The seas, "The Great Common," is no longer the wilderness between continents, susceptible to surface domination of routes and access points, as they used to be, but Mahan is not dead. Indeed, as the likelihood and credibility of conflict changes throughout the range of escalation from showing the flag to all out use of weapons of mass destruction, there will be situations where sea power, if not "command" of the world's oceans, is more useful than it has been in the past.

Hans Morganthau's <u>Politics Among Nations</u> is a mid-20th Century classic. He was an international political realist who saw the key role of the interests of nation-states, backed by all of the elements of power that those states could bring to bear. What those interests are and how those elements of power are applied were, in his view, the stuff of international relations. While, in later life, Morganthau added moral considerations to his thinking, his basic 1948 model remained intact.

The Three M's have been overtaken by several revolutions. Mackinder and Mahan, tied closely to the Earth's surface and 19th Century technology, never really had a claim to a universally applicable image of how politics, economics, geography, and military power interact. They were, however, briefly influential and highly relevant in history, and it is important to understand that they are not irrelevant today. We need to take great care to understand when and where their ideas in strategic calculations still have meaning.

Morganthau's thinking is not tied as tightly to geography and time. His model can be updated for modern technology, economics, communications, and even the tentative international attempts to impose enforcement of law and morality. This is worth doing, but it is necessary to understand that, no matter how carefully one takes into consideration the interests of the various actors and the kinds of power those actors bring to bear, the world and the regions that comprise it are more complex and changing faster than Morganthau ever envisioned.

It is true that the absolute sovereignty of the Nation-State has been eroded by the emergence of non-state entities, multi-state organizations, and superpower actors whose sovereignty at times credibly extends beyond a sovereign state's traditional spheres of influence. These non-state and super-state actors indulge in behaviors *on behalf* of states or groups, but there is no evidence that they deter acts to defend the true, vital interests *of* a state.

Vital interests of a sovereign state are still fundamentally different from any non-state interests. A sovereign state, if vital interests are at stake, will "pull out all the stops." Weapons of mass destruction punctuate this fact.

Economic interdependence has had an impact on Morganthau's ideas. Mutual economic dependence mitigates behavior and alters relative power calculations. Generally, interdependence serves to increase the influence of the less powerful and decrease the influence of the more powerful. Of course, Morganthau understood this, but he did not anticipate the degree of economic and even military interdependence that now affects even the most powerful states. In 1968, twenty years after Morganthau's seminal work, Harvard professor Stanley Hoffman, in his book Gulliver's Troubles, began to explore the complexities faced even by intercontinental nuclear superpowers during a time of Mutually Assured Destruction. This author sat in Hoffman's class that year, nearly half a century ago. Today we find ourselves in a new nuclear age with emerging Gullivers and restless Lilliputs of varying descriptions.

It is time to rethink the impact of interdependence on the exercise and nature of national power. Americans are far too used to thinking of interdependence in economic terms. It is very important to recognize the political and military aspects of interdependence in this century, how those are changing, and what potential for management of that change might exist.

Philosophy intervenes. Western notions of the relationship between man and government, laden with moral considerations and images of

God-created rights in a "state of nature" have been inserted into thinking about the conduct of international relations. We are now seeing Muslim influences in play, and it is clear that other competing formulations of "international morality," "human rights" and "crimes against humanity" will compete in international forums that would judge behavior on the world's stage.

There are, of course, some internationally agreed-upon practices that have a measure of legitimacy and longevity. However, a serious approach to a modern geopolitical strategy must not rely on "international law " or on the process of nurturing such law. International "courts" are a very long way from exercising the power of sovereign states, even those that support such tribunals. There is no effective international law enforcement. So far these "courts" have reflected western thinking but they cannot continue that way much longer. Attempts to arrive at punitive or behavior-modifying actions at the United Nations increasingly face philosophical perspectives outside the western ones that have long dominated the UN.

War used to be a last resort, and the decisive one, of the politico-military spectrum. War as an instrument of national power has changed dramatically. It is still changing throughout the spectrum of conflict. War's utility, and its relevance in some cases, among the elements of national power beg serious modern analysis and recalculation.

Military instruments, and the credibility of their use, have changed more than the strategies of nation-states have changed. Great danger of miscalculation and surprise lurk here. Command, Control and Communications have undergone revolutions. At the upper end, "He who controls the information" might dominate more than "He who controls the real estate." At the lower end of the conflict spectrum, shoe bombers and hijackers have penetrated geopolitical bastions. The credibility of the high end of military weaponry in global war has diminished while the credibility at the low end has been demonstrated. The middle is in flux. Dirty bombs and MIRVs are not the weapons they used to be.

A new international order is emerging to accommodate a powerful new reality. Humanity is rising to a new level. In a post-industrial era charged by ever-accelerating technological development, the average circumstances of human beings and the average capacities of states are steadily rising. There will always be haves and have-nots and some will never catch up with others, but the human species is "evening out." This is changing the relative power and influence of nation-states and the locus of regional power centers.

In Morganthau's day politics among nations were not completely static, but they could be captured by the naked eye. Today, calculations of the balance of the elements of national power must deal with many more changing elements at many more levels. Only in the coarsest way can the balance of power be understood. The most sophisticated geostrategic thinker can have only a gross, short-term understanding of the shifting geopolitical tectonic plates in Eurasia and the Americas. The obvious geopolitical faults and potential eruptions in the major regions are discernible, but hardly predictable enough for long -term planning and policy. We have to adjust to this opaque environment and stay flexible. America's traditional sanctuary between two oceans and two compliant bordering neighbors is less of an asset in this environment.

Policy, planning and preparation by nations will always be based on relative power calculations, but they must be far more flexible and dynamic than in the past. Gross calculations, like Command of the Seas for example, which require such huge expenditures that many if not most of the national "eggs" were in one basket, have long been out of date. Now the same applies to huge, complex force postures aimed at dominating the conflict spectrum across the board, but based on a fairly fixed image of world power relationships. It may be that no nation can afford this for very long, especially since the actual, necessary use of such power is infrequent and improbable enough, with careful management, to make the cost questionable. Military superpowers may already be things of the past.

A new Strategic Vision for America

It is easy to get wrapped around the axle on terminology when one talks about Strategic Vision, military doctrine and military strategy. It is a good entanglement to avoid by simply saying what you mean:

> *By "Strategic Vision" I mean the way that a nation*
> *perceives the world and how it proposes to array power*
> *to cope with that world. My primary interest here is in*
> *the way America proposes to array its military power*
> *but "Strategic Vision" encompasses all the elements of*
> *a nation's power. A nation's Strategic Vision determines*
> *its Military Doctrine.*

> *"Military Doctrine" is an articulation of a nation's*
> *views on the nature of modern warfare and the ways*
> *that military forces are used in that warfare. Military*
> *Doctrine is the foundation for military Strategy. (My*
> *commentary in this book is primarily about America's*
> *Military Doctrine.)*

> *"Military Strategy" involves the planning and*
> *development of military forces for uses that comport*
> *with Military Doctrine.*

A Holistic Strategic Vision

Our Strategic Vision must not just be "from the inside out." In the past, The United States of America has had the luxury of allowing foreign and domestic security concerns to be isolated from one another. We have treated war as something almost detached from our shores. Indeed, it is sometimes a strain to convince Americans that action abroad is necessitated by genuine concern about the security of the Homeland.

The Military Services and much of our intelligence capacity are carefully constrained from acting inside the country for good reasons that fit our history to date. The separate states have their own militias, outgrowths of the Founding Fathers appreciation of the domestic need for citizen militias, and the rationale behind the Second Amendment.

These arrangements have well served our unique republic, blessed as it is by its location between two oceans in a vast stretch of rich land in a temperate climatic zone. Long borders with a weak Mexico and a compatible Canada helped to perpetuate the notion that domestic and foreign security are separate things. A strong school of thought jealous of the separation of federal and state power in all things has retarded sophisticated thinking that might better address both the internal and external threats to the country.

Any attempt to focus on domestic economic and military security has quickly fallen prey to charges of isolationism. Attempts to focus on evildoing abroad because it is antithetical to our values, especially in the absence of specific threats to America, have brought forth charges of "foreign entanglements." Efforts to define foreign philosophies and behavior abroad in terms of an internal threat have been both properly rejected (McCarthyism) and badly received (NSA surveillance.) We Americans, with Libertarians everywhere in our political spectrum, will always be skeptical of bogeymen. This is a good thing in the American way of thinking, but it needs to be attenuated to meet modern reality.

Because of this odd, insular strategic vision, some strange political manifestations have evolved to deal with strategic realities. We do not always know when or how or why to use force or declare war. We have, like ostriches, hidden our eyes and allowed remarkable latitude to an elected Commander in Chief, something that bothers thoughtful Americans. We suffer schizophrenia in trying to find legislation that balances civil liberties with very real civil dangers, again befuddling both political and military thinkers.

Modern communications and technology have made obsolete our old bifocal Strategic Vision with its odd separation of domestic and foreign security. It is obvious that we must, like other countries have long had to do, arrive at a *Strategic Vision which integrates the entire range of threat to our homeland and our way of life, and which applies all of our domestic, foreign and military policy tools throughout that range of threat.*

This has enormous implications. It means substantial growth of federal power at the expense of the states. (A growth foreshadowed by the federal funding and control already in the National Guard.) It means a new understanding of domestic security and immigration that, while not giving up on the notion that new blood has strengthened America, recognizes the real dangers that can penetrate our borders. It means that our loose attitudes about the need to protect our power grid and water supplies need to be tightened up. Individual privacy and anonymity, already eroded by new technology, will be challenged by ever more recognition of the need for intelligence on enemies extremely difficult to identify and track.

This sounds like an America that is less carefree and less fun. It is. Many citizens, not just Libertarians, will rightly be concerned that we are moving in the wrong direction and giving up too much in the name of national security. They must not be ignored. They must be allowed to serve as a proper brake on needed change.

Two questions are critical. Can we develop an approach to strategy and security that preserves as much as possible of America's free and open approach to life based on individualism free of government regulation? Can we balance traditional American openness to international trade and discourse with a needed 21st Century approach to domestic security from modern international threats?

The answer to both questions is yes. But it is affirmative only if we confront the complexities and the divergences from our history directly. This requires leadership in both Congress and in the White House, something lacking these days. We are now drifting toward a new approach to strategy and security because new security realities are palpable. Action is needed. Without leadership that can articulate the need and ensure sensible change, there is a danger of getting this terribly wrong.

3.) American Military Power and the Second Nuclear Age

"...our technology has exceeded our humanity"
Albert Einstein

The reader should be reminded that the foregoing and following comments are those of a Hoosier boy marinated in old-fashioned American attitudes, a submariner, a Cold Warrior, and an educator who grappled extensively with national security policy. The strategic vision that emanates from this background includes an appreciation of the capabilities and limitations of conventional military power and the calculations involved when considering the potential use of nuclear weapons.

The nuclear landscape has changed, but our nuclear strategy and policy has not kept pace. Nuclear weaponry caused a genuine Revolution in Military Affairs over half a century ago. Military thinkers, scholars, and policymakers labored mightily and produced something new and terrible in the history of warfare – a set of international military concepts based on the threat to incinerate the planet. The most amazing thing about this is not that it was outrageous, but that it worked!

The First Nuclear Age will occupy and amaze historians forever, but it is over. What was understood and accepted by nuclear powers about the relationships between political and military behavior at all levels of potential conflict no longer applies.

We are in a Second Nuclear Age where the old understandings and expectations about when, how, and where nuclear weapons are relevant have changed. Those old understandings and expectations stunted the growth of military strategy by limiting sophisticated thought about the use of and reaction to nuclear weapons at lower and intermediate levels of conflict. We have been playing it by ear at lower levels of conflict for a long time. Beware of those who say differently: ad hoc plans do not constitute policy that can be called on in a time of great tension and confusion.

The Early Days: Nuclear Terror and Good Luck

The early years of the Balance of Terror are remembered today as the "Duck and Cover" years when children were told to duck under their school desks on hearing an air raid siren. This quaint memory, a vestige of the days of German and Japanese subs and ships off our coasts and of the London bombings, glosses over a sinister fact. *We really did not understand the new strategic environment.* It took well over a decade to arrive at strategic concepts and models to deal with the new intercontinental nuclear realities.

It also took time to develop confidence that both emerging intercontinental nuclear superpowers understood and accepted the evolving rules of the game. They were arcane rules, and new in strategic thought. While policymakers were climbing a steep learning curve and technology and production of weapons was advancing, it was a dangerous, uncertain time.

Nuclear deterrence was radically different from conventional military deterrence. Homelands and top command centers were in play throughout a range of nuclear conflict. Armageddon, or something like it, was believable. Dialog between the parties that had to grasp these realities was oblique. Military and political leaders of the time had cut their teeth in a strategic era without true weapons of mass destruction.

We were lucky. The Taiwan Crisis of 1958 was with a still-emerging China and not with a Russia that was also still getting used to a world with hydrogen bombs. The Cuban Missile Crisis of 1962 *almost* came too early in our understanding of the relationship between shorter range, "theater," nuclear weapons and intercontinental nuclear weapons. Both sides learned vital lessons in 1962. Perhaps the most important one was that mutual understanding of the arcane theories and vocabulary of intercontinental nuclear strategy was essential to the survival of both sides.

The Right Number of Nuclear Wars

During this uncertain and dangerous initial Nuclear Age, a generation of nuclear strategy and policy advisors, analysts, and writers evolved. They were devoted to a crucial but negative concept: NOT exercising the vast, awful capacities that America had while, at the same time, being sure that we could. They were dedicated to the proposition that, while maintaining instruments of war was critical, success in Military Strategy lay in NOT using them.

Very important, the prospect of nuclear cataclysm would deter the use of nuclear weapons at all levels by all players. This deterrence extended into conventional warfare that would probably necessitate escalation to nuclear devices.

The legacy of this first generation of nuclear age thinkers and strategists is this: ***We had the right number of nuclear wars!*** It can be argued that major conflict between nuclear powers was deterred by the threat of escalation to nuclear conflict.

This first-generation nuclear age thinking has gotten long in the tooth. It has been extended into a Second Nuclear Age where the nuclear players have multiplied and time and technology have eroded the stark paradigms on which first generation nuclear thought was based.

War in a new nuclear age

Twentieth century thinking about the strategy of nuclear warfare focused on two intercontinental nuclear superpowers and the relationship of various levels of conflict to the probability of escalation to higher levels. Tight, hyper-rational models called "Escalation Ladders" were used to explain how lower levels of conflict were connected to higher ones, and vice-versa. At the lowest levels, nations merely "showed their flags." At the highest levels, all-out intercontinental nuclear exchanges ended the world for our failure to heed the warnings built into the model. It was a model characterized by rational behavior and order, rather than by the horrendous terror it purported to represent. It was the stuff of movies.

We are not in Kansas anymore. *Twentieth-century nuclear escalation theory is no longer valid.* The credibility of a threat to escalate from lower levels of conflict, even to the highest levels of nuclear warfare, has been eroded by time and experience. The ability to deliver nuclear weapons thousands of miles is just not as relevant to the entire range of conflict as it used to be.

The change may mean that the chances of *global* incineration have decreased, but it is not unmitigated good news. There was a kind of MAD stability in Mutually Assured Destruction and a Manichean world with two dominant players. The twenty-first century is evolving multiple competing power centers where lower levels of conflict, sometimes very large and very prolonged conflict, is ever more likely. These power centers possess various levels of military capability, some of it nuclear, and their attitudes about the use of their capabilities are unlikely to conform to the outdated notions developed in an age of two nuclear superpowers.

In early thinking about nuclear escalation, a threat to cross the nuclear threshold at the tactical, or" theater," level of conflict was a threat to cause uncontrollable escalation that, although dramatic and highly risky, was reasonably credible. Smaller US forces that would "have" to use tactical nuclear weapons would deter huge Soviet conventional force of tanks and infantry. Incredibly, national treasure was spent on force structures designed to play this game of inability to avoid escalation. In NATO one policymaker was asked how many Americans were really needed to deter Russians from driving their tanks through the Fulda Gap. His answer, "we only really need one American soldier, but he has to be sure to be killed on the first day." This writer argued at the time that the Soviet Navy on the high seas, like NATO forces at the Fulda Gap, was a limited force dependent on the credibility of escalation to nuclear war.

A perceived "need" to use tactical nuclear weapons in Europe or at sea, credibly threatening all-out nuclear war, was believable in the last century. At least, it was believable enough that no one dared test it. In this century, it no longer makes any sense to posture oneself to "have" to use nuclear weapons as a means of deterring conventional attack. The threat to escalate to mutual suicide levels is no longer credible.

The proliferation of nuclear weapons did not fit into the concepts of escalation that were applied to intercontinental nuclear powers. "Other" nuclear powers were either subsumed into superpower nuclear conflict (England, France, China) or were treated as individual, separate conflict scenarios tenuously disconnected from traditional escalation theory. (Israel, India, Pakistan, North Korea).

Iran and the other nascent nuclear powers (Brazil, Saudi Arabia, etc.) add new, complicated, separate conflict scenarios that are ever more disconnected from traditional escalation theory. They add to the combinations and permutations of nuclear war scenarios and increase the probability that nuclear weapons will be used in a 21st Century version of "limited" war. Regional conflicts, especially in the Middle East or

South Asia, with "limited" use of what used to be called "weapons of mass destruction," might well become a new reality. Such conflict is made more likely by the presence of "loose nukes" left in former Soviet Republics and the existence of nuclear weapons in the hands of sovereign states, like Pakistan, that could be taken over by extremist leaders.

To date, regional nuclear threats have been weakened by a lingering connection to traditional thinking about nuclear escalation and its doomsday implications. That connection has dissipated with time and proliferation. Very important, the <u>threat</u> of conducting regional nuclear warfare may become more credible as back up to local and regional policies of the new nuclear states.

The chance of accident or of irrational use of nuclear weapons also increases greatly in the new nuclear warfare context. So does unplanned use of nuclear weapons in the chaos and fog of war at conventional force levels.

The Balance of Terror was an awful basis on which to conduct international politics. The possibility of causing a global nuclear wasteland diminished the capacity for human beings to conduct civilized policies and try to better the lot of mankind. Unfortunately, the current state of nuclear weapons strategies may prove to be worse, and fraught with dangers of miscalculation, as the three power centers of this century, Europe, China, and the United States, compete for positions of influence.

The New Nuclear Age and America's Homeland

Once the nuclear genie was released from the bottle of Mutually Assured Destruction, all bets were off on "delivery systems." In fact, the nature of a "nuclear device" and the character of the potential nuclear attacker cannot be estimated with certainty. The source of a nuclear threat may not be a state or even a revolutionary movement. These frightening realities, which had been with us for some time, came home to roost on September 11, 2001. No one doubts today that there are non-state actors, and terrorists who might act at the instigation of some state, who would visit any "device" they can obtain on the American Homeland.

On first hearing that the World Trade Center Buildings had been attacked, many thought it was some kind of ruse. Our disbelief and surprise was rooted in an ostrich-like American attitude toward domestic aspects of national security.

America had been safe and snug between two oceans for two hundred years. We dealt with the new vulnerability to intercontinental nuclear weapons with the now-outdated strategies of the First Nuclear Age and returned our thinking to the safe and snug refuge on the North American Continent. In spite of attacks on our embassies, the USS COLE, and even on the World Trade Center in 1993, we did not think about an attack on America.

We did not think of strategy to deal with threats to the homeland until the 9/11 Bolt from the Blue. New, vital, domestic elements to the American concept of war appeared overnight. A major element involves nuclear and other weapons of mass destruction. For America, which had become accustomed to separating its domestic and foreign strategies and force postures, this was revolutionary change.

Our first instinct, to create a Department of Homeland Security and perpetuate the artificial domestic/foreign categories of thought, was understandable but imperfect. What is needed is a comprehensive national strategy that takes into consideration both domestic and foreign military contingencies. It must also be realistic about the possible use of nuclear weapons and it must correct the longstanding myth that domestic and foreign force structures can be kept separate.

The Total Force concept is in the right direction of thought, but was a band-aid applied to provide forces overseas, not to integrate domestic and foreign military threats. Guard and Reserve forces must seriously be integrated into a comprehensive, coherent force structure and strategy.

Needed: A Strategy for the Second Nuclear Age

Time, technology, and a changing international environment have made the world vulnerable to nasty, prolonged, "limited wars" under nuclear umbrellas, and for "limited nuclear wars" divorced from powers with intercontinental nuclear delivery systems. This is a dangerous world. Those who dismiss this reality as far-fetched are making a terrible mistake.

A new revolution in Military Strategy, based on new realities, is needed. It is far past due. Our thinking, and our force postures, have been too slow to adapt to a world with increasing ways that nuclear weapons can be used. Sophisticated, measured responses are going to be unlikely if the policymakers and nation-states are awakened to the Second Nuclear Age by an event that should have been considered, if not predicted. It will be a bad time to be Rip Van Winkle.

Are we prepared for an embassy, or a ship moored in a foreign port, to go up in a mushroom cloud? For Atlanta to be hit by a dirty bomb? For Riyadh, Teheran or New Delhi to disappear? For a "conventional" war in sub-Saharan Africa to reveal access to weapons we did not know about? For Israel to cease to exist? For a Taiwan Straits confrontation to cross the threshold? Are these far-fetched? Maybe. But no more so than an attack by civilian aircraft on the World Trade Center. Each one of these disasters, and a thousand more, is at least as likely as the intercontinental nuclear exchange that our nuclear policy has been focused on since the dawn of the First Nuclear Age.

Strategic arms talks have made progress in tempering the capabilities and intentions of major powers to use nuclear weapons. For two-thirds of a century, a few powers that generally shared thinking on nuclear weapons have avoided their use. This is very positive and, again, may reduce the probabilities of incinerating Planet Earth. But we must not let this lull us to sleep. The combinations and permutations of possible use of nuclear weapons are growing. History shows clearly that men will go to war, and eventually they will resort to the terrible capacities that they have made to kill one another.

History suggests that nuclear weapons will be used in this century. It is negligent to base strategy and policy on any other judgment. *America must develop its strategies and capabilities to cope with the numerous, and increasing, ways that it can happen.*

4.) American Military Doctrine for the 21st Century

America must reform its military doctrine and its force posture. We have drifted away from the kind of war that Americans support and can afford. We have failed to keep pace with change in global political, economic, and military reality.

The prospects for the use of nuclear weapons have changed faster than our thinking about them. Uses of non-nuclear military force in the last half-century have taught us some very expensive lessons about the misuse of force. Our past mistakes and the changing nature of nuclear war need to be taken to heart. A domestic dimension of national security threat has evolved that requires thinking that should be integrated into a comprehensive, integrated foreign and domestic US Military Strategy, something new to Americans.

Economic realities accompany the military ones. America can no longer afford to buttress outdated thinking with nearly open-ended military acquisitions. The abuses of the past, where politicians push military equipment that the military does not want or need, cost overruns are accepted as part of an out-of control acquisitions "game," and the Executive Branch decides unilaterally to use force outside The American Way of War, are facing a stark economic reality. We cannot afford it.

Our current military policies are out of tune with the philosophical and moral outlook of the majority of Americans. Most understand that this nation's greatness lies in being a beacon of freedom and opportunity, not in being an arsenal.

At our best, we import democracy into our melting pot. We do not export our ideas, or impose them on other cultures by force. For over fifty years, politicians have ignored these basic American concepts and the American military has tried to obey. We have been dragged into military quagmires where public tolerance eventually wears out.

A silver lining: past mistakes can lead us to The Edison Insight. Thomas Edison was asked early in his quest if he had succeeded in making a light bulb. He responded, "No, but I know a hundred ways not to do it."

By now, politicians have a mountain of data on how *not* to employ force. It is obvious that we need to return to the American Way of War. [1]

The American Way of War is to answer genuine threats to the nation's security by mobilizing massive force and crushing the enemy. We do not dabble with our children's lives and the nation's treasure. Politicians are quick to "play" with military "instruments" but the American people are not. Our doctrine and our force postures must be adjusted for The American Way of War, not for being a plaything of diplomats and politicians. The military element in our country's power lies in the "Well-Regulated Militia" that the Founding Fathers understood must be rooted in the population. This point is even more salient now that the threat to our national security has a much more credible domestic component.

The good news is that we can deal with all of this. Reform of our strategy and force posture at costs that can be sustained is possible. The country is in the mood to do it. There are leaders in Defense who are quite capable of it.

What needs to be done?

First, current strategy and policy must be changed with a return to the American Way of War in mind.

This requires a non-assertive, deliberate, and defensive mindset. Politicians and Politico-military thinkers and diplomats must be disabused of the notion that our children in uniform, our missiles, and our aircraft carriers are "arrows" in their quiver or "tools" in their toolbox. This arrogant and ill-advised idea has been bandied around so long and so glibly that policymakers actually began to believe that nice, clean, "surgical" applications of the instruments of death are in consonance with American views of the use of force in international politics. They are not.

---

[1] An essay by this author entitled "Return to the American Way of War" appeared in the issue of The U.S. Naval Institute <u>PROCEEDINGS</u>, May 2011. pp. 40-43.

Americans see the military "tool" among the nation's instruments of power more as a sledgehammer than as a scalpel. Americans, through their elected representatives in Congress, must formally declare a war that is in The American Way. When war is declared by due process, it will not be controversial. Americans do not need to be "led" for a just, moral use of force. Presidents have neither the duty nor the moral authority to declare war. They cannot justly substitute reasons, however "humanitarian" or "democratic" those reasons, for the Will of the People.

Policymakers have violated the American Way of War repeatedly for decades. The demand for due process before committing our troops will frustrate and annoy Presidents and Secretaries of State who want to play with toy soldiers. Americans have eventually rejected these violations, sometimes after enormous loss of life and treasure and after a diminution of America's moral standing in the world.

Clearly, a major departure from the attitudes and behaviors of the last half-century is needed. It is time to change our thinking about the instruments of diplomacy, about the American role in the world, and the place of military force in both of these.

By the way, it is not only Presidents and Secretaries of State that must be reined in. "Hawks" are ever present throughout the political spectrum. They are motivated by economic greed, ideological conviction, political ambition, or just plain old-fashioned "bubba" mentality. These, when combined, are loud and powerful voices that can seem to suggest public support. They must be put to the test of due process. This is a minimum requirement: smart policymakers will remember that prolonged, indecisive conflict soon loses American support even when there seems to be consensus at the beginning of it.

None of this is meant to suggest that America should stop being a great military power. Military force should and will always be a crucial instrument of our diplomacy. Our military power is a large part of who we are on the world stage. The potential of that power lay behind our diplomacy. It has huge, inherent military impact on calculations of friends and adversaries. "Show of force" has utility because it relates the totality of our awesome potential to politico-military situations. America is at its best on the world stage when we speak softly and carry a big stick. The Shining City on the Hill is not the world's arsenal, but it is also not a pushover.

We err when we think that little sticks work well for us. Our awesome military capacity is not easily divisible. We cannot take the military elements of that power and pick and choose how to apply them to force other nations to behave the way we want them to behave. Even if it works in the short term, it cannot be sustained for long in American public opinion.

Standoff use of military force, where we try to disconnect killing from dying, fails

to uphold American morality. Unmanned drones, cruise missiles hurled from afar, and "no-fly" zones are attempts to kill without dying. Americans will die, and kill, for their country if it is in danger, but we are not killers.

An All-Volunteer Force is a kind of standoff weapon. Privileged Americans are insulated from both the killing and the dying. This diminishes the soul of American power, and is not The American Way of War. Policemen are hired as volunteers and have a moral and just duty to kill if necessary without dying, but the American military is not a police force. Policies that permit a political class to keep its own children safe from war and educate them to join the class and send other people's children to war are very fundamentally un-American.

We must come to grips with the fact that the economic, social and political "arrows" in our quiver, though they are slow and sometimes ineffective, are the tools that we have to use. We need to get better at using these in a world where new power centers are evolving.

American goals in the international environment should be long-term goals that are aimed at promoting and preserving our national security. Such goals rarely require the instant gratification of the use of force. They almost always require the patience and perseverance of diplomacy. Diplomacy requires tolerance of a world always in flux and almost never the war we Americans would like it to be. If it were, we would not be The Shining City on the Hill.

We have been off track for a long time and it will take a major effort to get back to The American Way of War. Strong leaders with courage and conviction need to come forward. It will take great courage *not* to resort to weapons and to conduct our foreign policy with frustratingly slow and often less effective instruments of power. It would require strong conviction to start the process of changing military strategy, force planning and budgeting to fit The American Way of War. It would be revolutionary change.

This change includes a totally different approach to the relationship of domestic and foreign forces and strategies. The Total Force approach has already exposed the fallacies in separating domestic and foreign forces. The American Way of War, and the Founding Fathers, understood that *we are a reserve and militia nation at heart. A clearly articulated Doctrine that recognizes this is a good place to start.* Making defense budget justifications and broad military policies and strategies conform to that Doctrine would be next.

Second, we must come to grips with the new nuclear age. The landscape for the potential use of weapons of mass destruction has changed dramatically while concepts for the conduct of war involving nuclear use have lagged behind. Our minds are still in the First Nuclear Age, but a Second Nuclear Age has already dawned. We are in danger of facing High Noon unprepared.

The old concepts, based on a Balance of Terror and dependent on a precarious acceptance of logic based on theories and "ladders" of escalation, are out of date. The potential players have changed, the weapons are not the same, and the probable scenarios are markedly different from the past.

Very important, the passage of time has combined with the new circumstances to erode the credibility of threats to use intercontinental nuclear weapons. A threat to commit mutual suicide is no longer believable between nation states, and it means nothing at all to rogue elements and terrorists. American domestic vulnerability to the latter has increased.

"Isolated" nuclear exchanges, separated from intercontinental nuclear arsenals, were considered in the First Nuclear Age, but most serious thinkers put little stock in them even at that time. Nuclear War at Sea or "Limited Nuclear War" in Europe or the Middle East, fanciful creations of the Sixties and Seventies, could become the nightmares of the 21st Century. Such wars, especially without initial involvement of major nuclear states, are clearly more likely.

Time, progress at nuclear arms control, the global reach of non-state movements, and tectonic shifts in global and regional power centers, have dramatically altered the nuclear weapons landscape. *New plans and policies, and new public understandings, need to be in place before we are faced with a catastrophic nuclear event.* We cannot predict what that event will be, the combinations and permutations grow steadily, but we can be far more prepared than we are now.

Third, we must adjust and modernize our force structure to serve an updated American approach to the use of force tailored to the way Americans understand and will support war. We have a strong base from which to begin.

Modernization and tailoring to fit a new American Military Doctrine can be done at a reasonable pace. Basically, we need to use up what we have while building and tailoring forces judiciously with lean structures and far more limited use in mind.

The implications of this to other state and non-state players in the world are huge and must not be misunderstood. It means we will not be the world's policeman, and we will not be trying to make anyone over in our image. It has an element of "let the chips fall where they may" in it. It places vast responsibility on regional actors for their own neighborhoods.

It does NOT mean America ceases to be a leader in the world and does NOT mean that we fail to speak up on issues of morality and human rights. It DOES mean a reduction in our willingness to try to change behaviors with military force. This will be unsatisfying to ideologically inspired educated elites in America, but it will be just fine with the vast majority of our population and it will in the end increase the credibility of The Shining City on the Hill.

Forces for countering guerrilla warfare or "limited" interventions would be deemphasized. Forces built for "projection of military power" would exist to show the flag, but would not seek to plant our flag or impose our way of life somewhere else. Generally, forces for uses of military instruments short of war would be "spinoffs" of *forces justified and maintained for war in defense of genuine threats to the homeland.* Strategy, planning, and force building would be carefully tailored to The American Way of War.

This is not as simple as it might seem or as simplistic as detractors might charge. Some conflict with major adversaries short of direct, immediate threat to the American territory could certainly be seen as a genuine threat to the Homeland. For example, China will almost surely want to dominate trade and politics at its perimeter and on Asian seas in a manner intolerable to interests of the United States that could be considered "vital" in this century. Deterring or countering such a threat must be part of strategy, planning, and force building tailored to The American Way of War. This reality will affect the needed balance between standing and reserve forces, but it will not change the fact that an important shift toward the latter is clearly now in order.

The significant caveat in the previous paragraph is not meant to justify perpetuation of "domino thinking" where one setback inevitably leads to total failure. It is also not meant to justify repeats of trumped-up plans to use the American addiction to foreign oil as a reason to go to war. It is high time that America understands that we really do have the best political system on Earth and need not fear temporary popularity, even successes, of other ideas. Our energy addictions are indeed national security vulnerabilities, but they clearly can and must be addressed at home. They cannot be fixed by force of arms.

The capacity to mobilize must be re-thought and strengthened as capabilities and intentions to use military force at lower levels of conflict are reduced. This involves not just new approaches to reserve and

National Guard forces, but a new concept for "core" standing active duty forces that exist *primarily* to execute The American Way of War. These will be smaller, highly professional, high quality, and high tech forces. They will not by any stretch of the imagination be inexpensive, but they will be leaner, smarter, and far more efficient than what we maintain today.

A new Doctrine does not immediately require the new force that should be in place in the next decade or two. It *requires first and foremost a change in behavior.* America needs to extract itself from ongoing conflicts, even at some costs. Deployments and military exposures around the globe need to be steadily, and not too slowly, diminished. It is true that there will be cases where we will not like the results of pulling out, and hawkish detractors will hurry to say that the sky is falling, but we must learn to deal with this.

Our diplomacy must and will grow to cope with the world without the constant application of force. In terms of military posture, we will gradually but surely find ourselves with more forces than we need, and we can retire, or mothball, forces in an orderly way.

A Military Doctrine that clearly relates our use of force to unambiguous, direct threats to our national security and survival would give us the time and resources to update our military posture for the middle of the 21st Century.

Chapter XX
EPILOGUE:
America's Future

> *"You are the light of the world.*
> *A city that is set on a hill cannot be hidden."*
> *Jesus Christ - Sermon on the Mount.*

The future of American Democracy was questioned in its youth at the beginning of the Nineteenth century by the prescient writings of Alexis Tocqueville who travelled America in 1830. He was impressed with much of America, for example the built in checks and balances and the State and Federal political machinery, but he decried the nastiness of party politics and significant role that pursuit of material wealth plays in American thinking. Tocqueville feared that a American democracy might degenerate into tyranny. A growing, ignorant majority might suppress thought.

More fundamental doubts about the staying power of democracy as a form of government existed before Tocqueville. Until the last half-century such thoughts about the limited life span of democratic experiments seemed to have no relevance to the United States of America, a global superpower that seemed destined to grow and prosper. In the early 21st Century, this has changed.

It is not clear who first articulated the "death spiral" of democracy throughout history, but the notion is worth our attention today in America. Basically, the notion is that democracy does not endure because, eventually, a majority extracts entitlements from the public wealth and sustains public servants that perpetuate and extend those entitlements. Fiscal collapse is accompanied by dictatorial policies. Democracy thus contains the seeds of its own devolution to dictatorship.

The "death spiral" is often attributed to Alexander Tytler (1747-1813) a Scottish Lord and professor at Edinburg. Whether he originated it or not, he based his thinking on a detailed knowledge of attempts at democracy in history. Most thought-provoking are the stages that democracies are said to pass through:

> *From spiritual faith to great courage;*
> *From courage to liberty;*
> *From liberty to abundance;*
> *From abundance to complacency;*
> *From complacency to apathy;*
> *From apathy to dependence;*
> *From dependence back into bondage*

This writer would have scoffed at this in his youth. It would have seemed as outrageous, irrelevant speculation to a student of politics at Louisville in the Happy Days of the late Fifties or even to a graduate student at Harvard in the tumultuous late Sixties. It does not seem so far fetched at this writing. The descent from "abundance" in the spiral has been alarmingly fast. The erosion of what Tocqueville admired and the rise of what he feared has accelerated.

Looking back, I am struck by the fact that the future of our country has never really been in doubt until now. Every generation has said that the next one is going to the dogs, but it turns out to be the inability of passing generations to process the change that comes with the march of time. Older generations and Chicken Little have something in common. One of these days Chicken Little is going to be right. Is it now?

Change: Bend but do not Break

Two centuries ago the great Scottish poet Robert Burns, who corresponded with Lord Tytler, was speaking to one of the lowliest of God's creatures in his poem "To a Mouse." Looking to the future, Burns was pessimistic: *"an' forward, tho' I canna see, I guess an' fear!"* Burns had reason to fear the future. He might not like how it turned out but the sky did not fall in Burn's day. Americans guess and fear today. They, like Burns, have reason to fear.

Western societies are gravitating toward a least common denominator. There is growing agreement that America should go gently into the good night with Europeans who have gravitated toward Socialism and the tyranny of an entitled majority. Sadly, there is joy in some circles at the spectacle of seeing America become less than it has been.

The fact is that the world has changed and the role of America must change. We must confront change and deal with it. Does change mean submergence in an international mixing bowl and abandoning our position in the world? Does it portend the decline and fall of the unique American experiment with democracy?

Change in the material world is inevitable. Philosophers and social commentators have plenty to say about changes in technology and process, but no one expects material and technical things to stay the same. Changes in ideas are not accepted as easily by our species, which has made uneasy, sometimes hard-fought, compromises with governmental power and with each other and is not quick to adapt. It is extremely difficult for those with high stakes in a current political order to accept the fact that change is inevitable in society, too. Material change causes social change, and the march of time causes societies that endure to widen the mainstream of social thought and values. The question is not whether there will be social change but the pace of change and the way that social institutions adapt to that change.

Here lies the essence of sociopolitical conflict of our time. Grossly simplified, Progressivism insists on change faster than stability demands and the most conservative elements (currently called the Tea Party) want to maintain a mainstream of social thought and values that so completely rejects change that it too threatens instability. Our political machinery only coarsely articulates differences so severe and has reached a point where it hardly functions at all. Americanism is rooted in individualism so social "machinery," not codified, is in flux and harbors the possibility of a tyranny of a majority. Edmund Burke would be frustrated but Alexis Tocqueville would not be surprised.

Cultural mainstreams are always under pressure as time marches on and change takes place. Attitudes toward skin color, gender, mental illness, economic class, sexual preference, etc., are always evolving, especially in a society like ours that holds up the ideals of individual freedom and equality as absolutes. Change is normal and inevitable and we must adjust to it. We must at the same time work hard to preserve what we know is right and what we know that works. It is valid and sensible to fight *change aimed at destabilizing the very core of American culture and its form of democracy.*

Not all change is good. The American Family is no longer the accepted social role model. The American Melting Pot has become politically incorrect. Innovation and productivity have given way to a consumer economy. Checks and balances in government are failing, and confidence in democratically elected representatives is at an all-time low. The gap between rich and poor widens as greed at the top cheats workers at the bottom. A sober look at all this suggests that the decline may be irreversible. American innovativeness and productivity, based on recovery of the American work ethic, could be resurrected, *but the will to restore America is not visible.*

Hedrick Smith, quoted earlier, correctly identified the decline of the American Dream. It is true that American big business has, as it did at other times in our past, betrayed the American working person and caused great damage to the American Way of Life. This recurring disaster, which is not a partisan matter, must be taken on and set right. It must be done with full understanding of the change that has taken place already in technology, productivity, and global economics.

There is an uncritical acceptance of international economic interdependence and an unwillingness to recognize American Exceptionalism. Leftists and Progressives who see the submergence of America into a great common denominator as victory should heed the lessons of the fall of the Soviet Union. A supposed monolithic superpower crumbled quickly. When its material and economic base failed, its political and social culture had been compromised and could not prop it up. Military power was irrelevant.

America can bend, but She can also break. There are limits to which She can be a consumer economy in a productive world. There are

***also limits to the compromises that our society can make to its core
institutions.*** If we do not pull up our socks and restore the American
work ethic, cultural stability, and economic vitality and viability, the
best we can hope for is that, like Britons, we are able to enjoy being
mediocre. The worst would be the death spiral of democracy ending in
chaos and even dictatorship.

Change, but Remain the Shining City on the Hill.

So far, the decline of America has been exaggerated. The global Balance
of Power is in flux as always, but America's geographic, climatic, and
resource blessings make her a natural superpower, even though the
relative importance of military power, especially nuclear military power,
is declining. So far, our lead in technology and innovation has reinforced
our primacy in global affairs.

Images of America abroad are in flux as ideological challenges to our
social and political model rise, new power centers evolve, and modern
communications mitigate the huge gap between global poor and rich.
We are envied, and hated, by extremists who see that America is still
the Shining City on a Hill to most of the world, even if Americans
themselves do not know it, or if they insist on being ashamed of it.

America remains the go-to nation, but we must pay attention to the
shifting correlation of forces in the world, and especially to a new
relationship between domestic and foreign security. We can, and should
distance ourselves from many world issues, but we cannot act as if our
territory and culture are isolated.

America can still lead. It is not time for us to "lead from behind" or
apologize for our leading position either now or in the past. We do need
to understand and work effectively in a world much different from the
past. Our role in the world is primary but not determining in many cases.
Our military power is far less determining than in the past. This fact is,
properly understood and managed, in our national interest.

America for over a century has been called upon for projection of
virtually unlimited power. We can and should be a global power, but

we cannot expect to unilaterally rule the globe. We cannot duplicate America in the sand or jungle and we should not want to. Our greatest strength and our greatest argument is that we are an example to follow--- the Shining City on the Hill. We need to limit our expectations to what is necessary to secure our homeland and focus on the projection of limited power with emphasis on non-military instruments.

Prognosis: America in The 21st Century

At this writing, America is in the 21st Century's second decade. We have endured the terrorist attack of September 11th, 2001 and a War on Terrorism that ensnared American troops and spawned even more terrorism. The limits of our superpower status are becoming clear to a world facing nuclear proliferation, dramatic economic change, and the emergence of disaffected and extremist movements that find new license in a world where power is diffused. New technological innovations, especially a thoroughgoing revolution in global communications, make all the problems on Earth instant "news" and cast bright light on America's inability to cope, much less lead.

Domestically, America is in a blue funk. For over a hundred years, the country steadily compromised with Progressivism, sometimes based on large majorities and often with tolerable results, until America approached the limits of this compromise. In other words, *the modification of raw capitalism and 19th-century flaws that had been absorbed into the American Frontier model had run its course by the turn of the 21st Century.*

Remember that my generation, and those generations that followed it, did not oppose most of the change of the latter half of the 20th Century. We did oppose abuses of liberal programs as discussed earlier in this Story. *A crucial point to make here is that we began to balk when the limits of compromise with Progressivism began to be clear.*

This juncture in our history has been marked by heated debate among those who would have normally found much common ground. This is not unusual: at significant points in the evolution of a nation's outlook, contending schools of thought vie for followers. Even Mao Tse Tung proclaimed: "let a hundred flowers bloom!"

"Compassionate Conservatism," a slogan of the second Bush Administration that began the 21st Century, was a sign of the emergence of a conservatism that still retained some acceptance of the drift toward Progressivism at the end of the 20th Century. It did not take long for this more moderate image of conservatism to lose support, not just in the base of the Republican Party but in the broader population. A decade of Terrorism and two questionable wars was not a time of moderation.

So, we got the Tea Party. Many, probably very many, of my generation took this conservative road. They did not articulate very well the end of compromise with Progressivism, but they certainly said clearly and militantly: "This far and no farther!" On this point even those less conservatively inclined agreed. Progressivism had been poorly disguised rather than hidden for decades, and it finally came out of the closet. Savvy observers saw that this split the traditional support of the Democratic Party, which had always embraced a wide swath of

American thought from Reagan Democrats to fairly open Socialists.

Philosophical funk is no surprise when a hundred flowers bloom. When established social norms are vigorously challenged by articulate and passionate spokesmen, many in the government, this is particularly true. When such voices are loud, contentious, and very different, *the mainstream of American thought seems narrower than its fringes.* Relativism dominates social and political intercourse. Clarity is impossible. Values seem to be up for grabs. There is political gridlock.

The checks and balances needed to moderate competing views of governance can come under attack. No one anticipated that the very foundations of our constitutional structure would be in question, but competing images of the relationship of society, the individual, and government have challenged Separation of Powers, a key constitutional principle. The American form of democratic governance is under far more pressure than is commonly understood by a public that is much more engaged with material considerations than with conceptual ones.

Only a fabulously rich and blessed country could afford such a mess without starting to fall apart. We are currently held together more by our inheritance than by our actions or our thoughts. Truly vital questions are: can this last until we resolve our current malaise? And: how will we resolve it?

It is no exaggeration to say that we are on the brink a Second Civil War, a conceptual conflict that, to paraphrase Lincoln, will test whether the nation will long endure.

This is not simply a disagreement that, as hoped by many observers and "talking heads," can be solved if only rational politicians will get together and find a suitable compromise. Past disagreements, including some huge ones, have lent themselves to compromise, but the impasse now is looking like the beginnings of a Manichaean struggle. Political compromise will not work if that is what it is.

Our current impasse is so deeply rooted that it may take strong action to surmount it. This, frankly, is a sinister thought. Strong action implies fierce dissent. Loud protests, violence, and riots arise from the frustration of not being heard and not being heeded, particularly when the unheard and the unheeded are a huge segment of the population. It isn't far-fetched to envision widespread rebellion.

Leftists and Revolutionaries do not need to be told this because it has been the stuff of their thinking, and their fervent hopes for the chaos necessary to end the American experiment, for two centuries. The Founding Fathers even envisioned the possibility of an enraged citizenry and saw an armed population as insurance against tyrannical government.

The rest of us need to contemplate what this means and what can be done about it. Can we avoid it and put our house in order without giving in to a leftward decline through constant compromise with Progressivism? Or, must we embrace the reality that the time has come for a stand against the erosion of the political, social and economic values and practices that have defined us? If the latter, can we stand firm without falling into a reactionary abyss that could be worse than the intellectual, economic and moral squalor of Progressivism-cum-Socialism?

Like the poet Burns, "I guess and fear." I guess that the current malaise will lead to no good, and I fear that there will not be a peaceful solution.

The truth is that these are huge questions that my life's journey has not equipped me to answer. Maybe no one is equipped to answer questions so big. Perhaps history has to unwind by itself, propelled by the forces coiled up in America's past.

If this is so, I hope there is another Officer who will tell his story.

This book is an intellectual journey. It is based in the fundamental middle-American values and opinions, good and bad, of the "happy Days" of the Fifties. These values and opinions are dragged kicking and screaming through a rich and varied set of experiences as a young man is, amazingly, nurtured and tolerated by a usually hidebound Navy. The journey ends with summaries about Russia, US Military Policy and Strategy and the prospects for social and political turmoil in America.

An Officer's Story
A political-military Journey
By
Steve F. Kime

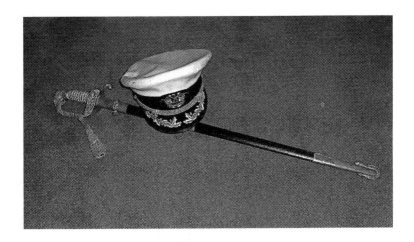

Steve F. Kime, a retired Navy Captain, is not a cookie-cutter product of a military academy. His unusual career led him from his roots in Indiana to submarine duty, a doctorate at Harvard, service in Russia during treaty negotiations and the shootdown of an airliner, and responsibilities in strategy, intelligence and higher education.

His was a politico-military Coming of Age. He pulls no punches in relating his mid-America upbringing and the experiences of his unusual career to current social, political and military issues.

Printed in the United States
By Bookmasters